AF213421

KEEPING HOLD OF JUSTICE

Keeping Hold of Justice focuses on a select range of encounters between law and colonialism from the early nineteenth century to the present. It emphasizes the nature of colonialism as a distinctively structural injustice, one that becomes entrenched in the social, political, legal, and discursive structures of societies and thereby continues to affect people's lives in the present. It charts, in particular, the role of law in both enabling and sustaining colonial injustice and in recognizing and redressing it. In so doing, the book seeks to demonstrate the possibilities for structural justice that still exist despite the enduring legacies and harms of colonialism. It puts forward that these possibilities can be found through collaborative methodologies and practices, such as those informing this book, which actively bring together different disciplines, peoples, temporalities, laws, and ways of knowing. They reveal law not only as a source of colonial harm but also as a potential means of keeping hold of justice.

Jennifer Balint is Associate Professor in Socio-Legal Studies in Criminology, School of Social and Political Sciences, at the University of Melbourne. **Julie Evans** is Principal Fellow of Melbourne Law School and Criminology, School of Social and Political Sciences, at the University of Melbourne. **Mark McMillan** is Deputy Pro Vice-Chancellor of Indigenous Education and Engagement at RMIT University. **Nesam McMillan** is Senior Lecturer in Global Criminology in the School of Social and Political Sciences at the University of Melbourne.

Law, Meaning, and Violence

The scope of Law, Meaning, and Violence is defined by the wide-ranging scholarly debates signaled by each of the words in the title. Those debates have taken place among and between lawyers, anthropologists, political theorists, sociologists, and historians, as well as literary and cultural critics. This series is intended to recognize the importance of such ongoing conversations about law, meaning, and violence as well as to encourage and further them.

Series Editors: Martha Minow, Harvard Law School
Austin Sarat, Amherst College

RECENT TITLES IN THE SERIES

Keeping Hold of Justice: Encounters between Law and Colonialism
by Jennifer Balint, Julie Evans, Mark McMillan, and Nesam McMillan

The Jurisprudence of Emergency: Colonialism and the Rule of Law (with new Foreword and Preface)
by Nasser Hussain

Archiving Sovereignty: Law, History, Violence
by Stewart Motha

The Holocaust, Corporations, and the Law: Unfinished Business
by Leora Bilsky

Curating Community: Museums, Constitutionalism, and the Taming of the Political,
by Stacy Douglas

Refining Child Pornography Law: Crime, Language, and Social Consequences,
edited by Carissa Byrne Hessick

The First Global Prosecutor: Promise and Constraints,
edited by Martha Minow, C. Cora True-Frost, and Alex Whiting

Hybrid Justice: The Extraordinary Chambers in the Courts of Cambodia,
by John D. Ciorciari and Anne Heindel

The Justice of Mercy, by Linda Ross Meyer

Dying Inside: The HIV/AIDS Ward at Limestone Prison,
by Benjamin Fleury-Steiner with Carla Crowder

Sacred Violence: Torture, Terror, and Sovereignty, by Paul W. Kahn

Punishment and Political Order, by Keally McBride

Lives of Lawyers Revisited: Transformation and Resilience in the Organizations of Practice,
by Michael J. Kelly

Among the Lowest of the Dead: The Culture of Capital Punishment,
by David Von Drehle

Punishing Schools: Fear and Citizenship in American Public Education,
by William Lyons and Julie Drew

Suing the Gun Industry: A Battle at the Crossroads of Gun Control and Mass Torts,
edited by Timothy D. Lytton

Transformative Justice: Israeli Identity on Trial, by Leora Bilsky

Keeping Hold of Justice

ENCOUNTERS BETWEEN LAW AND COLONIALISM

Jennifer Balint
Julie Evans
Mark McMillan
Nesam McMillan

University of Michigan Press
Ann Arbor

Copyright © 2020 by Jennifer Balint, Julie Evans, Mark McMillan, and Nesam McMillan
All rights reserved

For questions or permissions, please contact um.press.perms@umich.edu

Published in the United States of America by the
University of Michigan Press
Printed and bound by CPI Group (UK) Ltd, Croydon, CR0 4YY

A CIP catalog record for this book is available from the British Library.

First published February 2020

Library of Congress Cataloging-in-Publication Data

Names: Balint, Jennifer, 1968– author. | Evans, Julie, 1952– author. | McMillan, Mark David, 1969– author. | McMillan, Nesam, 1979– author.
Title: Keeping hold of justice : encounters between law and colonialism / Jennifer Balint, Julie Evans, Mark McMillan, Nesam McMillan.
Description: Ann Arbor : University of Michigan Press, 2020. | Series: Law, meaning, and violence | Includes bibliographical references and index.
Identifiers: LCCN 2019039052 (print) | LCCN 2019039053 (ebook) | ISBN 9780472131686 (hardcover) | ISBN 9780472126279 (ebook)
Subjects: LCSH: Aboriginal Australians—Legal status, laws, etc.—Social aspects.
Classification: LCC KU519.I64 B35 2020 (print) | LCC KU519.I64 (ebook) | DDC 342.9408/72—dc23
LC record available at https://lccn.loc.gov/2019039052
LC ebook record available at https://lccn.loc.gov/2019039053

Cover image of petition photographed by Giordano Nanni. Public Record Office Victoria, VPRS 3991/P0, Unit 834, Item 75/H12439. Petition written and signed by William Barak and Coranderrk residents, 20 October 1875. Reproduced with cultural permission from Wurundjeri Woi Wurrung Cultural Heritage Aboriginal Corporation.

CONTENTS

Digital materials related to this title can be found on the Fulcrum platform via the following citable URL: https://doi.org/10.3998/mpub.11323120

ACKNOWLEDGMENTS

As the following pages will attest, this book is an inherently collaborative endeavor that is part of a much larger, cross-sectoral, and interdisciplinary engagement that became known as the Minutes of Evidence project. There are therefore many people to thank, and processes to acknowledge, in recognition of an extraordinary partnership that took place between 2009 and 2016, and whose legacies continue to unfold.

First, we acknowledge the Traditional Owners of the land on which we live and write, the Wurundjeri people of the Kulin nation. We pay our respect to their Elders, past and present, and in extending that respect to Indigenous peoples across Australia, we acknowledge that their sovereignty was never ceded. We particularly thank Wurundjeri Elders Aunty Joy Murphy Wandin, Aunty Diane Kerr, and Uncle Bill Nicholson—and their communities—who so generously shared knowledge and stories and provided ongoing advice and guidance for the project as a whole. We are grateful to the Wurundjeri Woi Wurrung Cultural Heritage Aboriginal Corporation for cultural permission to reproduce the 1875 petition that follows these acknowledgments and features on the front cover of this book, and stands as an enduring testament to Indigenous activism and sovereignty.

Thank you to everyone who gave material and intellectual support to the ideas developed here. Minutes of Evidence was funded through an Australian Research Council Linkage Project grant that brought our work at the University of Melbourne into conversation with twelve government, community, and university-based partners: VicHealth, Victorian Department of Education and Early Childhood Development, Victorian Aboriginal Education Association Incorporated, Koorie Heritage Trust, Arts Victoria, Ilbijerri Theatre Company,

La Mama Theatre, State Library of Victoria, Regional Arts Victoria, Deakin University, University of Sussex, and Royal Holloway, University of London. The particular insights, perspectives, and practices of our cross-sectoral partners helped shape our ideas about structural injustice and justice while many conversations with our academic colleagues on the project—Joanna Cruickshank, Pat Grimshaw, Zoe Laidlaw, Alan Lester, and Giordano Nanni—further informed our thinking. We are especially grateful for Pat Grimshaw's gentle but firm encouragement to realize our ambitions to write a coauthored book about our collective concerns. Tony Birch's and Dianne Otto's engagement with the project as a whole also enriched its framing and contribution.

We are grateful to Leigh Day & Co. and Richard Hermer QC for allowing access to files on the "Mau Mau" case brought to the British High Court of Justice, and also to Eleanor Gilbert of the Aboriginal Tent Embassy for access to files from the "genocide" hearing at the Supreme Court of the Australian Capital Territory in 1998. Thank you to Steven Rhall for permission to republish the photos of *Coranderrk: We Will Show the Country*. Thank you to Tsari Anderson from Public Record Office Victoria for her assistance in accessing the 1875 petition.

Chapter 5 has appeared in different form in the *International Journal of Transitional Justice*, and we are grateful to the publishers for their permission to reproduce this material: Jennifer Balint, Julie Evans, and Nesam McMillan, "Rethinking Transitional Justice, Redressing Indigenous Harm: A New Conceptual Approach," *International Journal of Transitional Justice* 8, no. 2 (2014): 194–216.

We have had the privilege of working with many excellent research assistants during this process and express particular thanks to Matthew Mitchell for his considered attention to the book as a whole and to Charlotte Mertens for her close engagement with its ideas. The assistance of Marty Bortz, Mark Evenhuis, Tessa Fluence, Cameron Louis-Gleeson, Cosima McCrae, and Maria Rae was invaluable during the writing of individual chapters. Thank you to Caryn Sobel for her indexing. In the final stages, we very much appreciated the generosity of anonymous reviewers whose detailed comments on the manuscript helped us clarify the overall arc and contribution of the book. We are also grateful for the guidance and support provided by the 'Law, Meaning and Violence' series at University of Michigan Press, and the editorial team including Elizabeth Demers, Danielle Coty, Mary Hashman, and John Raymond.

Through Australian Research Council and University of Melbourne funding we have been able to present our ideas on this work in Australia and around the world and to benefit from the feedback from fellow researchers and practitioners at conferences and symposia organized by the University of Sydney, the University of Technology (Sydney), Swinburne University, Monash University, Flinders University, the Australian National University, Australian Institute of Aboriginal and Torres Strait Islander Studies, the Institute for Postcolonial Studies, History Teachers' Association of Victoria, Australian and New Zealand Critical Criminology Conference, Australian and New Zealand Society of Criminology, the Law and Society Association, Socio-Legal Studies Association, Royal Holloway University of London, the University of Kent, the University of Liverpool, the London School of Economics, Sheffield-Hallam University, the International Institute for the Sociology of Law (Oñati, Spain), the University of Toronto, KU (Katholieke Universiteit) Leuven, the University of Copenhagen, Queen Mary University of London, and the University of Sussex.

We have also enjoyed the support of our institutional homes at the University of Melbourne (the School of Social and Political Sciences, and the Criminology Discipline in particular, and Melbourne Law School) and RMIT University, and we have been grateful to the Faculty of Arts and the School of Social and Political Sciences at the University of Melbourne for their financial support throughout.

Finally, we extend our gratitude to each other as coauthors for the longstanding commitment required by this collaborative endeavor and to those friends and family for their support and generosity throughout the project and the writing of this book, with special thanks to Remi, Lucy, and Benjamin; to Dave and Alice; to Peter and Zane; to David, Jack, and Will.

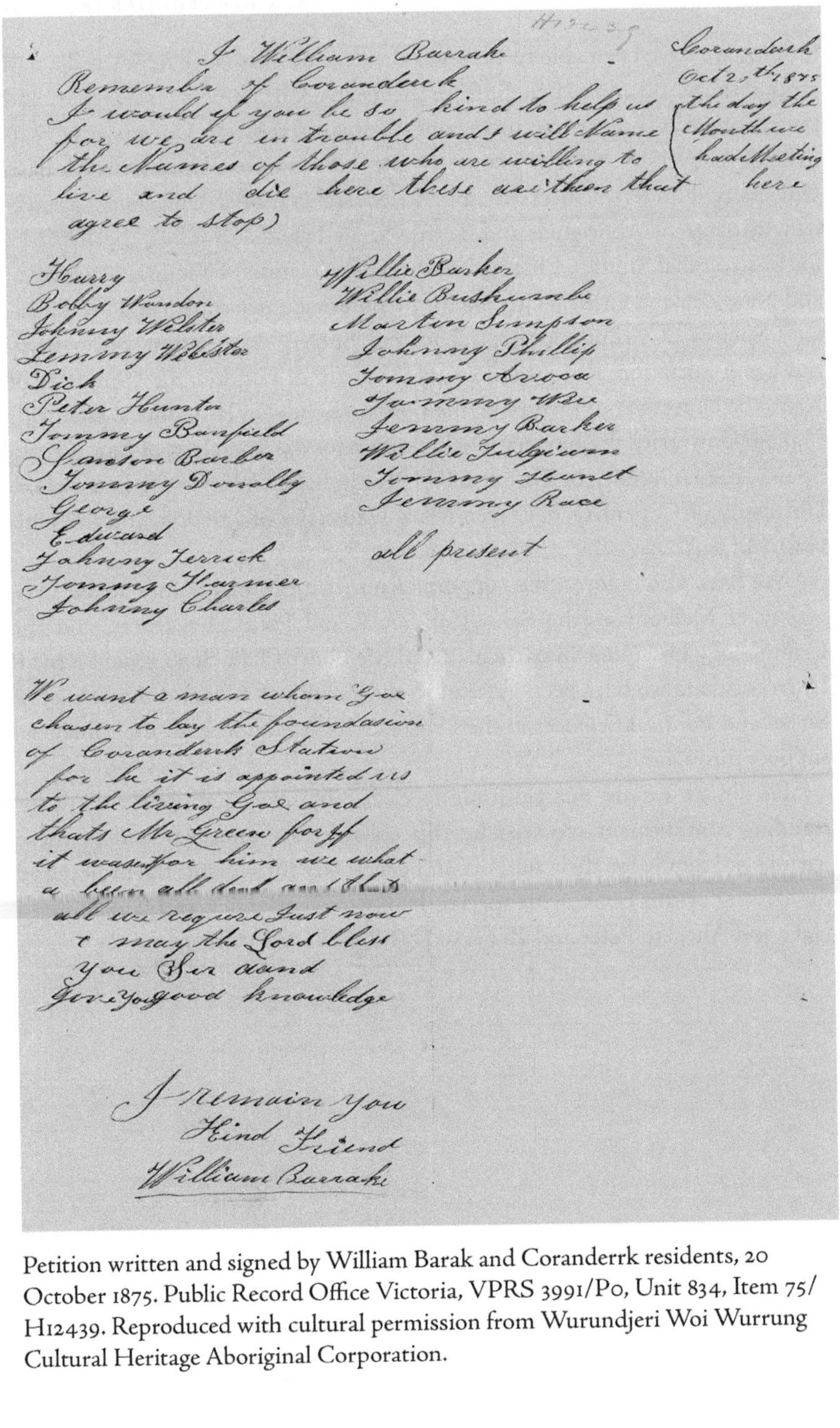
I William Barrak
Remember of Coranderrk
I would if you be so kind to help us
for we are in trouble and I will Name
the Names of those who are willing to
live and die here these are them that
agree to stop)

Coranderrk
Oct 20th 1875
the day the
Month we
had Meeting
here

Harry
Bobby Wandon
Johnny Webster
Jemmy Webster
Dick
Peter Hunter
Tommy Banfield
Sanson Barber
Tommy Dunolly
George
Edward
Johnny Terrick
Tommy Farmer
Johnny Charles

Willie Barker
Willie Bushurnbe
Martin Simpson
Johnny Phillip
Tommy Arrora
Tommy Wie
Jemmy Barker
Willie Fulgium
Tommy Hunter
Jemmy Race

all present

We want a man whom God
chosen to lay the foundasion
of Coranderrk Station
for he it is appointed us
to the living God and
thats Mr Green for if
it wasn't for him we what
a been all dead and that
all we require Just now
& may the Lord bless
you Sir and
Give you good knowledge

I remain you
Kind Friend
William Barrak

Petition written and signed by William Barak and Coranderrk residents, 20 October 1875. Public Record Office Victoria, VPRS 3991/P0, Unit 834, Item 75/H12439. Reproduced with cultural permission from Wurundjeri Woi Wurrung Cultural Heritage Aboriginal Corporation.

Chapter 1

INTRODUCTION—ENCOUNTERS BETWEEN LAW AND COLONIALISM

From Structural Injustice to Structural Justice

1881: In the British settler colony of Victoria, John Green—a Scottish Presbyterian lay preacher and respected founding manager of the Coranderrk Aboriginal reserve—explained his decision to resign a few years earlier rather than follow the direction of his superiors to remove residents from the home they had sought to establish following their initial dispossession in the wake of "settlement" almost fifty years earlier. Green was required to declare his position before an official inquiry into the growing unrest surrounding the evident determination of the Board for the Protection of Aborigines to break up the reserve and sell the profitable land to settler farmers. He testified: "I know that I could move the Aborigines if I could assure them it was for their good to do so . . . but I will not try—decidedly not."[1]

Green's thoughts and actions were supported by the testimonies of other prominent colonists who openly condemned the devastating impact of British settlement, rejecting prevailing views that Koori peoples had no stake in the land or future in the colony, and calling on settler law to support ways for everyone to live together justly in light of the circumstances in which they now found themselves. William Barak, the *Ngurungaeta* (clan head) of the Wurundjeri people of the Kulin nation and leader of the various men, women, and children who were residing at Coranderrk, used the forum to bring their case before colonial officials. This was just one of many episodes in Barak's long and powerful campaign for social and political relations between Koori and settler communities to be

Figure 1. Uncle Jack Charles playing William Barak and Tom Long playing John Green in *Coranderrk: We Will Show the Country*, a dramatic reenactment of the testimony at the 1881 Parliamentary Inquiry into the Coranderrk Aboriginal Reserve, Victoria, Australia. From a 2011 performance by the Ilbijerri Theatre Company at La Mama Courthouse Theatre: Isaac Drandic (director), Rachel Maza (dramaturgy), Giordano Nanni and Andrea James (script), with actors Syd Brisbane, Uncle Jack Charles, Jim Daly, Peter Finlay, Greg Fryer, Liz Jones, Tom Long, Melodie Reynolds and Glenn Shea. Photograph: Steven Rhall.

conducted according to the laws, values, and interests of both groups, rather than by simply imposing European ways of knowing and being in the world. In so doing, Barak was following in the footsteps of Kulin leaders Billibellary and Simon Wonga, who had previously sought to forge ongoing sovereign relations between the different peoples whose lives had been brought together through the violence and immediacy of the broader settler colonial enterprise in Australia where the need for formal legal engagement with Indigenous peoples was not acknowledged.[2]

Calls for Indigenous and non-Indigenous laws to be brought overtly into relation to agree on social order were unusual at this time in the Australian colonies where settler interests had commonly assumed precedence by the mid-

Figure 2. Melodie Reynolds plays Caroline Morgan in *Coranderrk: We Will Show the Country*, a dramatic reenactment of the testimony at the 1881 Parliamentary Inquiry into the Coranderrk Aboriginal Reserve, Victoria, Australia. From a 2011 performance by the Ilbijerri Theatre Company at the La Mama Courthouse Theatre, Carlton, Victoria: Isaac Drandic (director), Rachel Maza (dramaturgy), Giordano Nanni and Andrea James (script), with actors Syd Brisbane, Uncle Jack Charles, Jim Daly, Peter Finlay, Greg Fryer, Liz Jones, Tom Long, Melodie Reynolds, and Glenn Shea. Photograph: Steven Rhall.

nineteenth century.[3] But, in this case, the findings of the Coranderrk Inquiry—formally known as "The Board Appointed to Enquire into, and Report upon, the Present Condition and Management of the Coranderrk Station"—left open the possibility of advancing more equitable relationships between Koori and settler peoples, their worldviews, and systems of law. For even though colonization continued as a grave injustice imposed upon Koori peoples, the local influence of humanitarian sentiment in Victoria meant that successive administrations had early on acknowledged their obligation to provide at least a degree of safety and cultural autonomy through a system of land-based "protection" on missions and reserves.[4] The 1881 Coranderrk Inquiry went even further. Through inviting the testimonies of Koori residents, publicly hearing and recording their assertions of self-determination and belonging, and ultimately finding that the station was indeed ill-managed following Green's departure, the Inquiry held out an official opportunity to consider possibilities to accommodate pluralist expressions and practices of law, governance, and landholding in the colony. Within five years, however, a new government, bolstered by an increasingly self-interested electorate, passed landmark legislation designed to entrench the racialization and assimilation of Koori people, deny their sovereign claims, and uphold the kind of exclusive settler jurisdiction that eventually unfolded throughout the Australian colonies. Even though their success was commonly short-lived in settler colonies across the British Empire, such potentially productive encounters between law and colonialism in the past maintain profound significance in the present.[5]

Law, Colonialism, and the Question of Justice

This book focuses on a series of such encounters between law and colonialism across time and space. It is concerned with questions of justice and injustice, particularly questions of structural injustice and the possibility of structural justice. Through our analysis of different types of engagements between law (plurally conceived) and colonialism—including the settler colonial context we have introduced above—we seek to underscore the distinctively structural nature of colonial injustice. Such injustice becomes embedded in the social, political, legal, and discursive arrangements of certain polities where it continues to have a material impact in the present. Yet we also draw attention to the possibilities for justice that nevertheless remain. These possibilities include, quite clearly, the importance of structural reform and legal redress for past harms; but they are also more expansive, implicating and involving law in different ways. We argue, for example, that possibilities for justice can also be found in a greater recognition by law (as a discursive field) of colonial harm, in the legal record of colonial injury and its ability to be reactivated in the present to pursue just ends, and in an acceptance of our individual responsibility for our own laws and practices. Ultimately, we show that law is not only a site and source of colonial harm but also a potential means of keeping hold of justice.

The book focuses first on identifying the role of law in instantiating structurally unjust relations in colonial contexts; second, reflecting critically on the limits and capacity of law to recognize and redress the past and enduring harms of colonialism; and third, considering the possibilities for structural justice that may arise and that can still be generated within the colonial encounter. We discuss a diverse selection of encounters between law and colonialism to demonstrate how such encounters generate new ways of understanding law and possibilities for new modes of interrelation. Our methodology, as we draw out below and in the conclusion, is to bring together different experiences, perspectives, temporalities, and laws (including ways of knowing law) in order to spark new ways of understanding colonial harm and the potentiality for justice.

For us, keeping hold of justice means working within unjust structures in ways that at once acknowledge, challenge, and diminish their hold. It means keeping hold not only of prospects for structural justice existing within past and present colonial orders but also of the responsibility this entails for each of us in bringing about their more fulsome expression in the future. Our central concern is thus the complex relation between colonialism, law, structural injustice, and structural justice, its manifestation in the past, present, and future, and the possibilities for justice that remain.

This book is part of a larger interdisciplinary, cross-sectoral, and Australian-based research endeavor called the Minutes of Evidence project. This unique collaboration brought together Indigenous and non-Indigenous researchers, performing artists, educators, and community and government agencies interested in promoting new ways of comprehending structural injustice and the possibility of structural justice across the spheres of research, performance, and education.[6] Comprising eleven organizational partners from Victoria and two from England, the project drew on the 1881 Coranderrk Inquiry to foster greater awareness of local colonial injustices and increase public understanding of constructive ways forward. Using the medium of live performance to make this task engaging and accessible, and with the generous support and involvement of descendants of the Coranderrk community, the project produced a verbatim theater play called *Coranderrk: We Will Show the Country*.[7] Based on the Inquiry's archived "minutes of evidence," comprising the actual record of testimony from the Inquiry, and drawing on letters, newspaper articles, and petitions from the time, the play created a number of "meeting points" to share and interrogate Victoria's (and Australia's) past in schools and universities, in theaters, in other public venues, and on Country in Aboriginal lands.[8] These "meeting points" were designed to foster proximity,[9] creating space for new forms of relational engagement.

Situated in the colonial encounter of Victoria, and unusually for the time including testimony from Aboriginal residents of Coranderrk reserve along with settler supporters and opponents, the Coranderrk Inquiry was uniquely suited to conveying the meaning and significance of complex socio-legal phenomena (such as structural injustice and colonial injury) to public and school audiences, while the play brought to life more abstract theoretical accounts of settler colonialism. The broader story of the Inquiry also informed the collaborative development of new modules and classroom resources for the History and Civics and Citizenship curriculum in secondary schools, with protocols for engaging appropriately with local Koori communities. The project further transcended the conventional academic sphere through its commitment to sustaining respectful personal relations and professional partnerships between Indigenous and non-Indigenous peoples, organizations, and communities.

In terms of its methodology, the Minutes of Evidence project sought to connect different Indigenous and non-Indigenous knowledges, insights, and perspectives on our shared colonial past, and to highlight the significance of working collaboratively toward structural justice in the present and the future. The creation of such meeting points made the project innovative in both nature and scope. And this book is an attempt to apply this same methodology—of bringing together the past, present, and future; different disciplines and perspectives; and Indigenous and non-Indigenous ways of knowing—within the academic sphere to further develop some of the broader project's intellectual concerns with structural injustice and structural justice.

Our book is interdisciplinary and collaborative in orientation, addressing scholars working across criminology, history, and law. It thus represents another "meeting point": between a criminological concern with hidden and structural harms; an historical studies commitment to acknowledging the nuanced complexity of the past and its relation to the present and future; and a socio-legal focus on understanding the intricate connection between law, structural inequality, and questions of justice. While we each took initial lead on separate chapters (Julie Evans for chapter 2, Mark McMillan for chapter 3, Nesam McMillan for chapter 4, Jennifer Balint for chapter 6), their arguments and conceptual frameworks emerged from our conversations, debates, and interactions on the Minutes of Evidence project over several years, and are shared intellectual products. Moreover, this introduction, the conclusion, and chapter 5 are purposively cowritten. The book as a whole therefore sits alongside the broad body of work produced by academic and practitioner collaborators on the project while also making a specific contribution to more wide-ranging scholarly consideration of the relation between law, history, and colonialism.[10]

Like the broader Minutes of Evidence project, we also draw on the Coranderrk Inquiry to ground our own analysis and concerns. Accordingly, the next section of this introduction provides further details of the Inquiry, and its re-performance in the present, as a way of explicating our key themes and locating our analysis of law, colonialism, and structural injustice in time and place. In the chapters that follow, we expand our gaze to the experiences of British settlement in other parts of Australia; to claims for justice made by the Kenyan Mau Mau both under the colonial administration and later in the United Kingdom against the British state; and to contemporary international justice institutions and their willingness and ability to recognize the impact of colonialism in the context of the 1994 Rwandan genocide and more broadly. In so doing, we bring historical episodes of structural injustice into contact with contemporary justice frameworks such as transitional justice, and with reference to new and emerging global institutions. We do so not to conflate or to offer a prescriptive Western-centric or universally applicable agenda for the future. Rather, we engage with our different case studies in their specificity to deepen our consideration of the continued influence of the colonial past in the present and of the extent of law's potential in helping realize structural justice in the future. Indeed, as drawn out more fully in chapters 2 and 3, our discussion is informed by the importance of bringing normative European frameworks into meaningful relation with Indigenous ways of knowing and being in the world, and the significance of dialogue and collaboration in recognizing and addressing entrenched historical harms and promoting lawfulness.[11] It is this methodology of establishing productive meeting points between different historical experiences, temporalities, forms of law, and, significantly, ontologies of law that we consider a key contribution of our work.

Through our interdisciplinary and creative method, however, we do seek to advance a central argument: one that demonstrates both the structurally unjust nature of colonial harm and also the possibilities for justice and just relations that continue to exist despite the advent of colonialism. Our discussion thus speaks directly to an enduring socio-legal concern with the relationship between law and justice, with our focus specifically on the relation between law and justice within the colonial encounter. Socio-legal theorists have both acknowledged and interrogated the common association between law and justice.[12] They have demonstrated that although justice is often conceptualized as a legal end, law in practice has frequently functioned to reflect and embed dominant social, political, and cultural power dynamics and uphold and legitimate an unjust status quo in many modern Western democracies.[13] The debate about whether law itself can redress structural inequality, or is too deeply implicated in it, is a seminal and ongoing socio-legal concern.[14] Meanwhile, calls to "decenter" law as the site of analysis have also given rise to an exploration of the different ways of conceiving of and enacting justice as not only legal but also social, symbolic, economic, and even transformative.[15]

Our intervention in these debates is to explore the complex nature of the relationship between law, justice, injustice, and colonialism with reference to a range of times and contexts. We focus quite specifically on colonialism as a structural injustice—one that continues to affect people's lives and opportunities long after apparent declarations of "postcolonial" independence—and the possibilities of a structural justice. Our emphasis on the enduring significance of "past" colonial harm is accordingly informed by postcolonial theory's attention to the resilience of colonial forms of knowledge and forms of social, political, and legal arrangements that continue to influence global and national relations and affect the life experiences and aspirations of the groups and individuals they encompass.[16] This conceptualization of colonialism as a distinctively structural injustice also draws on explanatory frameworks offered by historian Patrick Wolfe and political theorist Iris Marion Young, whose work we elaborate below. Meanwhile, our overall approach acknowledges law as plural and diverse and is attentive to possibilities for improving the quality of relations between the different peoples and laws involved in continuing colonial encounters. In this respect, we are indebted to the specific understanding of lawful relations articulated by Shaunnagh Dorsett and Shaun McVeigh in their book *Jurisdiction* and to the writings of other critical scholars whose work attends to the quality of engagement between Indigenous and non-Indigenous ways of knowing, including ways of knowing law.[17] Meanwhile, our expansive consideration of structural injustice and structural justice as both discursively and materially manifest—involving questions about the social, political, and legal recognition of colonial harm and its practical redress—draws on the work of cultural theorists and critical criminologists that demonstrates the ethical salience of *how* experiences of justice are socially and publicly regarded.[18]

These diverse literatures are used alongside and in conversation with other

Half-Caste Act in 1886.[26] Henceforth, Koori people deemed not to be "full blood" were no longer entitled to live on reserves or receive government support. The Act foreshadowed similar racializing legislation in other Australian colonies with the effect of breaking up and dispersing Aboriginal families, and subjecting individuals and communities to lasting regulation, surveillance, and control.[27]

The story of the Coranderrk Inquiry testifies to the strength and resilience of Koori people in the face of the injustices that were becoming structurally embedded in Victoria, and is also an important demonstration of strategic alliances between Indigenous and non-Indigenous peoples in search of better ways forward. This history, and its restaging in the present, grounds our examination in this book of four main conceptual concerns: the complex relation between law and colonial injustice; the distinctively *structural* nature of colonial injustice; the intertwined nature of the colonial past, the present, and the future; and the possibility of just ways forward.

Colonial Injustice and the Law

First, for us, the Coranderrk story exemplifies the complex nature of the relationship between law and the structural injustice of colonialism. On the one hand, as a clear instrument of governance of the colonial state, law is deeply implicated in colonial harm. In this case, legislation is used as a framework for entrenching separation and repression, and is a collaborator and companion in injustice. Law and the state have a particular relationship: law is dependent upon the state for its power, but also exerts its own. And as an instrument of colonial power, it exerts a particular force. As Zoë Laidlaw has pointed out, "The law was a medium within which the practices, priorities, and nature of British colonialism were debated; it served both to enable and to constitute colonialism."[28] Violence and the law are bound together: as Elizabeth Kolsky has noted, for example, in the context of British colonial rule in India, "law itself was part of the structure of violence."[29] This is clear also at the international level, where it is international law, and its predecessors, that historically produced Indigenous peoples per se as categorically ineligible for sovereignty on the basis of their perceived departure from religious, cultural, or economic norms.[30] The profound discursive effects of this centuries-old relation between law and colonialism were evident in the lived historical experiences of Indigenous people across the British Empire, including those residing at Coranderrk and elsewhere in the Australian colonies. They still prevail in contemporary Australia where settler law commonly fails to come into meaningful relation with Indigenous sovereignty.

Yet on the other hand, for Coranderrk residents and their settler allies, and for other Indigenous communities such as the Kikuyu in Kenya, settler law offered a language and a process for making justice claims about the everyday realities of settler colonial rule, the "everydayness of injustice."[31] It is this conceptualization of law, as a tool of injustice yet called upon for justice, that we draw upon in the book.[32] Regarding Coranderrk, it was through using one of the mechanisms of settler law—an official public inquiry—that residents highlighted to a broader community the inequity of life in the colony and asserted their own perspectives on what needed to be done. And it was that Inquiry's hearings that pointed to the contradictions of settler law's claims to fairness and exposed its complicity in legitimating and entrenching settler interests. In turn, it is also settler law that created an enduring record of the violence and discrimination it condoned, a record that can be drawn upon in the present to facilitate new conversations about lawful and just futures.

Colonialism as a Structural Injustice

Second, we emphasize that colonialism is a distinctively structural injustice, a normalized form of harm that becomes entrenched in the social, political, legal, and discursive arrangements of individual polities. To understand the enduring impact of colonialism and begin to move toward its redress, we argue that it is crucial to appreciate colonialism as a structural harm. Political philosopher Iris Marion Young conceptualizes structural injustices, such as socioeconomic inequality, as different from forms of injustice that are more readily attributable to identifiable perpetrators either through "the wrongful action of an individual agent or the repressive policies of a state."[33] For Young, structural injustices are a "kind of moral wrong" whose sources are commonly so multifarious, widespread, diffuse, or located in a distant past that it is misplaced to seek to blame any set of individuals or institutions.[34] Young's conceptualization also benefits from earlier work in related fields, including that of Johan Galtung, founding scholar of peace and conflict studies, who defined the term "structural violence." Galtung explained "direct" violence as associated with an individual actor and "indirect" (or "structural") violence as that which "is built into the structure and shows up as unequal power and consequently as unequal life chances."[35] While the work of anthropologists Nancy Scheper-Hughes and Philippe Bourgois is informed by localized ethnographies, it too adopts a similarly broad purview, claiming that structural violence should be understood as "the violence of poverty, hunger, social exclusion and humiliation." They explain that "the social and cultural dimensions of violence are what give violence its power and meaning."[36]

The structural injustice of colonialism was revealed in the Coranderrk Inquiry—for example in Taungerong clan head Thomas Bamfield's statement that "I think they have done enough in this country to ruin the natives without taking it from us anymore."[37] Bamfield testified to the poor management of the station since John Green had been forced out, but also importantly took the inquiry from being about the conditions on the station to the structure of dispossession.[38] Indeed, colonialism is an archetypal structural injustice. As political theorist Catherine Lu explains:

> Like most political, social, and economic injustices that affect large groups of people, colonial injustices involved not simply wrongful acts by individual or state perpetrators. They also relied on social structural processes that enabled and even encouraged individual or state wrongdoing, and produced and reproduced unjust outcomes. Acknowledging colonialism as structural injustice does not displace assessments of individual or state liability for wrongful actions, but identifies other contributory agents in the production of colonial injustices, and raises the question of their remedial responsibilities.[39]

Moreover, when arising in the particular context of settler colonialism, structural injustice remains inherently associated with the historical foundations of contemporary nation-states. Patrick Wolfe's influential articulation of settler colonial theory identifies the unique structural relation between colonizer and colonized in settler societies such as Australia, Canada, New Zealand, and the United States of America where the colonizer never leaves and where (in contrast to slave or franchise formations) the economic interest lies primarily in permanently "settling" the ancestral lands of Indigenous peoples and claiming them as their own.[40] Settler colonial theory therefore seeks to account for the unique nature of settler states where the continuity between the colonial past and the present is more literal: with a lack of any official transition to a decolonized state, such polities effectively remain colonial formations.

Wolfe's historical analysis illuminates the structural nature of settler colonial harms where the violence of the dispossession of Indigenous peoples and their ongoing subordination to colonial interests helps to constitute an exclusive settler sovereignty, which seeks continually to fortify its legitimacy by repressing or marginalizing Indigenous claims. His schema characterizes settlement as "a structure rather than an event" that unfolds in stages according to a persistent "cultural logic of elimination" in support of settler hegemony.[41] This never-ending process is therefore evident not only in the initial periods of invasion and dispossession but also in subsequent periods of incarceration on reserves and in relentless racializing efforts to assimilate Indigenous peoples into no longer counting as sovereigns.

In Australia, for example, as a range of scholars have shown,[42] the 1992 *Mabo* High Court decision (which recognized a limited form of Indigenous land rights) and resultant native title legislation have yet to produce a comprehensive point of rupture given the difficulties many claimants have had in bringing their cases before the courts, and in securing legal determinations in their favor. Similarly, in the international legal order, enduring structural injustice is manifest in the continued primacy of Western notions of sovereignty that were produced and developed not only within Europe but also through the colonial encounter.[43]

While settler colonial theory highlights the insistent privileging of settler interests we note, too, how such analytical insights clarify the urgency of meaningful change in such societies rather than denying its possibility. Indigenous and non-Indigenous scholars have observed of the Australian case, for example, that despite the seriousness of its constraints, the *Mabo* decision nevertheless still signals the capacity of settler law to acknowledge its potential to improve the quality of its relations with Indigenous peoples and laws.[44]

A key problem, however, regarding the recognition and redress of structural injustice is making it visible and appreciable. That is, the nature and power of structural injustices is traceable to the way in which they become significantly naturalized over time so that populations commonly perceive their manifestation in entrenched inequalities persistently suffered by particular groups as taken-for-granted, if regrettable, social norms. Young emphasizes that in contrast to willfully imposed harms, structural injustices can be perpetuated through the mass of the population simply taking part, for example, in a market economy that is structured to benefit certain groups at the expense of others. Such generalized structural inequalities are reproduced over time not just through the material structures of a society but also through the ways in which unequal relations between different groups are continually rationalized through persistently privileging certain narratives. Contemporary economic and ideological processes therefore "carry the effects of past assumptions, decisions, and interests with them," inevitably either supporting or constraining the actions and aspirations of individuals and groups "even as we try to transform them."[45]

The hidden nature of structural injustice is importantly constitutive of the harm it causes. That is, the social, political, and legal nonrecognition of any injury is not simply a barrier to its redress but also a form of violence. Scholars from diverse disciplines have been at pains to highlight and problematize the lack of public attention to certain experiences of suffering and to draw attention to the inequalities that mark whose suffering is acknowledged and whose is not.[46] Here, critical scholars, notably Judith Butler, emphasize the political and affective significance of the way in which—or the frames through which—people's suffering is publicly regarded. She argues that the frames we use to conceptualize and rationalize certain violence (such as war) and understand its effects are politically and ethically salient, shaping "what 'can' be heard, read, seen, felt, and known" in the sociopolitical sphere.[47] These insights underscore the problematic nature of structural historical injustice and its contemporary legal and political obfuscation, which is itself intrinsically injurious.

To sum up this theme of our analysis, we argue that a conceptualization of colonialism as a distinctively *structural* injustice is thus crucial in recognizing it as materially and individually experienced and yet inextricably connected to and occluded by seemingly neutral and objective social, political, legal, and discursive structures. As will become evident throughout the book, it is such a recognition of the structural character of colonial injustice that compels a greater contemporary engagement with the enduring significance of the past (chapter 2) and the necessity of structural reform (chapter 5) as well as the importance of legal (and social and political) recognition of colonial harm alongside its concrete redress (chapters 3, 4 and 6). Hence the significance of the Coranderrk Inquiry in hearing and recording the testimonies of so many Indigenous witnesses to the injustice they experienced on a daily basis and of their rearticulation before public, student, and academic audiences in the present through the Minutes of Evidence project; again, demonstrating the potentialities of justice within colonialism and through law.

Bringing the Past into the Present

Third, and relatedly, the Coranderrk Inquiry sheds light on the intertwined and nonlinear relation of the past, present, and future. Through the Minutes of Evidence project, testimonies that were delivered originally in 1881 were brought back to life in the verbatim theater play *Coranderrk: We Will Show the Country*. It is in these testimonies, which outline both the structural injustice of colonialism and the just alternatives that remain, that the potential for lawful and just relations in the past is made visible in the present and available for the future. The reactivation of these testimonies created a "meeting point" for consideration that the past is not solely a site of harm but also holds the possibility of establishing *just relations*.

Introducing one of the early performances, Koori academic, novelist, and poet Tony Birch asked the audience to reflect on what it means to *hear* these voices from Victoria's colonial history, to learn at once, and in such a personal way, about the nature and scope of past and present injustices; the bravery, strength, and resilience of Aboriginal people in speaking openly to a legal and political system that sought to oppress them; their alternative visions for justice that were shared by named settler supporters; and the possibilities such historical examples of interpersonal collaboration continue to represent for an ethical future. Birch explained further that for all his intimate familiarity with the written records of the Inquiry,

> to hear these words *spoken* for the first time . . . was something completely different . . . the power of the spoken word for me was something remarkable and I firmly believe that we are witnessing another historical moment to have this hearing . . . spoken to us. And I think that to consider when you listen to these men and women that over . . . 130 years later . . . some people would be sitting here and appreciate those voices, and that struggle, is something that we should be so pleased to be involved in.[48]

Indeed, during question and answer sessions held after the performances, some audience members drew parallels between this historical record of structural injustice and contemporary examples, including a 1998 Federal Court judgment (upheld by the Australian High Court in 2002) that denied native title to Yorta Yorta people on the basis that the pastoralist and member of the Board of Protection Edward Curr, who testified to the Inquiry, had already dismissed their sovereign entitlement to land in his 1883 memoir of life in colonial Victoria.[49] Parallels were also drawn to the coercive national emergency legislation that was hastily enacted in 2007 by the Australian Government in response to widespread accusations of sexual abuse of Aboriginal children in the Northern Territory. Known colloquially as "the Intervention," the exceptional Northern Territory National Emergency Response legislation overrode the authority of the Northern Territory Government and local community organizations and was supported by the deployment of soldiers and the suspension of the Racial Discrimination Act.[50] Such observations highlight the ways in which the structural injustices of colonialism have endured in Australia, and specify the capacities of settler discourses and institutions to reproduce exclusivist notions and practices of sovereignty.

The analyses presented in this book suggest that any attempt to address the enduring structures of injustice inaugurated through colonial discourse and practice demands an acknowledgment of the relation between the past, present, and future. Legal theorist Ratna Kapur argues, too, that a linear conceptualization of time as "progressive" can act as a further means of exclusion, suggesting that "the 'post' in postcolonial does not merely mark an end to the colonial moment. It provides the opportunity to interrogate and elaborate on how the past continues to inform the present."[51] Historical theorist Berber Bevernage also insists on the "radical contemporaneity" of the past, present, and future, resisting their conceptualization as distinct or temporally striated states.[52] Stewart Motha, in his analysis of sovereign violence has shown how the "archaic forms and assertions of sovereignty persist in the present," and are sustained by law.[53]

As observed in our discussion of the 1881 Coranderrk Inquiry and its contemporary reperformance, we see possibilities for just relations in the past, even as structural injustices are being embedded. We suggest that the colonial past is not simply a site of injustice, but an essential basis upon which to make sense of the present. It is only through understanding this interconnection that we can appreciate the full significance of colonialism as a structural injustice.

Ways Forward: Keeping Hold of Justice

Finally, the book draws on the Coranderrk Inquiry to raise future possibilities for justice—what we term a structural justice—within and despite enduring colonial structural injustice. Coranderrk residents and their settler allies powerfully used their testimonies to offer alternative ways forward, including through pushing Inquiry commissioners to move beyond asking questions about the everyday conditions of the station and to focus on structural issues of land and self-determination. They spoke to the common questions being asked at the time, of how to *live together justly*.

Asked "Would you like the Government to give you all the food you want, and all the clothing, and no work?," *Ngurungaeta* William Barak responded:

> If they had everything right and the Government leave us here, give us this ground and let us manage here and get all the money. Why do not the people do it themselves—do what they like, and go on and do the work.[54]

Meanwhile, in roundly condemning official attempts to undermine the reserve, Coranderrk's founding manager John Green spoke directly to the importance of respectful relations: "If the Aboriginal is put into the question, he will strive to keep his own law. That is where I consider you have failed."[55]

The "meeting point" of peoples, communities, and laws created through the Coranderrk Inquiry countered the predominant settler colonial narrative of Aboriginal peoples as lawless, lazy, uninterested in work, and as having no stake in the colony's present or future. It thereby challenged, too, those racializing discourses and practices that increasingly sought to naturalize discrimination by linking perceptions of somatic differences between populations to their eligibility for full sovereign freedom and humanity.[56] In highlighting the destructive rationale of the colonial enterprise, Koori witnesses asserted their sovereign willingness to be partners in a colony that recognized pluralist expressions of sovereignty.

In this book, we explore ways to *keep hold* of justice, imaginatively, affectively, cognitively, and practically. Keeping hold of justice is an active orientation; it is something that individuals, communities, and societies must keep pursuing. Our overall argument is therefore specifically attuned to recognizing both the possibility and the necessity of a structural justice that is grounded in a comprehensive knowledge of colonial harms, a keen appreciation of their lived experience and effects in the past and present, and a respectful commitment to working collaboratively toward meaningful structural change.

CHAPTER SUMMARY

Our collaborative understanding of structural justice arises within each of the chapters, and through reading the book as a whole. Each of the following chapters considers the significance of the colonial past in the present, drawing out the ways it has shaped contemporary national and international communities and laws (chapters 2, 4), led to ongoing encounters between Indigenous and Western laws (chapter 3), is a necessary partner to structural change and reform (chapter 5), and has produced a legal record that continues to speak powerfully in the present (chapter 6). In so doing, they also emphasize the ways forward that emerge from a greater engagement with these pasts.

The book begins with a focus on case studies defined by a distinct form of legal order—namely, that in which there has been no official point of rupture with the colonial past, no formal process of decolonization. To this end, chapters 2 and 3 offer contextualized analyses of structural injustice in Australia as a settler society. They highlight the relation between the past, present, and future, and how taking responsibility for one's own law can bolster possibilities for justice. Chapter 2 presents an historical case study of life and law on a settler colonial frontier in Wiradjuri country in New South Wales in 1824 when dispossession was beginning to unfold in the context of *terra nullius* (a legal myth deeming Australia to be a land "belonging to no-one"). It charts how, no matter what the abstract claims of settler law, it fell to colonial officials on the ground to grapple with the (often violent) actuality of ordering relations between Indigenous and non-Indigenous peoples and of instantiating structural injustices in support of settler interests. It suggests that in times of crisis in the colonies, localized pragmatic understandings of what might be considered "legal" came to prevail over more fulsome, ethical understandings of what might be considered "lawful" as Indigenous lands were increasingly brought within settler jurisdiction. Through explicating the structural inequity of colonialism, it also teases out the potential for a greater appreciation of such enduring injustice, including ways "to live justly with law"[57] that may be found in engaging with the lived experience of colonial encounters.

Chapter 3 then gives practical insight into what it means to engage with and between different worldviews and laws, enabling a deeper appreciation of what a meeting of laws, as a practice of structural justice in settler societies, may entail. This chapter demonstrates, for example, the disjuncture between the connection settlers commonly have with their law and the alternative legal position of Wiradjuri peoples as holders of law. It also underscores the ethical imperative of the relationality of Aboriginal and colonial legal systems, which are always in relation despite the overt denial of colonial legality. It thus develops our conceptualization of the past, present, and future by demonstrating continued relationality between Western and Indigenous systems of law and knowing and the possibilities for a more just future that this entails. Accordingly, building on chapter 2, it contends that there is a responsibility for non-Indigenous peoples to think more reflexively and expansively about what it might mean to make a commitment to come more consciously into relation with Indigenous peoples, nations, and laws.

The book then engages with another type of legal order, one where there has been a notional point of rupture, or a purported shift from colonial rule. These analyses demonstrate how such a shift has resulted in a "linear conceptualization" of the past, present, and future through Western and international laws' disavowal of the continued significance of "past" colonial structural injustice in the present. Chapters 4, 5, and 6 also demonstrate the possibilities for keeping hold of justice in these contexts through a commitment to engaging with the past, acknowledging the past, and reactivating the past.

Chapter 4 focuses on a case study of contemporary international criminal justice. The discussion centers around two sites of encounter between law and colonialism: the jurisprudence of the International Criminal Tribunal for Rwanda, and the negotiations surrounding the potential inclusion of the crime of colonial domination in a Draft Code of Offences Against the Peace and Security of Mankind. Across both these sites, the chapter traces how colonial injustices and their enduring implications are simultaneously recognized and rhetorically and practically contained through their framing as "past," nonjusticiable, and matters of politics and history rather than of law. Leaving aside the question of justiciability, which is always-already shut down through the presentist and progressive orientation of international criminal law, this chapter considers how else past experiences of colonialism might be made, or enabled, to mean and matter in the international and other legal spheres. It invites further consideration of how international criminal justice might more comprehensively bear witness, discursively and practically, to the devastating and unjust nature of colonial histories and why this might be an important, if not indispensable, gesture of structural justice.

Chapter 5 then engages with transitional justice, a contemporary legal framework taken up internationally that currently facilitates the acknowledgment and practical redress of mass harm. Transitional justice is an internationally endorsed program of legal and social initiatives designed to sustain peace and achieve justice in countries that have experienced genocide and other forms of widespread conflict. This chapter considers how a field of theory and practice such as transitional justice, which has also been critiqued for its presentist nature and its neglect of structural inequalities, is nevertheless an existing "tool" through which colonial harm can be acknowledged and through which the need for a comprehensive "justice agenda" can be envisaged and even pursued. It does so by bringing together the two previously disconnected academic fields of settler colonial theory and transitional justice to consider how they collectively shed light on the possibility of a structural justice and the nature of law's relation to it.

Opening out further on the possible relations between structural justice and the law, chapter 6 then considers the power of the claims made to law and the record they create. Focusing on the use of law in the colonial Kenyan state during the "Emergency" from 1952 to 1960 alongside claims of genocide advanced by Indigenous peoples in Australia, this chapter demonstrates that despite the role of law as a collaborator in historical injustice, particularly within colonial structures, law continues to be turned to as a site of justice. It shows how law's capacity to respond to justice claims in the colonies, as elsewhere, is socially and politically determined. Yet it also shows how law contains the possibility of change through the claims made to it, and the ability of such claims to persist and be reformulated over time and place. The record of law, and its limitations, can be referred to as a means for constituting a structural justice that may unfold outside of law. The record of law can be used to *reactivate* claims and create a space where structural injustice is appreciable and a structural justice possible.

Our conclusion brings together our diverse considerations of the structural injustice of colonialism and of the remaining possibilities for structural justice by elaborating further on this methodology of bringing together different encounters, perspectives, and temporalities to chart new ways forward. Our method is relational in bringing and holding together diverse imperatives, orientations, laws, disciplines, and temporal states as a means of raising awareness of structural injustice and sparking new modes of engaging with it. We return to the Minutes of Evidence project as a way of explicating the key contributions of our analysis, namely our demonstration of the continued possibilities for just relations that persist even within situations of enduring colonial injustice and our method of recognizing and realizing such possibilities.

Keeping Hold of Justice seeks to show that the possibility of a structural justice is found in the productive nature of encounters. It is through a method of establishing "meeting points" that just possibilities in the present and the future can be found.

Chapter 2

SETTLER SOCIETIES

The Making of Legal Order in Australia

> If we direct attention to the event or activity that called jurisdiction into existence, the wrongs are not abstract, they are particular wrongs associated with lives lived in relation with others.[1]

> We need to shift the burden of carrying the memory of colonial violence on behalf of the white community. . . . We live with this because the wider community refuses to take on its responsibilities; because governments in this country have been historically deficient—morally, legally, and ethically.[2]

> As a law professor, he knew that framing what was at issue in a case made a huge difference to its reasoning. A decision-maker always had a choice in this regard.[3]

In contemporary times, many critical legal scholars have explored how law continually denies the actuality of its past even as it seeks to ground its authority in time immemorial—an openly historical allusion whose vagueness places it nevertheless "beyond the imaginings 'of the best historians.'"[4] The reiterative dynamics of such ironies in law explain how certain legal narratives come to prevail over alternative everyday understandings and experiences. Far from fostering appreciation of law through knowledge of its lived effects, as Peter Goodrich writes, such "mythical" legal history provokes "an escape from memory, a flight from the past as it was spoken and lived."[5]

By way of contrast, the idea of a living law embraces rather than flees its past. Through engaging critically with history, a living law not only acknowledges the actual circumstances in which matters of normative law unfold. It also enables new possibilities to emerge, making it easier to recognize the capacity of law to respond more expansively to matters of justice and conscience, including in circumstances where the quality of relations between settler states and Indigenous peoples is concerned. In *Drawing Out Law*, John Borrows shows how continuing to resist the link between life and law also suppresses the visibility of, and engagement with, Indigenous laws and ways of knowing, further bolstering the propensity of dominant law to produce narrow understandings of what counts as justice in the past, present, and future.[6] Finding ways to "share, monitor, and resolve disputes through a negotiated protocol," on the other hand, "is a hopeful sign. It reveals the potential for change that exists when First Nations in Canada bring their law out from under the shadows of the courts."[7]

Shaunnagh Dorsett and Shaun McVeigh bring a related perspective to their critical work on jurisdiction in Australia where they note the transformative potential of distinguishing between abstract acknowledgments of past wrongs and coming to consider them as "particular wrongs associated with lives lived in relation with others."[8] They suggest that elaborating understanding of how social order between different peoples is actually produced through law works both to improve wider community recognition of historic injustices and to release rather than subdue law's withheld or subordinated capacities to foster lawful relations that are "meaningful or adequate to the tasks that need to be addressed as a matter of justice (legal or otherwise)."[9]

With these helpful contributions in mind, this chapter also turns to the past but brings a historian's perspective to bear on how law was lived by Indigenous and non-Indigenous peoples on a settler colonial frontier in the early nineteenth century. Geographically focused on southeast Australia, the analysis draws attention to "particular wrongs" arising from the instantiation of British sovereignty in the intersecting space of Wiradjuri country and the "newly settled" Bathurst districts of colonial New South Wales. While the international legal notion of *terra nullius* was invoked to justify British sovereignty in Australia on the basis that it was a "land belonging to no-one" this chapter considers how the practical process of realizing exclusive jurisdiction in this part of the colony exposed the dissonance between Britain's legal claim and the actual sovereign presence of Wiradjuri peoples and their law. In relatively remote areas such as Bathurst, colonial authority had yet to be tested and officials continued to struggle with their task of asserting sovereignty over the lands of others, with some individuals (at least rhetorically) claiming to balance the "welfare" of Indigenous people with their wholesale dispossession.

Throughout this book, we contend that appreciating the structural nature of such colonial harms—it was not until 1992 that the High Court of Australia denied the applicability of *terra nullius* in Australia[10]—helps explain certain continuities between the historical experiences of colonized and colonizing peoples in the past and present, in both settler colonial and postcolonial contexts. This chapter and the next discuss, from different perspectives, how scrutinizing examples of the meeting of Indigenous and non-Indigenous laws in settler societies can shed light on the relation between law, colonialism, and structural injustice and on the possibilities for justice that nevertheless remain. While focusing here on instances of unlawfulness in the Australian colonies, we note certain variations in jurisdictional forms and practices that also existed in the early decades of British rule. These alternative understandings and expressions of law, which were locally responsive to prevailing circumstances, at the very least identify historical capacities for accommodating (if only temporarily) pluralist legal frameworks, understandings, and practices.[11]

In these ways, this chapter presents a detailed consideration and justification for the call to history that we advance in the book as a whole.[12] With reference to the contested process of establishing socio-legal order in southeast Australia we explore the legal and ethical significance of the past and present as lived experience. While we acknowledge both the urgency and the magnitude of the need to find ways to live together lawfully in settler societies (as our opening quotes implore), we start with the past to underscore that understanding how settler law was imposed and lived in the formative years of colonial rule—and how Indigenous peoples and laws responded—is a vital part of meeting that challenge. We begin by providing a brief account of the defining features of settler colonialism before turning to the particular policies and practices of dispossession that both assumed and inaugurated colonial authority in newly settled regions and whose effects persist to this day.

THE DISTINCTIVENESS OF THE SETTLER STATE

As former British settler colonies, contemporary settler polities such as Australia, New Zealand, Canada, and the United States of America share similar histories as distinctive forms of colonial enterprise whose fundamental features endure into the present. As discussed briefly in the introduction, theorists of settler colonialism contend that unlike other nations where colonial rule was formally—if not actually—surpassed in the independence movements of the mid-twentieth century, modern settler states largely continue as they were initially established: through the founding dispossession of Indigenous peoples, and by persisting in efforts to subordinate—if not erase—their sovereignty, laws, and jurisdictions.[13] As primarily land-based economic endeavors, settler colonies are understood to be structurally different, for example, from slave or franchise formations where economic concerns revolve principally around the exploitation of labor or resources and where colonial interests—for all their longevity, influence, and immediacy on the ground—remain relatively detached. The dominant economic and discursive conditions of settler formations, on the other hand, are conducive to colonists seeking to secure a permanent future outside their mother country through making the lands of others their own. Patrick Wolfe accordingly explains that settler colonialism cannot be consigned to the past but should be seen, rather, as an ongoing—and always incomplete—project whose structural characteristics and "governing logic" continually privilege settler sovereignty, worldviews, and interests over those of Indigenous peoples.[14]

That settler societies were constituted through territorial dispossession defines the uniqueness of Indigenous peoples' relation to the state when compared with settlers, or with minority immigrant or refugee populations whose manner of incorporation as citizens is qualitatively different.[15] In the present day, the structural nature of this relation, and of the violence that produced it, can be difficult for majority populations to appreciate as it is increasingly naturalized over time. Past colonial practices and preoccupations can be rendered remote or obscure, their nature and ongoing effects less tangible to mainstream interests and sensibilities. Nevertheless, the multifarious impacts of colonial harms continue to rebound within both Indigenous and non-Indigenous communities.[16]

While Indigenous and non-Indigenous peoples live with this history in diverse ways, its negative repercussions are commonly only made publicly available through formal indictors of dramatically disproportionate "social disadvantage" in Indigenous communities, from health to education to employment to matters of criminal justice. Viewed within what amounts to a deficit-based welfare framework, such official renditions of the contemporary effects of systemic injustices might well invoke seemingly ameliorative policy responses from governments yet all the while they may resist more thoroughgoing explanation and redress in structural justice terms. In the case of Australia, for example, bipartisan political commitments to recent policy frameworks that support a "practical" aim of "closing the gap" between Indigenous and non-Indigenous performance on a range of welfare measures have prevailed over so-called "symbolic" initiatives. Accordingly, support for modern-day treaty agreements or other considerations of pluralist legal forms and arrangements—which bear the capacity to bring Indigenous law and settler law into just relation—still tends to be expressed through local rather than national initiatives.[17]

While settler states, including Australia, have offered varying degrees of acknowledgment of historic injustices—whether through government apologies, constitutional recognition of first nations status, self-determination in decision-making, or land rights, for example—the extent to which, as we discuss further in chapter 5, state-based reforms are limited by the normative structures of justice within which they are framed influences the nature and quality of relations they envisage and support in the present and future.

COLONIAL AUSTRALIA 1816–1840: WHOSE LAW, WHO HAS AUTHORITY FOR LAW?

As already observed, and in contrast to the historical experiences of Indigenous peoples in the United States of America, New Zealand, and large parts of Canada, Britain considered treaties inappropriate in its Australian dominions.[18] But while this legal foreclosing of Indigenous peoples' rights to engage lawfully with the Crown presupposed an exclusive settler sovereignty, it could not determine it in practice: permanent settlement would not be secured through abstract pronouncements of entitlement alone.[19] The actuality of relations in frontier districts—between local Aboriginal peoples and increasing numbers of settlers, their servant workers, and governing officers—therefore vitalized the operations of *terra nullius*, forcing everyone to live out the disparity between law's explicit disavowal of Indigenous sovereignty in Australia and the evident disagreement of its holders on the ground.

In the absence of treaties, where disputes over jurisdiction took place, it fell to officials to decide precisely how relations would be ordered as various "crisis points" unfolded.[20] Colonial governors, who ultimately bore both personal and professional responsibility for "unruly" settlement and whose individual thoughts and actions routinely entered the written record, had therefore to confront the ways in which the silencing claims of imperial law were received by those whose lives and interests were affected in situ.[21] At times, they were also compelled to explain (to superiors in London) and to declare (to inhabitants in the colonies) exactly how and why it was that *colonial* jurisdiction over Aboriginal lands would prevail in newly settled regions, while also navigating the legal and ethical limits of their authority to order, or simply to condone, settlement by force.

Experiencing Life and Law in Wiradjuri Country/ Bathurst Districts, 1824

Discussion now turns to the specific circumstances surrounding the settlement of the Bathurst districts of New South Wales and to the events that culminated in a formal proclamation of martial law against Wiradjuri people in August 1824. It traces how settlers and officials called on law at this time and seeks to bring forth "that which must have been lived for a discourse to take the form that it does."[22]

The township of Bathurst became the first inland settlement in New South Wales in 1814. It was named after Earl Bathurst, Britain's secretary of state for war and the colonies (1812–27), to whom the sixth governor of New South Wales (1821–25), Major-General Sir Thomas Makdougall Brisbane, was obliged to report on matters of colonial administration. Bathurst was added to the collection of English names populating the correspondence and maps that had been making the long journey from the antipodes to officials in London since 1788 when Governor Arthur Phillip's arrival marked the formal beginnings of convict settlement at Sydney Cove.[23] At that time Phillip's instructions concerning the ordering of relations between Indigenous and non-Indigenous peoples in the fledgling colony had been minimal: to "open an intercourse" with Aborigines and to "conciliate their affections."[24] While some peaceful encounters did initially take place between colonists and Aboriginal peoples, instances of conflict also occurred. Disputes increased dramatically in the early years of the nineteenth century when farming and settlements began encroaching farther into Aboriginal countries to the north and west of Sydney along the fertile plains of the Hawkesbury and Nepean Rivers.[25]

Here as elsewhere in the Australian colonies, as discussed below, successive governors struggled to find a stable basis in law to control the actual and potential violence of such "frontier" encounters. The stipulations of government orders, proclamations, and administrative regulations shifted radically between assuring Aborigines of their protection before British law, offering them inducements to become "settled" and "civilized," outlawing individuals deemed particularly dangerous, banishing groups from visiting towns and dwellings, and, on the grounds of self-defense, authorizing the arming of individual settlers, "retaliatory" raids, and terrorizing campaigns to be led by magistrates and supported by the military.[26]

It was during this period that a crossing was finally forged through the rugged Blue Mountains that had formerly signaled the physical limits of colonial development to the west of Sydney, opening the way into Wiradjuri country.[27] At first, the establishment of farms proceeded slowly in what had become known officially as the Bathurst districts, but by the early years of Brisbane's appointment at the end of 1821 tensions between Wiradjuri peoples and settlers were growing. Brisbane had been charged with overseeing sweeping changes to the colony's first institutions, shifting away from a predominantly military administration and establishing a civilian form of government with civil courts and trial by jury, an advisory nominee council, freedom of the press, programs to encourage immigration of free settlers, and a regulated system of land sales and convict labor designed to stem the controversial favoritism of earlier practices and facilitate land clearance.[28]

Clashes in the Bathurst region became more serious from 1823. While many observers explicitly associate them with the effects of Governor Brisbane's new land acquisition policies, opinion varies on the precise causes of openly violent disputes: conflicts have been variously interpreted as localized acts of retribution for infractions of Wiradjuri law (such as the abuse of women and destruction of food sources) by settlers; as infractions of British law (such as the theft or destruction of property) by Wiradjuri people; as evidence of more systematic opposition to an ever-expanding program of dispossession through agrarian settlement; or as influenced by the high proportion of convicts or former convicts among the settlers.[29]

Our focus here, though, is on examining the ways in which officials, in the absence of treaties, turned to law in other ways to authorize their management of relations between those settlers and Wiradjuri people who found themselves living together in Wiradjuri Country. In seeking to regulate the "frontier violence," officials drew on certain repressive forms and practices of law, including those that had already been deployed elsewhere in the colony, to justify and eventually to enforce colonial jurisdiction and open up Wiradjuri lands for permanent settlement. At times, officials chose to dispense with ordinary legal forms altogether.

"That Which Must Have Been Lived . . ."

Over the last few months of 1823, stories reached Sydney that "Aborigines" had been stealing provisions and equipment and spearing sheep and cattle on several farms. By the new year, the *Sydney Gazette* reported further "Depredations by the Natives of Bathurst," advising readers that a retaliatory party had secured the capture of Windrayne, a Wiradjuri leader known colloquially as "Saturday," who had been sentenced to a month's imprisonment.[30] In June, the *Gazette* wrote of more altercations and that over a three-day period in May several stockkeepers and servants had been killed, huts burned, and livestock slain. The editor hoped, however, that a report that three Aboriginal women had been killed in retribution would soon prove incorrect.[31]

Governor Brisbane wrote to Earl Bathurst in London on 18 June requesting approval to raise more troops in "consequence of some violent outrages committed by the Aborigines against the Stock keepers in the neighborhood of Bathurst, in which no less than Seven of the latter have been murdered in the most cruel and barbarous manner."[32] The 22 July *Gazette* alluded to "a multiplicity of distressing accounts from Bathurst" but cast doubt on news of numerous deaths, including reports that "60 or 70 natives have been killed."[33] That same day, a meeting was held in Sydney between the magistrates and other "principal inhabitants" of the colony. The *Gazette* said that the object of the meeting had been

> to take into consideration the present adoption of certain resolutions that embraced the Native question: to express the grateful acknowledgment of the Public towards the Government, which had exercised the utmost promptitude and support in alleviating the distresses, and preventing the future inconvenience of the settlers, and their dependents, in the interior, from the incursions of the aboriginal tribes; and to reward several praiseworthy individuals, who had stepped forward, regardless of consequences, to preserve human life; and to save the stock of the country from total destruction.[34]

Meanwhile, earlier rumors that three Aboriginal women had been killed in a retaliatory raid in May had proved true. Five stockkeepers had been charged with manslaughter of one of the women and a trial date set for 6 August in the colony's new Supreme Court.

As recorded in the *Gazette*, the trial of the stockkeepers John Johnston, William Clarke, John Nicholson, Henry Castles, and John Crear fleshed out the local circumstances in which the crime had occurred.[35] Witnesses testified to specific times and places of attacks on settlers and stock and subsequent retaliations, emphasizing the prevailing state of alarm. William Lane, for example, an overseer on one of the farms, believed his "family and people were in imminent danger" and explained that as "consternation among the men on the estate increased" he agreed to the prisoners' request to supply them with horses and arm them with muskets and a sword "that they might go in pursuit of the natives, else they would all be murdered." Lane said that he had later heard, including from some of the accused, that an altercation had taken place and that some natives had "dropped," among them "an old woman." He reiterated that the "whole of the country was in great agitation from the violence of the natives" and he had allowed the prisoners "to go out in quest of the natives merely from motives of apprehension." Witness Magistrate William Cox also "enumerated the various acts of cruelty and depredation that had been committed, within his recollection" over the last eight months, stating that "the natives may now be called at war with the Europeans."

Defense solicitor Rowe argued as a point of law that his clients were "warranted" in undertaking violent reprisal, "having acted under the direction of" Governor Lachlan Macquarie's 4 May 1816 Proclamation.[36] In that proclamation, Macquarie began by outlining the context of his decision to authorize military action in response to "atrocious and wanton Barbarities" committed by hostile Aborigines including "indiscriminately murdering Men, Women, and Children, from whom they had received no Offence or Provocation" and destroying property and livestock while the Cumberland Plain (east of the Blue Mountains) was being settled. Macquarie declared that his previous lenient and humane efforts "to conciliate [Aborigines] to the British Government, by affording them Protection, Assistance and Indulgence," had failed to stem the violence of the previous three years, despite warnings of the potential consequences of continuing with such actions. He therefore had found himself "reluctantly compelled" to authorize "a Military Force to drive away these hostile Tribes from

British Settlements in the remote Parts of the Country, and to take as many of them Prisoners as possible."[37] Several Aborigines had been "unavoidably killed and wounded, in Consequence of their not having surrendered themselves on being called on so to do," but these would have included some of "the most guilty and atrocious of the Natives" involved in recent murders and robberies. While it was "unavoidable" that a few innocent Aboriginal men, women, and children "may have fallen in these conflicts," it was hoped that that such severity would strike terror into surviving tribes and deter further "Outrages and Barbarities." The Proclamation then laid out a series of preventative measures designed to protect settlers and their property in the form of "Rules, Orders, and Regulations to be observed by the Natives, and rigidly enforced and carried into Effect by all Magistrates and Peace Officers in the Colony of New South Wales."

Under the authority of the Proclamation, Aborigines were ordered not to come within one mile of a town or farm "occupied or belonging to any British Subject" if carrying "any warlike offensive Weapon or Weapons of any Description, such as Spears, Clubs" or they would risk being "considered in a State of Aggression and Hostility, and treated accordingly"; if more than six unarmed Aborigines came "to lurk or loiter about any Farm in the Interior" they, too, would risk "being considered Enemies, and treated accordingly"; the practice of large numbers of Aborigines assembling in or near Sydney with a view to "inflicting Punishments on Transgressors of their own Customs and Manners" was banned as "a barbarous Custom repugnant to the British Laws" and made subject to summary justice. They were commanded to abandon such practices "not only at and near the British Settlements, but also in their own wild and remote Places of Resort." On the other hand, if Aborigines chose to abide peacefully by the Proclamation, Macquarie would offer them the protection of the British government and, on application, issue them successive monthly certificates to that effect. In counterbalance to not allowing them to "go about the Country armed" he would offer small plots of Crown land and assistance with provisions and equipment to those willing to give up "wandering, idle, and predatory Habits" and become self-supporting and "industrious and useful" settlers, either as farmers or servants. He further entreated Aborigines to consider handing over their children to be educated and civilized in the Native Institution he had established two years previously and explained, too, his willingness to meet with them annually to discuss "the best Manner of improving their present Condition."[38] The Proclamation finished with Macquarie's explicit instructions to settlers:

> His EXCELLENCY the GOVERNOR hereby orders and directs, that on Occasions of any Natives coming armed, or in a hostile Manner without Arms, or in unarmed Parties exceeding Six in Number, to any Farm belonging to, or occupied by British Subjects in the Interior, such Natives are first to be desired in a civil Manner to depart from the said Farm, and if they persist in remaining thereon, or attempt to plunder, rob, or commit any kind of Depredations, they are then to be driven away by Force of Arms by the Settlers themselves; and in Case they are not able to do so, they are to apply to a Magistrate for Aid from the nearest Military Station; and the Troops stationed there are hereby commanded to render their Assistance when so required.[39]

Consideration of Macquarie's Proclamation benefits, too, from greater explanation of the context of the correspondence that surrounded it. On 18 March 1816 Macquarie had written to advise Earl Bathurst of his intentions "to Inflict exemplary and Severe Punishments" on hostile tribes and to drive them from settled areas. While still committed to his conciliatory plans to "domesticate and Civilize these Wild rude People," his proposed coercive measures had become "Absolutely Necessary" if settlers were to return to their abandoned farms.[40] Macquarie's instructions to the troops on 9 April were more explicit: all Aboriginal people they encountered, whether men, women or children, were to be made prisoners of war, should be shot if they "showed fight" or ran away, and their bodies hung conspicuously in trees to terrorize survivors.[41] He reported to Bathurst on 8 June that the operation had lasted twenty-three days, and while the troops encountered few of the hostile tribes fourteen had been killed and five taken prisoner in "the Occurrence of most importance." The Proclamation had been issued before "the return of the Military Party" to publicly explain the necessity of using military force in the present circumstances but also to encourage Aborigines ("so rude and unenlightened a race") to accept inducements to become settlers. There was reason to hope, the governor concluded, "that the examples, which have been made on the One hand, and the encouragements held out on the other, will preserve the Colony from the further recurrence of such Cruelties."[42]

By 20 July, however, Macquarie issued a "Proclamation of Outlawry Against Ten Natives" that significantly escalated operations. He reiterated how his previous measures represented a considered combination of using military force against Aborigines and inducements for them to submit to settlement, and he was at pains to say that they had been "fully acquainted" with his Proclamation to them two months previously. Violence against "unoffending and unprotected settlers" had nevertheless continued and ten individual instigators were now named as "in a State of Outlawry" and formally placed beyond the protection of the government. All British subjects "whether Free Men, Prisoners of the Crown, or Friendly Natives" were therefore "authorised and enjoined" to capture the outlaws and bring them to justice before a magistrate. If capture for that purpose was impossible, these same British subjects were "at Liberty by such Means as may be within their Power, to kill and utterly destroy them as outlaws and murderers." A reward of ten pounds would be paid for each outlaw brought in, or proven to have been killed. District magistrates were advised to assemble settlers who now were "authorised to repel attacks by Force of Arms," while making sure never to provoke such attacks themselves. Moreover, "with a View to overawe the hostile Natives generally in those Parts of the Colony where they have committed the more flagrant and violent Acts of Cruelty and Outrage," three military detachments, with others available as needed, were ready to support settlers whenever they advised the nearest magistrate of their requirements.[43]

In the 1824 trial of the five Bathurst stockkeepers, Macquarie's 4 May Proclamation was called upon anew to authorize the armed reprisal of the defendants (although no mention was made of the conciliatory proposals, such as they were).[44] In confirming the technical means of implementing the earlier Proclamation, witness William Cox confirmed that as a magistrate in 1816 "a military guard had been placed at his disposal" and that parties always had a "Magistrate at their head . . . and the settlers did never attack the black natives alone without a Magistrate." Moreover, "there have been no depredations, by the natives, on this [Sydney/eastern] side of the mountains, since the promulgation of that Regulation in 1816." In contrast, to the west of the mountains in the Bathurst districts, "outrages" had become more frequent in the last eight months, and in his opinion "resistance is justifiable." Cox spoke particularly for prisoner Johnson's "humane and unblemished character," adding that it "never was usual to fire upon the natives, unless in such emergencies as called for the interposition of the Executive, and times like the present."

Attorney-General Saxe Bannister and Chief Justice Francis Forbes both rejected the contention that the defendants' liability could be alleviated under the 1816 Proclamation. Saxe Bannister argued that, as only the present circumstances of the case under consideration could be considered, the earlier Proclamation did not apply. In summing up the case for the jury, Forbes observed "with all the due deference to the Authority from whence such edicts issue, that no Proclamation could furnish any protection to individuals committing outrages upon the natives of the Colony." Chief Justice Forbes, like Saxe Bannister, in any case doubted that the evidence supported a plea of self-defense. He considered that the immediate circumstances

> were sufficient to warrant the act, as it would have been too late to seek for that protection and assistance which they might otherwise have obtained. But, looking upon the subjects that had fallen victims, it seemed strange that these poor women should only have been killed.

Forbes advised the jury that it was for them to decide "whether the prisoners had acted with sufficient authority, or otherwise." After briefly retiring, the jury delivered a verdict of not guilty.

On 14 August, Governor Brisbane delivered his own Proclamation advising that legalized repression was in effect in the Bathurst Districts. Like his predecessor, Brisbane set out exactly how relations between settler and Aboriginal peoples and laws would be ordered and why the use of violence was "necessary . . . in Order to restore Tranquility."[45] On this occasion however—and perhaps alert to his responsibility to establish the institutions and practices of civil government or to the importance of seeking to indemnify the severity of his actions—Brisbane authorized a declaration of martial law. Despite its own uncertain legal grounding, it was nevertheless more robust than claims of settler self-defense.[46] No matter what the legal basis of his authority, the context and effects of his decision were similar, and this new proclamation effectively replicated in Wiradjuri country other Aboriginal peoples' lived experience of how they would be addressed by colonial law during the settlement of the Cumberland Plain.

Brisbane proclaimed that the "ABORIGINAL NATIVES of the Districts near Bathurst" had "for many Weeks past" indiscriminately attacked the stock station, putting some keepers "to cruel Deaths, wounding Others, and dispersing and plundering the Flocks and Herds; themselves not escaping sanguinary Retaliations." Although the ordinary powers of the civil magistrates had been "most anxiously exerted," they had failed to protect the lives of "HIS MAJESTY'S Subjects." Every conciliatory measure had also failed, such that "the

Slaughter of Black Women and Children, and unoffending White Men, as well as of the lawless Objects of Terror, continue to threaten the before-mentioned Districts."

Brisbane advised that "Experience" found that "the Use of Arms against the Natives beyond the ordinary Rule of Law in Time of Peace" would stop the mutual "Bloodshed" and "for this End, Resort to summary Justice has become necessary." On the basis of authority "vested by His Majesty's Royal Commission" and "in Order to restore Tranquillity," Brisbane declared "MARTIAL LAW TO BE IN FORCE IN ALL THE COUNTRY WESTWARD OF MOUNT YORK":

> And all Soldiers are hereby ordered to assist and obey their lawful Superiors in suppressing the Violences aforesaid; and all His Majesty's subjects are also called upon to assist the MAGISTRATES in executing such Measures, as any one or more of the said Magistrates shall direct to be taken for the same purpose, by such Ways and Means as are expedient, so long as Martial Law shall last; being always mindful, that the Shedding of Blood is only just, where all other Means of Defense or of Peace are exhausted; that Cruelty is never Lawful; and that, when personal Attacks become necessary, the helpless Women and Children are to be spared.

Within four days of this Proclamation a reward of 500 acres of land was offered to anyone "who will bring in SATURDAY, alive, to any Magistrate of the Territory."[47]

In contrast to Macquarie's swift communication to his superiors in London, Governor Brisbane waited almost three months to inform Earl Bathurst that martial law had been necessary in Wiradjuri country/Bathurst districts after "every other means of convincing the ill-judging Natives of the wrongs, they were committing, and our ample means of punishing them, had failed." Brisbane's dispatch was dated 3 November, by which time he was pleased also to report evidence of the success of the measure and that "the hostile Natives were hourly coming in to tender their submission and sue for peace and protection." Although still awaiting confirmation from Major James Thomas Morisset as to how many lives had been lost in the conflict at Bathurst, he had been anxious to advise the secretary of state of "a general view of the measure and its consequences" given that "the placing of a distant part of the Colony under Martial Law might be misrepresented and improperly understood."[48]

Martial law remained officially in force until 11 December when Brisbane once again proclaimed that "the judicious and humane Measure, pursued by the Magistrates assembled at Bathurst . . . have restored Tranquility without BLOODSHED." He would write more fulsomely to Earl Bathurst on the last day of 1824, explaining that martial law had regrettably been necessary "more from the want of legal intermediate powers to repress the aggressions of the Aborigines, than that of having recourse to all the powers conveyed by so strong a measure, which was sanctioned by the Attorney General and strongly recommended by all the Proprietors in that District of Country." He was now pleased to enclose the notice of repeal of martial law and to report that "during the four Months that Martial Law prevailed, not one outrage was committed under it, neither was a life sacrificed or even Blood spilt":

> This happy termination to the state of warfare may be mainly ascribed to the judgement, prudence, and moderation of Major Morriset, Commandant at Bathurst, together with the other Magistrates of that District, who themselves accompanied the Troops in their pursuit of the Aborigines.
>
> I found it necessary to augment the Detachment at Bathurst to 75 men; these were divided into various small parties, each headed by a Magistrate, and proceeded in different directions in towards the interior of the Country, and by previous arrangement were to form junctions at certain given points. This system of keeping these unfortunate People in a constant state of alarm soon brought them to a sense of their Duty, and I am most happy to have it in my power to report to Your Lordship that Saturday their great and most warlike Chieftain has been with me to receive his pardon, and that He, with most of His Tribe, attended the annual conference held here on the 28th Novr., which was more numerous than upon any former occasion.
>
> I hope on a future occasion to be able to give Your Lordship a pretty accurate return of all Individuals, who lost their lives during these disturbances, but hitherto we have not been able to ascertain it.
>
> I am digesting some plan for the bettering of the condition of the Aborigines, which I shall have the honor to submit for Your Lordship's consideration, and I trust it may meet Your sanction and approbation.[49]

Given the legal claim of *terra nullius*, it is painfully ironic just how explicitly official records explain the means by which exclusive colonial jurisdiction would come to prevail in the Australian colonies, and how particular modes of settler law would therefore be lived by Aboriginal and non-Aboriginal people in Wiradjuri country/Bathurst districts in the early decades of the nineteenth century. While Sir Thomas Brisbane was shortly to be relieved of his post—though this had nothing to do with his declaration of martial law—the new governor, Lt.-General Ralph Darling, would soon repeat the pattern Macquarie had earlier set in train. By 1826, while acknowledging that "some outrages, which have been committed by the Natives" were not entirely unprovoked,[50] he moved to approve settler self-defense[51] alongside the use of troops and mounted police against Aboriginal "aggressions" further to the north in yet another newly developing settlement project alongside the Hunter River. Attorney-General Saxe Bannister cautioned Darling about the need to proclaim martial law but the governor rejected the legal measure as unnecessary "to put down a few naked savages."[52] Darling's resolve had been fortified by the instructions he received on his appointment the previous year. Secretary of State Earl Bathurst appended the following advice "for his guidance" that "could not with propriety be embodied in your general Instructions":

> In reference to the discussions, which have recently taken place in the Colony respecting the manner in which the Native Inhabitants are to be treated when making hostile incursions for the purposes of Plunder, you will understand it to be your duty, when such disturbances cannot be prevented or allayed by less vigorous measures, to oppose force by force, and to repel such Aggressions in the same manner, as if they proceeded from any accredited State.[53]

Van Diemen's Land and South Australia, 1828–1840

The above discussion draws out some of the ways that official responses to disputes over the nature and mode of settlement came to distinguish the historical and legal experiences of Wiradjuri and other Aboriginal peoples from those of settlers as the "frontier" regions continued to expand in New South Wales.[54] Meanwhile, in other southeastern colonies, officials resorted to similar modes of legalized repression. In Van Diemen's Land (present-day Tasmania), Governor George Arthur approved coercive measures to dispossess Aboriginal peoples as settlement was extended throughout the 1820s. These culminated, too, in a formal proclamation of martial law—lasting from 1828 to 1830—and the subsequent removal of survivors to Flinders Island. Noted for his "humanitarian sentiments," Arthur remained committed to conciliation throughout, and despite the circumstances he oversaw, the governor's missives often reflected a kind of yearning for lawfulness, a hope that Indigenous peoples would choose to avoid the full force of settler law by simply submitting to their dispossession. In the latter stages of his strategy, he nailed illustrated proclamation boards to trees in an effort to convey his vision that the use of "illegal violence," whether by Aboriginal peoples or settlers, would be equally condemned by colonial law and that peaceful assimilation could still reasonably unfold in the island colony. Some years later, Arthur wrote of his regret that treaties had not been negotiated in Van Diemen's Land and strongly advocated their use if similar circumstances arose in the future.[55]

Within four years of the founding of the colony of South Australia in 1836, Governor George Gawler also chose to act according to the principles of martial law, while not making a formal declaration. Officials were already expressing concerns that settlers traveling overland from Port Phillip colony to the east (now known as Victoria) were becoming involved in "frontier conflicts" and when reports reached Adelaide that survivors of a shipwreck had met their deaths at the hands of Aboriginal people (in Ngarrindjerri country), Gawler sought legal advice from the chief justice about how best to bring them to justice. Charles Cooper declared, however, that as Aborigines in remote regions such as this had not submitted to British law, Gawler could not try them in the colonial courts. His opinion on the question of jurisdiction was shared in other contentious judgments during this period that challenged the assumptions of *terra nullius* and questioned the exclusiveness of British sovereignty.[56] Reluctant to issue an official proclamation for fear of deterring investment in the colony, Gawler wanted nevertheless to demonstrate the force of colonial authority even where settlement had yet to spread. He authorized a search party led by the commissioner of police, Major Thomas O'Halloran, to scour the countryside in search of perpetrators, hold a "trial in the field" for those accused, and perform exemplary executions before assembled onlookers. When Gawler's correspondence about the affair finally arrived in London, the Colonial Office's permanent under-secretary, James Stephen, was appalled. He advised the secretary of state: "It did not follow that because he could not try [the Aborigines] he might slay them."[57] The law officers were even more explicit. While rejecting Cooper's denial of jurisdiction, they stated that the summary execution of the supposed murderers "was contrary to Law; and that the legal character of the act [executed by O'Halloran and assisted by Gawler] was murder."[58]

LIVING TOGETHER LAWFULLY: APPRECIATING RESPONSIBILITY FOR LAW

Such lived histories of the imposition of colonial law demonstrate the importance of understanding what can happen "when sovereignty is the only language of authority and territorial sovereignty is the dominant mode of jurisdiction."[59] Settler colonial theory contends, too, that the normative linking of sovereignty to territory in settler societies exemplifies a governing logic of elimination that distinguishes settler colonialism from other imperial enterprises. Within Wolfe's schema, official efforts to deny the sovereignty of Indigenous peoples are seen to proceed in three interlocking phases, whether or not treaties were in play from the outset of settlement: the invasion of Indigenous lands (the subject of current concern), the incarceration of Indigenous peoples on reserves, and persistent attempts to assimilate them into the mainstream population.[60] In the Australian case, physical dispossession took place quite swiftly in the southeastern colonies with many Aboriginal people effectively coerced into living on government or mission reserves and their daily lives and future aspirations made subject to myriad administrative rules and regulations as the nineteenth century unfolded.[61]

Following the federation of the Australian colonies in 1901 and throughout the following century, such attention to mundane control at the local level was further supported by state-endorsed discriminatory policies ranging from constraints on civil and political rights to assimilationist legislation authorizing the removal of children and provoking further dislocation of families and disrupting connections to laws, lands, and cultures. Meanwhile, settler economic interest in gaining sovereignty over Indigenous lands was—and continues to be—bolstered by the force and ubiquity of particular racializing narratives whose basic precepts had been correlative with colonialism for centuries.

In the present, and as further discussed in chapter 5, deficit-based welfare models maintain their hold on public and political consciousness about so-called Indigenous issues in Australia, as elsewhere. This is despite repeated evidence, including in the reports and recommendations of government inquiries, that full redress of the complex legacies of historic injustices requires more than repeatedly implementing piecemeal policy-based initiatives alone.[62] The consequences of such failure to recognize and address structural injustices can be stark. For example, despite the comprehensive national review of the criminal justice system that was conducted from 1987 to 1991, the disproportionate representation of Indigenous peoples whether as offenders or victims is worsening: in 2018 Indigenous adults in Australia constituted 2 per cent of the population yet formed 28 percent of the overall adult prison population, and rates were much worse for women and children.[63]

The distinctively structural nature of colonial harm in settler societies continues to influence conditions of life in the present. Modes of governance and lived experiences have of course varied over time and place in Australia, including in response to hard-won social and political reforms, the formal rejection of *terra nullius*, the recognition of native title, and certain measures of self-determination.[64] Yet an overarching legal order that predominantly insists on exclusive sovereign authority necessarily limits prospects for permanently resetting the nature and quality of relations between Indigenous and non-Indigenous peoples.

For their part, as discussed in chapter 3, Indigenous peoples continue to practice sovereign autonomy, maintain connections to their laws, lands, and cultures, and hold out alternative understandings of how to live together justly in Australia despite the seemingly relentless inroads of settler discourse and practice that seek to render Indigenous jurisdictions "invisible to common law."[65] In terms of improving the quality of relations, Komumerri/Munaljahlai scholar Christine Black explains, too, why "young" European cultures need to understand "the sophistication of a continuous culture that goes back more than sixty thousand years":

> [A] newcomer needs to engage with the ancient history of the continent through the intellectual traditions of one or more of the two hundred clans in language, song, dance, and localized common law. Otherwise, newcomers are forever grafting themselves onto a landscape about which they have no real historical understanding, let alone a sustained relationship.[66]

As others have also observed, exercising responsibility for lawfulness requires settler states to facilitate ways for law to engage respectfully with Indigenous laws and jurisprudences while also finding its own "appropriate internal qualities . . . to meet the external realities it addresses."[67] This kind of official commitment is a necessary precondition to fostering more just and equitable relations within which settlers, as well as the state, assume responsibility for how their law was lived in the past, is lived in the present, and might be lived differently in the future.

A "living law" acknowledges its own history and particularity, it compels all of us whose national pasts were shaped through colonialism to ask: What do we know of our own law, of how we belong to that law, and of the different forms that our law might take? What is the importance of coming to know the history of our nation's law, the nature of its relationship with the laws of other peoples and jurisdictions, and the character of the justice it represents and upholds on our behalf? The next chapter elaborates the significance of these and related questions by offering a Wiradjuri perspective on questions of law, and responsibilities to law, before, during, and beyond the colonial encounter.

Chapter 3

HOLDING LAW

Bringing Indigenous and Non-Indigenous Laws into Relation

Nan's Story

Daphne Barnes (Nan) was born into the Wiradjuri world and the settler world on 4 September 1919. She was born on Wiradjuri country at Trangie, which by 1919 was a shared place given the assertion of settler jurisdiction in New South Wales. Nan was the daughter of Jesse Evans (Gran), a Wiradjuri woman, and a settler father (John Evans). Gran always said she been born into the Wiradjuri world on the banks of the Macquarie River (the Wiradjuri word is Wambool) at Dubbo on the day the first steam train came to town. That was in 1881. Gran was the Wiradjuri daughter of Elizabeth Baker, a Wiradjuri woman born on the Lachlan Valley Way in the 1860s. Nan passed on their Wiradjuri birthright—and ways of being and knowing Wiradjuri—to her eight Wiradjuri children with her settler husband Michael Barnes. My mother, Robyn McMillan (Barnes), was one of the eight Wiradjuri children. All of Nan's children were raised in Trangie—with brief periods of living in Wyong, New South Wales. My mother Robyn had five children. My siblings and I were raised and educated in Wiradjuri *and* settler law by Mum and Nan in Trangie.

Nan, and her mother before her, and her mother before her, were women of law. They *held* law, which was understood collectively but was the responsibility of the individual to know, hold, and practice. Law was always then in relation to those around them. As Wiradjuri women, they conducted lawful relations with other Wiradjuri. They also conducted lawful relations with non-Wiradjuri. Those relations with individual settlers (whom they ended up marrying) and the settler governing apparatus were attended to moment to moment. They could attend to the lawful relationship that was expected—and required—by the colonial encounter because they held law within themselves. It was their responsibility to their Wiradjuri world to not just hold law within but to act lawfully with others. They were, as individuals, a site of law, not merely an object or vessel to carry law.

This way of knowing how to be with law, how to hold law, and how to act lawfully was grounded in our Wiradjuri ontologies to place. We are a part of the law in totality. The Wiradjuri way of being and the Wiradjuri way of knowing law is that all things are connected. The place, the beings, the spirits are all connected and all things have a role and place in sustaining Wiradjuri law as a totally connected way of knowing. The authority to be Wiradjuri is understood through knowing that *all* things are connected. Wiradjuri cannot unknow that. Trying to unknow this disturbs the very Wiradjuri ontologies that bind the Wiradjuri world together in total. To know and hold Wiradjuri law is be constantly grounded in that way of knowing. That way of knowing means that we can *only* be with Wiradjuri law by holding and practicing law in each one of us; every "thing" does its part to maintain and sustain Wiradjuri law. So, when Wiradjuri people hold law, they are practicing law. It is the responsibility of Wiradjuri beings to hold law as individuals. Holding law as individuals completes Wiradjuri law. It is the responsibility of Wiradjuri people, post the colonial encounter, to practice and be in relation with settlers and settler law.

Nan was evidence of the practice of this permanent relationality. Daphne Barnes was more than just my grandmother. My grandmother was more than just an Aborigine. She was born into and with different laws. She was a Wiradjuri woman of law from birth and she existed with the law of the settler, even though the settler law tried to place her outside of its remit. Australian settler law could not know that it existed, and continues to exist, alongside Wiradjuri law. And yet settler law exists alongside all Indigenous nations' laws, and there are many.

Thus, the explanation of the connection with and between a Wiradjuri and settler past highlights that—for my family—law can only be relational. How we got to know Wiradjuri law and settler law was a practical reality. That reality was experienced day to day, moment to moment, as a way of being. We have never had to privilege one over the other. They exist within us as a way of being and therefore knowing. We have shared and practiced this relationality. We can be Wiradjuri *and* settler. These things are not dependent on each other to *be*. Nor are we hybridized as ontologies. They are distinct and separate ways of knowing and of being at law. The relationality between them is a practice of laws, and we are required to attend to this lawfulness by acknowledging that we cannot know settler law and ways of knowing by being a settler. We can only know how to be in a lawful relationship to settler law through our birthright and ontological connection to place through our Wiradjuri law.[1]

Like all Aboriginal people of Australia, the encounter of laws in 1788 established a permanent relationality of laws between Indigenous law and settler law. The relationality exists only because the settler exists *and* the Aborigines exist. The practice of the relationality is evident in the way in which Aboriginal people have conducted their lawful relationship with the settler since the encounter. However, Aborigines and settler have only existed in Australia since 1788. What is known for both Aboriginal people and settlers, as a matter of fact and of law, is that Aboriginal peoples were not a creation of their colonization. The Wiradjuri world that my Nan was born into and lived with was not dependent on settler law. There can be no doubt that settler law (and its way of knowing) impeded practices of Wiradjuri law. However, those interruptions did not impede how Wiradjuri people can know and practice Wiradjuri law. Thus, as a matter of fact and of law, the colonial encounter created a permanent relationality for settler law and Indigenous law(s), which includes our ways of knowing.

However, the settlers have not always acted as though their law was in relationship to my Wiradjuri ancestors. Why I focus on my grandmother as a woman of law is that during her lifetime she was treated physically, socially, and lawfully as being incapable of being *with* settler law.

For most of her life, the settler state saw her as "only" an Aborigine. She was placed outside of settler law and seen to not be capable of ever being able to hold settler law unconditionally, as this was only an expectation and requirement of people born into settler law. Not only did settler law see her as "merely" an Aborigine, she and all her family before and after her were treated as such. This means that the settlers, and their laws, were unwilling to recognize that she was a woman of law and that being a woman of law was inextricably linked and attached to how she could be seen as an Aborigine.

However, during her life, due to changes in settler law, she became "capable" of—and required to—hold settler law after 1965. That was her forty-seventh year of life—the very age that I am now. She was excluded from settler society from her birth in 1919 until "Aborigines" were granted participatory aspects of settler citizenship when

> in March 1962 the *Commonwealth Electoral Act* was amended to provide that Indigenous people could enroll to vote in federal elections if they wished. Unlike other Australians it was not compulsory for them to enrol.[2]

In the lead-up to the landmark 1967 referendum that amended two discriminatory clauses of the Australian Constitution, Gran and Nan, and Mum for a lesser period, were active witnesses to how settler law constructed and pursued a lawful relationship with Indigenous peoples and law.[3] Their lived experiences of how settler law undertook its lawful obligation and responsibilities of recognizing and responding to the relationality that existed illustrated the unwillingness of the settler to understand that it was obligated to be in relation to Indigenous law. The promise of the 1967 referendum was a mixed set of messages, actions, and plans for Aboriginal and Torres Strait Islander peoples and settlers. In the decades leading toward the referendum, there had been many instances of the continuing demand and practice of Aboriginal and Torres Strait Islander peoples for lawful relations. These were political and legal mechanisms that were deployed within the settler legal system and within varying Indigenous nations. Political institutions (where the members were all Indigenous) emerged. The political voices that sought to represent Indigenous peoples and experiences often called for better treatment of Indigenous peoples as well as the continued demand for lawful relationships.

When Nan was talking about what the referendum meant to her she was pleased that the settler law could be good to itself—that the referendum was to be of benefit and use to "them." As she was grounded in her way of knowing and being, she was just going to do what she had always done: be in lawful relations with settlers. She was hopeful that settlers now could understand their responsibility to the lawful relationship by understanding that they were actually in one. This is the fact she had always known, that settlers were not respecting themselves or their law. But this was hopefully an opportunity for the settler to be good to itself.[4] Nan was clear that the "equality" that was promised was only half of the equation. Indigenous peoples had, since the colonial encounter, practiced "equality" within the lawful relationship. The settlers' legal structure was just catching up to what Indigenous peoples had already known, lived, and practiced.

The settlers' unwillingness to recognize their obligation obscures the requirements of the relationship they created at the colonial encounter. This relationship that my ancestors had to live with remains part of their Wiradjuri lawfulness, as they had to meet this ambivalence.[5] Wiradjuri people had to participate in this ambivalence, not as a response to it, but as a necessary requirement of living up to their lawful relationship with the settlers. Because even though Nan was not considered a person of law in settler law, she was and maintained her position as a woman of law in the Wiradjuri way. She also acted as a reference point for how settlers understood their part of this relationality, in the way settler law and individuals treated her.

* * * *

This chapter focuses on the potentialities for both structural injustice and structural justice that are enabled through the "meeting of laws" symbolized by the colonial encounter. Through exploring and knowing Daphne's (Nan's) life, it is possible to see how a life of law can be lived relationally between settler law and Indigenous law. Her story, however, also raises similar questions to those posed at the end of the previous chapter about how settler law too can be known and can know itself to be in relation with Indigenous laws. It explicates the significance of the colonial encounter as establishing a permanent relationality between different systems of Indigenous and settler law. We acknowledge the structural injustice created by the Australian settler state's failure to understand its relationality to already existing Indigenous systems of law, as well as opening out the possibilities of doing so that remain.

We argue that there are possibilities of structural justice and lawful relations that can be found in the colonial encounter, as an enduring encounter between different legal systems and peoples that still exist and continually come into contact with one another.[6] The constant activity of these systems being in relation with each other may hold the prospects and possibilities of where structural injustice—continually occurring—is one site of transition to more just relations. Such structural justice is realized, and practiced, when the structures and the people that benefit from the structures reconcile that their law is in relation to and exists with Indigenous laws. These structures and people must recognize that their own continued presence can only be *with* Indigenous peoples. This includes an appreciation of the fact that Indigenous laws have never existed within their colonial framework, but alongside and independent to it. Such recognition creates a practice of meeting places—moment to moment—by making individual and structural ways of knowing how to be in *that place, their place,* as one of relationship and relationality to Indigenous peoples. It is an acknowledgment that their existence is *with* Indigenous peoples and not over them.

This will enable a further recognition that not only the structures of the colonial legacy have the obligation to be in relation to Indigenous peoples, but that individual people (individual settlers) also must conduct themselves as agents of the relationship. The state alone does not carry the obligation of the relationship—so too must the people. Equally, Indigenous people—as law holders—have always conducted themselves *as* law holders, and therefore in relationship with not only the structures of the settler state but also with settlers themselves as holders of settler law. The quality of the conduct of the relationship is then measurable and demonstrative of the lawful relationship itself.

To that end, the following discussion emphasizes the significance of the fact that there was a "before" colonization that gave way to an encounter.[7] In so doing, it explores how, at different points in time, it might be possible for Indigenous and non-Indigenous peoples to establish lawful relations through turning such an oppressive encounter between different laws into an expansive "meeting place" between them.

ENCOUNTER—COMING INTO RELATION

When the colonial state seeks to acquire new territories, it creates (and maintains) an encounter and meeting place of laws. The encounters between Indigenous populations and the colonial state that result are not contained or confined within one legal system or order "of law," but exist as relations *between* legal orders of different origins. Those different ways of knowing, those particular orders, are maintained, despite historical denials by one legal system of the full value, or even the very existence, of the other. Thus, colonialism can be understood as creating an environment—in the present—in which these distinct orders are always in relation to each other, rather than as simply producing the predominance of one order over the other. Both legal systems (Indigenous and colonial)—as matters of fact—*existed* prior to the colonial encounter.

Such "meetings of law" are common within and between legal systems. In national federal systems, for example, there is a specific requirement for a relationality between the laws of the provinces, territories, and the federal government in Canada; the fifty states of the union of the United States of America and the federal government; and the states, territories, and the Commonwealth of Australia government. The relationality of different legal systems is also a founding principle of the international legal order, which requires a recognition of the coexistence and interaction of laws. Moreover, and importantly, the colonial endeavor asked a question of relationality: legally, regarding particular countries, it asked whether there was a legal system already in that place that the colonial laws must relate to. If the answer was affirmative, the modes of acquisition that existed in international law required certain practices of making the existing and new legal systems relate.

When the continent that is now called "Australia" was colonized by the British Crown in 1788, the encounter inherently created many possibilities for lawful relationships with the Indigenous peoples who since time immemorial have been in lawful relation with their Country.[8] Indigenous peoples are much more than custodians of their Country. They are part of it. They form part of the law, which is the connection of all things. As seen through Nan's story, it is their very existence that makes Indigenous peoples holders of law. Accordingly, from the moment of first encounter in 1788, Indigenous peoples necessarily became—in law—in relationship with the settlers and their law. The settlers, on the other hand, did not understand themselves as required by their law to be in formal lawful relationships with Indigenous peoples and law(s). That is, because the possibility of relationship between colonial laws and the laws of Indigenous peoples and nations in Australia was overtly denied through the application of the doctrine of *terra nullius*, there is no history of treaty-making. This doctrine, which prevailed in Australia up until 1992, allowed the colonial power to take new territory on the basis that the land was empty of human capacity to govern ("belonging to no-one"). The doctrine was applied to Australia on the assumption that the Aboriginal people of the place were so low on the scale of "civilization"—and thereby governing capabilities—that the British deemed the place to be an empty land for the purpose of being *required* to treat with them.

The consequence of the application of the doctrine was that the settler state willfully failed to recognize Aboriginal peoples and nations as holders of law, as peoples and nations with existing legal systems that must continue to exist alongside the British legal system. From the perspective of settler law, in its application of *terra nullius*, in Australia, there was nothing—no law—and therefore *nothing* to share and *no-one* to share it with. According to settler law, settler law was the only law. This was not true and Australian settler law eventually, and very belatedly through the 1992 *Mabo* judgment, admitted for itself its error in this regard.[9] This long-held and willful denial to accept Aboriginal peoples as holders of law therefore impeded the development of structures—and more expansive ways of knowing the new place (for the British)—that could recognize and practice the relationship of laws. Instead, settlers and settler laws actively pushed Indigenous peoples outside of the scope of their law (and its protections). This was an official rejection (by settlers) of the prospect of lawful relations in the present (their present, now our past), and a disregard to the impact of this on the future of lawful relations.

The continued application and adherence to the doctrine has also impeded settler knowledge and legal acknowledgment of their existence in Australia as being in relationship with what was here before—and continuing. Individual settlers—who did not know that they were responsible as individuals to be in lawful relations with Indigenous peoples—dealt with Indigenous peoples with impunity and outright hostility. Without their being lawfully responsible for the relationship between Indigenous and non-Indigenous peoples and laws, there was an incapacity in settler law. This incapacity is reflected in the failure of individual settlers to appreciate that the colonial encounter *requires* ongoing lawful relationships. Thus, from the moment of encounter, the colonial structure of law in Australia has impeded the meeting places of law between colonial subjects and Indigenous peoples.

On the other hand, in this encounter, Indigenous peoples were simply extending their ability to conduct lawful relations with different sovereigns. This conception (and practice) was a rejection of invasion, which also necessitated adaptive strategies to maintain distinct ways of knowing. Indigenous nations have always practiced lawful relations between themselves and had negotiated sharing places of common interest among sovereigns. The development and adjustments of sharing places of law and coexisting jurisdictions was practiced among Indigenous peoples and polities both before and after the colonial encounter. These prior experiences were translated into sharing place with the settler. Yet such sharing was never understood as ceding authority.

Settlers, however, had *no* prior way of understanding Indigenous sovereign concepts and practices of sharing place at the moment of encounter, when settler law itself was unwilling to share place. The colonial project tried, and continues to try, to insist that Indigenous legal orders are only able to exist within the colonial legal system. This is wrong at settler law, wrong in fact, and wrong in practice. This is where the conflict between Indigenous law and colonial law has arisen. The problem that remains, however, is that the denial of the lawful relationship that was required by the colonial encounter has affected the relationship into the present. In the Australian case, when the laws of the Indigenous peoples and colonizers came into the same permanent orbit, there was a requirement that structures could recognize and make active the relationship must be developed. That is, that the colonial structures that emerged in the "new" place were required to do so with the express understanding and consciousness of the Indigenous relationship—as a fundamental principle of *how* they must mature. Yet this is also where in the Australian case (as discussed in the previous chapter) structural injustices were identified, initiated, and embedded. Instead of dealing with the requirements for relationship between laws and people that were already there, the Australian colonial state eventually moved to develop structures and ways of knowing and being in place that created structural injustices to Indigenous peoples.[10] Those structural injustices resulted in the immediate and continuing harm of Indigenous peoples; but the structural injustice has also affected the settler state's law for itself. The settler state and its peoples are now not familiar with its own system of laws as one of being in relation with Indigenous laws, and that has also served as a structural injustice to settlers in the present. There is a requirement for settler polities to appreciate how they and their law came to the present. It is through such an appreciation that they may also become responsible for their own law, as holders of settler law, and participate in the possibility of a lawful future.

MEETING PLACE—BRINGING INTO LAWFUL RELATION

If there is a claim that the colonial encounter constitutes a site of a structural injustice, there must also be an acknowledgment that the meeting places between laws that were created by this encounter remain as possible sites of structural justice. In the absence of formal, treaty-based relationships in Australia, Indigenous peoples have maintained a lawful stance that sovereignty has never been ceded. The consistent position of Indigenous peoples has been seen by settlers—and settler law— as merely a political discourse. However, it is not a political discourse at all. It is a legal one. This is particularly true given the High Court of Australia's recognition in 1992 in the *Mabo* case that Australia was not (in fact and law) *terra nullius* and not subject to correct modes of lawful acquisition of territory given the already existing Indigenous population. So where do the lawful relationships that Indigenous peoples have long demanded (and practiced) reside? Where are the meeting places? Where may the relationships rest—with the structure of law or with its individual citizens existing and acting as law holders? These are the questions we seek to engage with in this section, through a consideration of some of the meetings points of law since colonization and the possibilities that emerge through a more holistic understanding, on behalf of settler and non-Indigenous societies, for what it might mean to hold law and take responsibility for lawful relations.

CONTINUAL MEETING PLACES IN THE COLONIAL CONTEXT

After the initial colonial encounter, there has still been a constant and consistent meeting of laws in Australia and an overt witnessing of the relationship between settler and Indigenous law and ways of knowing. Among Indigenous communities, there was an enduring political imperative to demand that settlers act lawfully in their relations. This imperative was also traceable to an obligation of Indigenous peoples themselves to practice lawful relationships. As such, Indigenous political activity and demands for recognition of the relationality of laws in Australia were *not* demands for a settler recognition of Indigenous existence. They were part of the ongoing fulfilment by Indigenous leaders of the ongoing obligation on settlers and Indigenous communities alike to be in legal relation with one another. These were relations therefore of sovereigns fulfilling their obligations to the colonial encounter, rather than of the subservience of one party to another. We can see this demonstrated vividly in the statements by and petitions of Coranderrk residents to the 1881 Coranderrk Inquiry (discussed in our introduction) and in the letters by Kenyans to the colonial administration and in the testimony and affidavits by the Aboriginal Embassy activists (discussed in chapter 6).

Of note also are the actions of Yorta Yorta man William Cooper, founder and leader of the Australian Aborigines League. On behalf of the League, he petitioned the King and the Commonwealth and State crowns in 1937. Additionally, Cooper also called for a "Day of Mourning" on the 150th anniversary of settlement.[11] Like many moments of the demand for lawful relations, Cooper's petition was not one of begging. Nor was his petitioning only directed at the colonizer. He was sending messages to all Aboriginal people. A simplistic reading of Cooper's petitioning and calls for a "Day of Mourning" as only addressed to the settler state completely obscures the activity of his individual responsibility to his own law and to act lawfully in relation to the settler. He was in fact demonstrating *how* to execute the individual's responsibility to participate and be active in the lawful relationship that exists between Indigenous peoples and the settler.

Cooper was also demonstrating his status as a sovereign leader and law holder in who and where he petitioned, namely the monarch (a sovereign), the Commonwealth (a sovereign), and the state governments (also sovereigns). His actions are evidence that Aborigines understood where and how to engage sovereign to sovereign. Moreover, he was not just appealing to the settler state as a total entity. He was demonstrating that he understood the settler structure as a series of different but linked jurisdictions that operated over the same place and space simultaneously. This was also the way Indigenous peoples had always had a practice of sharing place while at the same time making distinctive sovereignties. The sophistication of Cooper's political and legal demands is evident here. He was acting lawfully as a leader of his nations and the collective Aboriginal peoples. These continued reminders and calls to arms were signs that sovereignty was not (and will never be) ceded. Cooper stated this as a law holder acting as a sovereign with other sovereigns and as an individual practicing his obligation to pursue lawful relationships.[12]

THE INDIVIDUAL AS LAW HOLDER AND MEETING PLACE

The possibilities of such meeting points transforming from signs of enduring structural injustice to steps toward a structural justice depend on a recognition by non-Indigenous communities of the status of the individual as a holder of law. Through a greater appreciation of Indigenous ontologies, the individual can be more fully seen as a jurisprudent and as a site for a potential meeting place of laws, capable of maintaining lawful relations and pursuing a structural justice. This raises the question of what it means to "hold" law. What is the difference between thinking of one's relation to law as inherently individual and thinking of one's relation to law in more detached terms? These questions are significant for enhancing understanding of the ways in which Indigenous and non-Indigenous peoples in past and present societies live with settler colonialism and for conceiving and practicing alternative ways toward a just future.

The question of how one may hold law—as an individual—is a difficult one in settler societies given the way that the vast majority of people have come to know their own law. For the majority, the ways of knowing law are rooted in how the structure of colonial law disavows the individual of their responsibilities as holders of law since the moment of the colonial encounter. In Western legal thought, the concepts of "the Crown" and "the law" have been privileged to exist beyond the corpus of a human actor.[13] A belief that law and jurisdiction exists outside of the individual human body has allowed two perceptions to prevail: first, that the "law" and "the Crown" are beyond the reach of any human actor, and, second, that the responsibility of the practice of law and the behaviors of the Crown is a metaphysical one and beyond the responsibility of the individual subject.

This aspect of the devolution of authority and responsibility "up" to the Crown—or any other recognized sovereign authority—has in the Western tradition laid the foundation for abdication of the responsibility of the individual invader to an ongoing lawful relationship with any colonized peoples and, in particular, Indigenous peoples. Moreover, Aileen Moreton-Robinson also observes how the separation of body from place invokes deep-seated and deeply held views that "place" can only be "owned" or "possessed," that it is only through the laws of possession of place that subjects exercise their legal rights.[14] Those legal rights, however, are granted by the state. There is no conception, whether in settler law, legal theory, or political theory, that situates the individual citizen as the holder of law. Rather, the individual only has rights of participation within a legal framework.

Through Nan's story, this recognition of place within a Western legal order—and the lack of acceptance of lawful responsibilities of the individual—can be seen to be in stark contrast to that of the ontological connections of the Indigenous peoples to not only place but also to their place *within* that place. Further, that the place within place is conceived ontologically as being one of responsibilities "to" law, rather than a sense that "law" is something that happens to them, from outside their corpus.[15]

A greater appreciation of the responsibility of the individual to participate in lawful relations with Indigenous peoples (and vice versa) may illuminate how structural justice can be pursued through the establishment of sustainable lawful relations between Indigenous peoples and settlers. The settler state has an obligation to ensure past injustices committed against Indigenous Australians and their antecedent legal orders have the possibility of being recognized, addressed, and redressed. This obligation can never be implemented if it is not accompanied by the objective of connecting those past wrongs with present experiences of Indigenous peoples.

Structural justice demands that historic wrongs committed by the nation-state in the name of "the people" toward Indigenous peoples during the colonial projects be identified by the present day for the possibility of better future relationships. Such processes can enable the individual citizen to be informed, not only of the wrong itself but also its status as a barrier to lawful relationships that has impeded the present conduct of lawful relations. This historic impediment of the present must be made clear to the individual citizen and law holder, so that the individual citizen can influence their own future lawful relations with Indigenous peoples and, as collectives, influence the nation-state in carrying out its lawful relations with Indigenous peoples. Meanwhile, it is Indigenous peoples who have the right to determine what justice is in relation to these wrongs and the site at which it is to be done.

Situating the individual as a holder of rights that are only expressed with respect to the human dimension of law is not something new. However, situating the individual as a possible site of justice for Indigenous peoples and their ongoing relationship with the state can be understood as a future possibility. The individual holds a crucial role of recognition of responsibilities to ongoing injustices experienced by Indigenous peoples due to prevailing state structures. These are not solely discharged through their participation in democratic institutions but through their intention to act lawfully with respect to the structural injustices that presently exist between Indigenous peoples and the state. This role goes beyond the identification of historic injustices toward Indigenous peoples by the state. It is imperative that the individual citizen must be able to act, as an individual, as a mechanism through which justice can be at least—in the present—articulated by and with Indigenous peoples.

QUALITY OF LAWFUL RELATIONS—BEING IN LAWFUL RELATION

In the 1992 *Mabo* case, the highest court in Australia recognized the relationality of different laws that had existed in Australia since British settlement. At the state level, this has not been reflected in substantive political, legal, social, structural, and economic change.[16] So once there is recognition of the requirement for lawful relation, how is that to be conducted and evaluated? For Nan, the question of how settler law could be good to itself was one that rested with individuals. For it was not the state that was committing despicable acts (often criminal) on Aboriginal and Torres Strait Islander peoples—it was individual members of society. Those individuals in many (though not all) respects operated *with* lawful authority granted by the governing apparatus. However, they acted as if law was given to them or bestowed upon them. This is the paradigm that Nan and many people of past generations could not work out. Their appeals to settler "office holders" were not calls on the settler legal system itself. They were calls to these individuals as holders of their law. This is an important, yet nuanced, distinction.

The significance of individuals in the quest for a structural justice is also illustrated by the concrete acts of individual settlers since colonization who sought to influence their law. These individuals did not hold law, but simply sought to shift their laws and their operations (or, as discussed briefly in the previous chapter, at least acknowledge its inequity). Returning to our first case study of the 1881 Coranderrk Inquiry again, of note were the actions of settlers Ann Bon and John Green. Ann Bon was especially important in exerting her influence so that the Parliament of Victoria instigated a formal inquiry in 1881. How Ann Bon is recalled in the settler archive has varied. This is how she is described by the Australian Dictionary of Biography:

> Devoutly religious, imperious in her manner, a loving but stern mother, an autocrat with her domestic staff and station hands, Ann Bon held firmly to her course even if it meant defying authority. Lonely and in many ways shy, she made few close friends, but to those in need, especially the Aboriginals, she showed compassion and generosity. Dispossessed members of the Taungerong tribe had found a refuge at Wappan; in the 1860s they were resettled at Cor-

> anderrk near Healesville, but on their annual return for shearing they kept Mrs. Bon informed of their treatment by the Board for the Protection of the Aborigines. Her home at Kew was a refuge for the sick and needy and she regularly visited Aboriginal patients in Melbourne hospitals. When her efforts to provide jobs and clothing were rebuked as "interference" in 1879, she began to support Aboriginals who opposed protection board policy, notably Thomas "Punch" Bamfield, henchman to William Barack. Using her influence with leading Presbyterian clergymen and politicians, she persuaded the government to investigate conditions at Coranderrk in 1881; she accepted membership of the inquiry and succeeded in reversing policy. The antagonism of officials prevented her appointment to the protection board but she continued her direct intercessions with government members. In 1904 she became a board-member and attended regularly until 1936. She maintained a voluminous correspondence with Aboriginals all over Victoria, remaining uniquely responsible to them; she earned reprimands for "disloyalty" in 1921, 1923 and 1936 when she protested to the minister that her colleagues' decisions had caused injustice or hardship.[17]

This description perfectly captures how settler law placed confines on the ability of the individual to act with law and impede the requirement for lawful relations. Ann Bon influenced others that were *office holders* (not law holders)[18] to conduct an official and lawful inquiry into the relationships that were being threatened at Coranderrk. What was initially challenged *within* Ann Bon—the individual—was that her law was incapable of filling its own obligations to itself, and this was manifest in the treatment of the Aborigines at the Coranderrk Reserve. Thus, she was a holder of law; however, she could not express that at the time. It is simply unattainable in the settler system *unless* the individual is deemed to be conferred with such a position (as, for example, a legislator).

Yet Ann Bon did directly influence the law. And Indigenous residents of Coranderrk were not deterred from asserting their understanding and demands for the lawful relationship that existed between them and the settlers. The final petition stated:

> We want the Board and the Inspector, Captain Page, to be no longer over us. We want only one man here, and that is Mr. John Green, and the station to be under the Chief Secretary; then we will show the country that the station could self-support itself.[19]

The Coranderrk residents did not want the Central Board for the Protection of Aborigines to have "control" over their lives. Instead, their demand was to be in a lawful relationship with people that were office holders. This was because relationships were conducted and practiced by people *of law*. As the Protector of Aborigines, John Green was in a position where he was seen as holding the law of the settlers and as an individual could influence the practice of settler law.

Like Ann Bon, Mr. John Green—as founder and first manager at the Coranderrk Reserve (and former Inspector of the Central Board for the Protection of Aborigines)—understood the requirement to have a lawful relationship with the Aboriginal peoples. He did everything he could—through practice—to ensure that his law and its movement toward the removal of the Aborigines could not be enacted. Unlike Bon, who influenced her law through connections and operation of laws, Green refused to conduct his law through the act of resignation from his official post. His influence was not about others or the operation of his law, but about his individual capacity not to enact it, for its enactment would be a breach of his obligations to the Aboriginal peoples that he was in lawful relations with. And there are accounts that Aborigines understood that they were in relation with him:

> The Coranderrk residents valued these qualities in Green and described their relationship with him in terms of friendship and collaboration. "Mr Green is very neighbourly," Thomas Bamfield informed the Inquiry, and "Mrs Green was like a mother to all the natives, and was good to the women when they were confined, and she used to look after the sick."[20]

The relationship expressed by the Aboriginal people at Coranderrk was understood well through the practice of Mr. Green and his wife. When other settlers and office holders of the colony were trying to influence Mr. Green he refused to abide by those directions. Instead, he publicly called out the seemingly unlawful pressure and stated that he would not follow the law, and abuse or damage his relationship with the Aboriginal people of Coranderrk. Moreover, he was using legal process to state that his law was an anathema to itself. He could not follow his law because it was wrong for itself and would be incapable of being in the lawful relationship with the Aborigines that he practiced. He said at the Inquiry:

> I may state that on one occasion Mr [Robert] Smyth [then the Board Secretary] came to Coranderrk, and told me that there were influences being brought to bear upon the Board and the Government to have the Aborigines removed from Coranderrk . . . and he believed that they would be well inclined to give way.
>
> But, he said, "If we give up the station we will be handsomely paid for our improvements. . . ." He [also] said: "Of course we know we cannot move them without you. You know you can easily move them."
>
> I stood and listened to him. I said, "Mr Smyth, I know that I could move the Aborigines if I could assure them it was for their good to do so, because I could speak to them as men and brothers and I know they would go, but I will not try—decidedly not."[21]

In 1992, individual legal officers of the High Court of Australia sought to influence (and make) settler law acknowledge and reflect its relationship to Indigenous laws. One century after the 1881 parliamentary Coranderrk Inquiry, there was a distinct alteration to how settler law should be in relation with Indigenous law. It took an individual—Eddie Mabo—to alter what had been 204 years of incorrectly applied settler law to this relationship. Moreover, it meant that each person who for 204 years had developed ideologies, practices, and structures to subvert the lawful relationship would now have to look to their own behaviors and attitudes toward Indigenous peoples and Indigenous laws. The legitimacy of the settler to their place within the territory was unsettled. Settler law was now unrecognizable to itself without first recognizing that a lawful relationship must exist with Indigenous peoples for it to exist.

Justice Gerard Brennan, as a single justice of the High Court of Australia, had been conferred the responsibility, like all judicial officers, to state what the law is. They do not hold law, they only state what the law is. The law—according to Justice Brennan in the *Mabo* decision in 1992—had been applied incorrectly. He said that settler law could no longer deny that Indigenous peoples' previous normative systems of laws and customs preexisted and survived the acquisition of British sovereignty. This means that the settler legal system was bound (as a matter of its own existence) to be in relation with Indigenous people. Justice Brennan stated in *Mabo*:

> Whatever the justification advanced in earlier days for refusing to recognize the rights and interests in land of the indigenous inhabitants of settled colonies, an unjust and discriminatory doctrine of that kind can no longer be accepted. . . . It is contrary both to international standards and to the fundamental values of our common law to entrench a discriminatory rule which, because of the supposed position on the scale of social organization of the indigenous inhabitants of a settled colony, denies them a right to occupy their traditional lands.[22]

The relational aspect of the overturning of the doctrine of *terra nullius* can be seen in the following judgments of Justices William Deane and Mary Gaudron:

> It follows from what has been said in earlier parts of this judgment that the application of settled principle to well-known facts leads to the conclusion that the common law applicable to the Colony in 1788, and thereafter until altered by valid legislation, preserved and protected the pre-existing claims of Aboriginal tribes or communities to particular areas of land with which they were specially identified, either solely or with others, by occupation or use for economic, social or ritual purposes. Under the law of the Colony, they were entitled to continue in the occupation or use of those lands as the holders of a common law native title which was a burden upon and reduced the title of the Crown. . . . The combined effect of (i) the personal nature of those rights, (ii) the absence of any presumption of a prior grant to the Aboriginal title-holders, and (iii) the applicable principles of English land law were that native title would be extinguished by a subsequent inconsistent grant of the relevant land by the Crown which was not invalid on its face. That extinguishment would, however, involve a wrongful infringement by the Crown of the rights of the Aboriginal title-holders.[23]

Examples in settler history exemplify the confusion of the lawful relationships between settlers, settler law, and Indigenous peoples. The settlers do not see themselves, as individuals, as holders of law. Rather, some settlers may hold office that transacts law. It is this flaw in logic that allows individual settlers to be unthinking about their role in the lawful relationship with Indigenous peoples that the application of their law demands.

The role of the individual in influencing their law and legal system in pursuit of a just and lawful relationship with Indigenous peoples—as holding this law and these meeting spaces—cannot be undervalued. It is one way in which the "meeting of laws" facilitated through the colonial encounter can give rise to just and lawful relations rather than the contemporary situation of enduring structural injustice.

ENDURING RELATIONALITY AND THE POSSIBILITY OF MORE JUST RELATIONS

It is the enduring relationality between Indigenous and non-Indigenous laws in settler contexts like Australia that continues to hold the possibility of just relations. To this end, this chapter has demonstrated the inherent relationality of laws in settler colonial and postcolonial contexts, but also the structural injustice created through the ongoing failure of settler colonial law (in this case) to fully come to terms with this relationality. In explicating the relationality of laws, it has sought to provide practical insight for non-Indigenous peoples into what it means to engage with and between different worldviews and laws, thereby opening out onto a more substantive consideration of what a practice of structural justice may entail. It has also drawn out the meeting points between colonial and Indigenous laws and peoples that have unfolded in the Australian context throughout time that continue to speak powerfully to the possibility of more lawful relations in the past and in the present.

For non-Indigenous peoples and polities, a greater acknowledgment of and engagement with the enduring relationality of their own law may enable them to better know and understand their own law and be responsible for it. As with chapter 2, we posit that a move toward greater structural justice might be found in the potential for, and responsibility of, non-Indigenous peoples to think more reflexively and expansively about what it might mean to make a commitment to come more consciously into relation with Indigenous peoples, nations, and laws. This involves an engagement with their own past and present and can occur through official state structures as well as individual practice, enabling non-Indigenous peoples and polities to know their own law, as well as its positionality and its past. It is the central importance of the recognition of the colonial past to a practice of structural justice that we continue to consider in the next chapter—which stays in the contemporary moment, but considers the field of international criminal justice and the potential for law to more fully "bear witness" to the colonial past and its ongoing implications.

Chapter 4

CRIMES AGAINST HUMANITY

The Appreciability of Colonial Harm

> Impunity is no longer an option for the perpetrators of atrocious acts. Accountability for the gravest crimes has become a real possibility and, most importantly, a global expectation'[1]

> Confronting this world, the European nations sprawl, ostentatiously opulent. This European opulence is literally scandalous, for it has been founded on slavery, it has been nourished with the blood of slaves and it comes directly from the soil and from the subsoil of that underdeveloped world. The well-being and the progress of Europe have been built up with the sweat and the dead bodies of Negroes, Arabs, Indians, and the yellow races [*sic*]. We have decided not to overlook this any longer.[2]

At the moment, on the global stage, an international justice project is unfolding. It is premised, in part, on the notion that certain harms constitute crimes against humanity as a whole and as such must be addressed. Those harms that are deemed to be "*the most* serious crimes of concern to the international community,"[3] and hence the proper subject of international justice, are predominantly state crimes (crimes perpetrated by states, or state-like entities, against their own or other people) including genocide, crimes against humanity, war crimes, and aggression. Past impunity for these crimes is vehemently denounced by international criminal justice advocates and great emphasis is placed on the importance of acknowledging and redressing the crimes of the past, both to satisfy the demands of "justice" and to ensure the possibility of a less violent and injurious future.[4]

Given its commitment to acknowledging and redressing the most serious, large-scale, and state-implicated crimes, the sphere of international criminal justice appears as an ideal legal space in which colonial injustice—as large-scale, state perpetrated, and devastating harm, ironically justified in the name of humanity[5]—might be acknowledged and redressed in the present. Along with the practice of transitional justice, to be discussed in the next chapter, international justice offers a language and architecture through which the enduring structural violence of colonialism could be more comprehensively recognized and addressed. Thus, building on the explication in the last three chapters of the grave and enduring injustice of structural colonial harm and its continued nonacknowledgment, this chapter and the next turn respectively to consider the capacity of contemporary justice processes (namely international justice and transitional justice) to more justly and ethically *recognize* structural colonial harm and *address* it. This line of inquiry moves us from a close engagement with the particular legal order associated with settler colonialism (discussed in chapters 2 and 3) to broaden our gaze to consider both settler colonial and postcolonial legal and social orders (the latter in which there has been a notional shift, unlike in settler colonial contexts, from a situation of colonialism to *post*colonialism).

This chapter in particular considers the encounter between international criminal justice and colonialism. It focuses on two examples of this encounter: first, the meeting of law and colonialism in the work of the International Criminal Tribunal for Rwanda (1995–2015), and, second, the debates regarding the legislation of the crime of colonial domination in a proposed Draft Code of Offences Against the Peace and Security of Mankind (particularly those occurring from 1984 to 1995).[6] It considers how, with what commitment, and with what effects the colonial past surfaces, disappears, and resonates in the sphere of international criminal justice. As such, it is concerned with the *appreciability* of the colonial past and colonial harm in the present—and with the law's recognition of colonial injury, as both a prelude to legal redress and as an act of structural justice in its own right. The next chapter then engages more closely with the possibility of the practical use of law to advance a more comprehensive "justice-based" agenda of structural reform.

This chapter, however, argues that the question of how the colonial past appears and is framed discursively in the law is crucial to any consideration of the complex relation between law, colonialism, structural injustice, and the possibility of a structural justice. We establish questions of representation as central to both colonial harm and a practice of structural justice. In so doing, we are informed by the work of postcolonial theorists, critical criminologists, and cultural theorists who have underscored the profound significance of representation. Postcolonial theorists continue to draw attention to the ways in which colonial discourses can enable the obliteration of the identity of those about whom they speak;[7] form part of narcissistic attempts to deny the uniqueness of others in order to build an authoritative version of the colonial self;[8] and downplay the cultural and historical particularity of colonial knowledge as they are projected as objective and value-free.[9] Meanwhile, in other fields, criminologists have drawn attention to the unevenness of dominant socio-legal acknowledgments of harm—the way in which certain injustices, but not others, are publicly recognized as crimes.[10] And, as mentioned briefly in our book introduction, cultural theorist Judith Butler has powerfully underscored the importance of the cultural "frames" through which the suffering of others is represented that shape and constrain its affective and sociopolitical resonance.[11]

Drawing on Butler's analytical framework, in this chapter, we are thus interested in whether colonial injury can "be heard, read, seen, felt, and known" through and by international criminal justice, as well as taking up a criminological line of inquiry as to whether it can be "seen" and "known" specifically as an experience of harm and injustice.[12] We demonstrate that the colonial past does appear in both the Tribunal's work and the negotiations around the draft international criminal law code. Moreover, its structurally unjust nature is made apparent in the way that it is described. At the same time, however, the harmful character of colonialism, its potential status as a justiciable crime, and its implications for the present and future are downplayed and disavowed. So, colonialism is unjust, but not a crime. It is repudiated, but it is placed firmly in the past.

In the International Criminal Tribunal for Rwanda's judgments and materials, for example, the colonial past is not visible as an injustice but as an objective historical context that helps understand the criminalized injuries of the 1994 Rwandan genocide. Meanwhile, across both the Tribunal and International Law Commission deliberations, the enduring social, legal, and political implications of colonial history are occluded through its demarcation as a closed or completed event, separable from the present and the future. Represented and engaged with in this way, the event of colonialism is seen, yet its potentially criminal character and its hold on the present and the future remain beyond view.

As well as critiquing the restrictive character of existing modes of recognition of colonial harm, we also endeavor to think more creatively and expansively about how else international criminal justice may acknowledge and address the colonial past in the present. In line with our broader focus on potential ways forward within and despite structural colonial harm, this chapter emphasizes the importance of the enhanced appreciability of colonial harm and its specific characteristics in the present. We consider the potential for international criminal justice to more comprehensively "bear witness" to the crimes of colonialism, by recognizing its inherently harmful, unjust, and criminal nature, and its ongoing effects. This is an important, justice-based intervention that recognizes law's status as a powerful discourse, an authoritative statement of societal values and transgressions.[13]

THE INTERNATIONAL CRIMINAL TRIBUNAL FOR RWANDA: COLONIAL CONTEXTS AND CONTEMPORARY CRIMES

The International Criminal Tribunal for Rwanda (ICTR) was established in the wake of the 1994 Rwandan genocide. Authorized by the Chapter 7 powers afforded to the United Nations Security Council under the Charter of the United Nations (1945) to respond to "any threat to the peace, breach of the peace, or act of aggression," this Tribunal was ad hoc, or temporary, in nature. Formally operational in 1995, the Tribunal has now closed with remaining cases to be dealt with by a new international institution (the International Residual Mechanism for Criminal Tribunals). However, during its operation, the ICTR was based in Arusha, Tanzania, and was tasked with the prosecution and punishment of the leaders of the Rwandan genocide. Its jurisdiction was limited to genocide, war crimes, and crimes against humanity committed between 1 January 1994 and 31 December 1994, either within Rwanda or in neighboring countries if Rwandan nationals committed the alleged crimes.[14] The Tribunal therefore had a limited and presentist jurisdictional mandate, reflective of a more generalized contemporary focus of extant international and transitional justice initiatives, as discussed further in the next chapter.

Throughout its life, the ICTR has had a variable relationship with the Rwandan government, which first endorsed its creation and later contested its operation on various grounds, such as its prosecution of certain parties to the armed conflict that accompanied the genocide in Rwanda, the Tribunal's location, and its maximum penalty of life imprisonment.[15] Moreover, there have been serious critiques of the inaccessible and remote nature of the Tribunal and its work to the Rwandan people who were most affected by the crimes with which it is concerned. These were exacerbated by the late establishment of structures of outreach and communication of the court's activities within Rwanda itself.[16]

Despite its limited temporal mandate, through both its judgments and its other informational materials (such as timelines and videos on its website), the ICTR acknowledges the event of colonialism in Rwanda and its structural characteristics.[17] Thus, in the first judgment of the Tribunal, an early and prominent section of text is devoted to the "Historical Context of the Events in Rwanda in 1994," which recounts—with reference to expert testimony—the occurrence of German and then Belgian colonization of Rwanda, the country's slow transition to full independence, and the postcolonial political and social situation preceding the genocide.[18] This account of Rwanda's history is then referred to in subsequent judgments[19] and set out anew in others.[20] Such jurisprudence is accompanied by other material available on the ICTR website, such as a timeline of the Rwandan genocide (borrowed from the Outreach Programme on the Rwanda Genocide and the United Nations website), which begins its narration of this contemporary mass harm with an image of a nineteenth-century colonial map and the heading: "November 15, 1884: Rwanda is assigned to Germany as part of German East Africa."

In both the ICTR judgments and ancillary materials, there is an emphasis on the Belgian colonial period, which came after German rule when Belgium "inherited" Rwanda as part of the post–World War I redistribution of Germany's colonial conquests. The Belgian colonial period is highlighted on the basis that Belgian colonial powers created, or at least shaped, the ethnic divisions and dynamics of Rwandan society that informed the genocide. In line with dominant academic and Rwandan accounts of the genocide,[21] the judgments (relying on the expert testimony of Rwandan and non-Rwandan academics) explain that prior to Belgian colonization divisions between those subsequently known as Tutsis and Hutus existed, but these distinctions were social and political rather than ethnic or racial in nature, and were malleable in the sense that people could move from one group to another. On this historical view, Tutsis were those Rwandan people associated with the aristocratic and cattle-owning class, while Hutus subsisted as cultivators. However, it was with Belgian colonial rule that such social and political divisions were first formalized, and second ethnicized through their notation on the ethnic identity cards that every Rwandan was required to carry. It was the Belgian colonial powers that officially classified the Rwandan people into three categories—"Hutu," "Tutsi," and "Twa"—which were also then transformed from social and political identifiers to signs of ethnic status. It is these ethnic divisions and identity cards that continued in existence until the 1994 genocide in which Tutsis and moderate Hutus were deliberately targeted because of their "ethnicity," often identified through the ethnic identity cards that all Rwandans were mandated to carry.

The colonial past, and specifically Belgium's colonization of Rwanda, is therefore framed in the ICTR's judgments and accompanying materials as significant to the more recent occurrence of the 1994 genocide. As such, despite the ICTR's jurisdictional mandate, both German colonialism and Belgian colonialism are introduced into the sphere of visibility of international criminal justice. Moreover, the distinctively structurally unjust nature of Belgian colonial rule also becomes evident through judicial descriptions of the ethnic categorization system on which it was premised. In *Nahimana et al.*, the judges highlight the material consequences of this structure of ethnic classification, noting how it enabled both the "differential distribution of social and political privilege along ethnic lines" and "ethnic prejudice" in Rwanda.[22] Meanwhile, this role of the identity card system in enabling and perpetuating structurally unjust arrangements in Rwandan society is even more explicitly acknowledged in *Kayishema and Ruzindana* in which the judges observe that "[f]rom its inception, the identification card has been used to facilitate discrimination against one group or another in Rwanda, be it in the implementation of an ethnic based quota system in educational and employment opportunities or in implementing a policy of genocide as was done in 1994."[23] The Belgian system of ethnic categorization is thus elaborated as a sign and means of a national system of political, social, economic, and ethnic inequality, through which certain groups in Rwandan society—on the basis of discriminatory and discredited biological race science—were respectively privileged and subjugated in ways that had negative implications for both.[24]

Moreover, it is not only the structural injustices of Belgian colonial rule that can be discerned through the ICTR judgments and secondary materials. Tribunal depictions of Rwandan history can also be read as testaments to the structural injustice that defined and resulted from an unequal system of international law and governance that only recognized the sovereignty of certain states that were, in turn, permitted to deal with other states as their own property to dispose of and dispossess as they saw fit. The chronological narration of the Rwandan genocide contained in the timeline on the ICTR website, for example, reveals (albeit perhaps not intentionally) a seamless continuity of colonial dispossession that had many disastrous stages, starting first with the events of "November 15, 1884" when "[a]t the 1884 Berlin Conference, the territory of Rwanda was assigned to Germany as part of German East Africa" and then proceeding to "October 20, 1924" when "Belgium is granted League of Nations mandate to govern Ruanda-Urundi" to "December 13, 1946" at which time "Ruanda-Urundi became a UN trust territory governed by Belgium until 1962 when it became the independent states of Rwanda and Burundi," with Rwanda tellingly not being admitted to the United Nations as a formally recognized sovereign state until 18 September 1962.[25] In contrast to dominant discourses that frame the international as a site of justice and humanity in the face of nationally located harm and injury,[26] here international governance mechanisms themselves are foregrounded as centrally implicated in processes of colonization and the social, political, economic, and legal structural inequalities they entailed and were premised upon.[27]

Yet while the ICTR frames locally and globally configured colonial practices as crucial to the 1994 genocide, it also downplays the significance of the colonial past and its enduring social and legal implications. First, in terms of the question of significance, the ICTR recognizes the formal global project of colonialism but not its innately harmful nature. In stark contrast to the quote from Frantz Fanon that opened this chapter, which refers to the "dead bodies" of colonized peoples, the "blood of slaves," and the "ostentatiously opulent" contemporary position of European countries that stands as testament to the enduring structural injustices established through colonial rule, the colonial past does not appear in the Tribunal judgments as an injustice in its own right. Indeed, in the few judgments that do discuss Rwanda's colonial history, the judges openly state that they aim to provide a factual and nonemotive account of it—to use "neutral language" to narrate these historical events.[28] The lengthy history of colonialism in Rwanda, its unjust nature, and its harmful effects are condensed into supposedly objective, factual, one-line sentences, obtusely described as "historical difficulties" that were "faced by Rwanda" that will not be engaged with in great detail.[29]

Thus, instead of appearing as an example of mass harm that should be "of concern to the international community," colonialism is portrayed as a historical event with cognitive and explanatory import. It is from this perspective, for example, that colonial history is deemed to be "necessary"[30] and "important"[31] to "understand fully"[32] the event of the genocide. It is the colonial past that "may explain the otherwise almost incomprehensible level and intensity of violence that erupted in April 1994 and continued relentlessly for several months."[33] Colonial history is thus invoked here as an explanatory tool, capable of rendering comprehensible the incomprehensible, and as a way of making sense of the present.

This nonrecognition of colonial harm as harm cannot necessarily be excused as attributable to judicial modes of speech that are grounded in a respect for impartiality and objectivity. These descriptions of colonialism differ markedly, for example, from the more affective and emotional register through which other, more contemporary harms are depicted in the judgments and on the Tribunal website. Across these sites, the Rwandan genocide itself is described more emotively as "tragic," "horrific," and as "100 bloody days" in which "unimaginable violence overtook the country."[34] A video on the Tribunal homepage that was uploaded to commemorate the twentieth anniversary of the genocide and the winding down of the Tribunal seeks to emphasize the injustice of the Rwandan genocide, during which "for one hundred bloody days, Rwanda experienced one of the worst atrocities in human history and the international community stood by."[35] The deaths of the ten Belgian soldiers present in Rwanda as peacekeepers during the genocide are also described as "brutal,"[36] in ironically more affectively resonant terms than past practices of Belgian colonization themselves.

This approach to the colonial past that can be traced through the ICTR materials demonstrates the significance of the representational techniques that are used to engage with and depict suffering. These frames of representation, as Butler suggests, are inherently political and affective, and shape and constrain both what or whose suffering can be seen and how it can be seen.[37] Questions of representation are thus central, rather than secondary, as it is "[o]ur capacity to feel and apprehend [that] hangs in the balance."[38] In this sense, the ICTR's account of colonial history is problematic to the extent that it enables the colonial past to literally appear within the pages of international criminal jurisprudence, but as an objective historical fact that does not invite mourning or redress. Colonial injustice is not positioned as an injury that might demand ethical and affective engagement from contemporary communities (regardless of its justiciability).

ICTR engagements with the colonial past also problematically downplay its present social and legal implications. Colonial history is recognized at the same time as it is placed outside the realms of contemporary international criminal justice. Thus, the trial chamber in *Kayishema and Ruzindana*, for example, draws on expert testimony regarding the Belgian policy of establishing identity cards to conclude that the Tutsi constituted a discrete "ethnic group" capable of being targeted under the 1948 Convention on the Prevention and Punishment of the Crime of Genocide (hereafter the Genocide Convention).[39] They also consider the "intense ethnic tensions" that characterized postcolonial Rwanda as a product of "the legacy of Tutsi favoritism by the colonial powers"—both statements gesturing toward the enduring nature of the structural injustices that characterized Belgian rule.[40] Yet it is the same chamber that also disavows the implications of this history for the present field of international criminal justice by proclaiming that it is "of the opinion that an attempt to explain the causal links between the history of Rwanda and the suffering endured by this nation in 1994 is not appropriate in this forum."[41] In a similar vein, the Tribunal in the *Nahimana et al.* case also invokes the Belgian colonial past to "understand" the "level and intensity" of the genocidal violence, but also concludes the historical section of its judgment by stating that it "recalls and underscores that this history cannot be used to justify such violence" and in any way obviate the accountability of the accused.[42]

However, to recognize the enduring significance of the colonial past only within a framework of direct causality is, we argue in this book, to offer a limited understanding of the connection between the past, present, and future. Rather, there are many ways in which colonialism—as a distinctively structural injustice that established social, political, and legal frameworks that still exist in the present—is significant to a consideration of contemporary mass harm. It is in this vein that Ann Laura Stoler, for example, argues for the recognition of the "imperial ruins"—the environmental and cultural as well as socio-legal and political continuities of empire—that exist in postcolonial settings.[43] Relatedly, in her work on the Democratic Republic of Congo, Nancy Rose Hunt frames the complex relation between the past and present as one of "repetition" and "difference," in which the violence and atrocity of the colonial past and the structural injustices it inaugurated shape more contemporary experiences of harm in former colonial contexts.[44] Meanwhile, Charlotte Mertens uses Hunt's, Stoler's, and Achille Mbembé's works to understand both the connection between colonial uses of sexual violence in the Democratic Republic of Congo and more recent uses of rape and sexual assault in this context and the way in which this violence has been unevenly amplified and covered over in dominant global narratives.[45] Their work demonstrates how we can acknowledge the continued import of Rwanda's colonial history without reductively claiming that colonialism caused the genocide. This history, for example, had an impact on the sociopolitical divisions that characterized the genocide and was a prelude to Rwandese experiences of contemporary harm. Historical dynamics also shaped global responses to the genocide, with Belgium constituting one of the main contributors to the peacekeeping force in Rwanda at the time of the genocide. Indeed, the Rwandan government itself has always been interested in both acknowledging the import of colonialism and also emphasizing the responsibility and accountability of the Rwandan people for the genocidal killings, as evident in President Paul Kagame's speeches at successive commemorations of the genocide and the Rwandan government's emphasis on accountability for Rwandan perpetrators of the genocide through national criminal trials and the *gacaca* tribunals.[46]

In the legal sphere, Kamari Clarke has used such a variegated temporal framework to offer a new perspective on now pervasive critiques of the cultural bias of international criminal justice institutions, such as the International Criminal Court, which has largely focused on African conflicts and countries.[47] She situates such cultural bias as inherent in the current jurisdiction of international criminal courts, arguing that international criminal courts will inevitably focus on African countries due to, first, the forms of harm (genocide, crimes against humanity, and so forth) that they are concerned with that are predominantly occurring in countries living with the legacies of colonial oppression and neoliberal global intervention and, second, their limited approach to responsibility (as individual criminal responsibility). A more complex approach to the past and the present may also enable the ICTR to itself appreciate how it is implicated in the reiteration and hence relegitimation of problematic colonial frameworks of knowledge. Richard Wilson, for example, highlights the way in which ICTR jurisprudence evinces a contradiction that undergirds international criminal law, between its universalist promise and imagination of a global humanity on the one hand, and its emphasis on protecting particular groups—

such as those ethnic, racial, religious, and national groups referenced in the Genocide Convention—on the other.[48] He argues that "[t]here appears to be an intrinsic paradox: while the international court administering humanitarian law is highly uncomfortable with . . . any suggestion that it might be reproducing the categorizations of the *genocidaires*, it requires these vexed categories to secure convictions for the crime of genocide."[49]

Indeed, the Tribunal ultimately had to rely on, and hence endorse, the colonizer's and genocidaires' conception of "Hutu" and "Tutsi" as fixed and objectively discernable ethnically based categories in order to find that the Tutsi of Rwanda constituted an identifiable ethnic group that could be targeted under the Genocide Convention. Yet, as Mahmood Mamdani argues, to emphasize the relation between Rwandan Hutu and Tutsi as one of "'ethnic difference' tends to freeze the history of the Rwandan state at its colonial stage, turning a historical outcome into a primordial difference."[50] ICTR judges had to endorse and productively use what they themselves acknowledge as an artificial and problematic colonial framework, which was the root of a whole system of social, political, and economic inequity, to hold that the Genocide Convention could be applied to the cases coming before it. The failure to register colonialism as a harm and the related placement of colonial history outside the remit of the international criminal courtroom stymies a fulsome appreciation of the significance of the colonial past for the present—the way it shapes future and present relations, institutions, and possibilities—and for contemporary international criminal justice itself.

THE CRIME OF COLONIALISM: RECOGNITION AND CLOSURE

The colonial past and its harmful nature is immediately more apparent in our second case study, namely the negotiations around the recognition of a crime of "colonial domination" in an international criminal code (1949–95). While, as we will detail, there was vociferous debate between states and state representatives about whether colonial harm should be included in the code, the very act of formulating a legal definition of a crime of colonialism and the consideration of it as potentially constituting one of *the most serious* international crimes serves to position past colonial acts as injurious and capable of criminalization. Indeed, in the course of the International Law Commission (ILC) deliberations, the offense of colonial domination is even portrayed as constituting one of the "genuine" crimes against the peace and security of mankind.[51] The implications of this recognition are stymied, however, not only by the ultimate failure to enact this proposed section of legislation but also by the continued adoption by Commission members and states of an unduly limited approach to the relation between the colonial past and the postcolonial present and future.

Following World War II, there was an initial attempt to develop an international criminal code. In 1949, the International Law Commission commenced both its operation and its consideration and formulation of the Draft Code of Offences Against the Peace and Security of Mankind.[52] The Code was to include and define not all international offences, but those deemed to be the most serious ones,[53] that is, those in the reports of the Commission deemed to be of an "especially horrible, cruel, savage and barbarous nature."[54] The ILC was also mandated with legislating guiding principles of international criminal liability (such as individual accountability for international crimes) that could be found in the Charter of the International Military Tribunal (1945) (also known as the "Nuremberg Charter") and other sources of international law (such as treaties). In developing the Code, the Commission's tasks were both recording recognized legal notions and contributing to the "progressive development" of this legal sphere. The Code never came into independent and formal existence, but the idea for it and accompanying debates stand as socio-legally significant attempts to articulate what constitute the gravest crimes against all of humanity that should be the legitimate focus of international criminal justice.

The Commission's first draft of the crimes to be included in the Code was produced in 1954, but this draft was effectively shelved in succeeding decades to allow for the progress of complementary deliberations, including the United Nations' discussions regarding the crime of aggression and the development of a standing international criminal court. When the Commission returned to its work in 1981 and the special rapporteur offered his revised draft of the Code in 1984, the proposed text included both the crimes from the 1954 version, which encompassed crimes such as aggression, genocide, war crimes, and other violations of state sovereignty, and offenses deemed to have been "recognized by the international community since 1954."[55] Significantly, in this 1984 Code, the crime of colonialism appeared as one of the harms now recognized by the international community. In a later 1991 draft it was specified as the crime of "colonial domination and other forms of alien domination" (from here on referred to as the crime of colonial domination), and defined as follows:

> Article 18: Colonial domination and other forms of alien domination:
>
> An individual who as leader or organizer establishes or maintains by force or orders the establishment or maintenance by force of colonial domination or any other form of alien domination contrary to the right of peoples to self-determination as enshrined in the Charter of the United Nations shall, on conviction thereof, be sentenced [to . . .].[56]

The bases for the inclusion of this crime were General Assembly statements such as the Declaration on the Granting of Independence to Colonial Countries and Peoples (1960) in which colonialism was unreservedly condemned, as well as other legal statements, such as Article 19 of the Draft Articles on State Responsibility[57] and the broader General Assembly sentiments that those fighting against colonial regimes should not be prosecuted but protected.[58]

As noted above, this very proposal of the crime of colonial domination serves to situate colonial harm as a proper subject of international criminal law. Moreover, in terms of our specific emphasis on colonialism as a structural injustice, the ILC reports and discussions also acknowledge its connection to enduring social and political arrangements both locally and globally. Outlined in later Commission reports, contemporary manifestations of colonial domination are said to be evident in the "glaring disparity between the political and economic situation of the States of the North and that of the States of the South"—a statement that highlights economic and political structural inequality as symptomatic of colonial practice.[59] An implicit acknowledgment of the structural character of colonialism is also evident in its positioning as an archetypal example of state crime, in which the governance structures of the state are mobilized to criminal ends.[60] In this vein, one commentator therefore asks "how could anyone imagine that aggression, genocide, the establishment of an apartheid regime, the maintenance of colonial domination by force or the systematic use of torture as a means of government could be the acts of isolated individuals?," underscoring the inherently structural and state-based nature of this form of injury.[61]

However, this recognition of colonial harm is limited. It is limited, for example, by the fact that—as with the ICTR materials—both opponents *and* supporters of recognizing the proposed crime take a linear and progressive approach to the past, present, and future: both sides frame the past, present, and future as separate and consecutive states and thereby occlude the way in which structural colonial injustice complicates these categories. This is clearest, for example, in the statements of those opposing the recognition of the crime of colonial domination who place colonialism as an event in a closed and completed past. Colonialism, as an experience and harm, is described as "abhorrent"[62] and yet "virtually extinct"[63] or "a thing of the past."[64] The special rapporteur thus describes colonialism as a "crime dated back principally to the sixteenth and seventeenth centuries."[65] There is a sense of closure afforded through this representation of colonialism as a past historical occurrence, a matter of history. From this perspective, the crime of colonial domination (along with apartheid) is described as addressing "insufficient existing practice or problems now solved."[66]

Indeed, in its strongest form, in this line of argument, colonialism is depicted as a foreign or meaningless concept in the contemporary social, legal, and political environment. It is in this spirit that in the 1993 debates about the crimes to be included in the Draft Code, the United Kingdom describes colonialism as "an outmoded concept redolent of the political attitudes of another era,"[67] while another spokesperson in the debates describes the language of colonial domination as "anachronistic,"[68] framing it as a concept best situated in another time and place, and not relevant in the contemporary world. Through such statements, colonialism is placed firmly in a past that is distinguished from a future or present, and a problem now solved or no longer amenable to legal redress. The ongoing legal and ethical implications of past colonial harm are thereby rendered unappreciable within the field of contemporary international criminal law.

Yet, as alluded to above, there are open and vehement contestations of this placing of colonialism in the past. Some Commission members, for example, draw attention to the continued existence of colonialism as a harmful global practice. They query "who could guarantee that colonial domination and apartheid were definitely a thing of the past?"[69] while others more definitively assert that it is not.[70] In making such observations, there are members who locate colonialism as a current and contemporary event, cautioning against "any premature optimism as to the final disappearance of all forms of colonial or neocolonial domination"[71] given the endurance of global socioeconomic inequality. Meanwhile, the continued relevance of the crime of colonial domination was also positioned as traceable to its possibility as a future occurrence, a mode of relation that "could resurface at any time."[72] From this perspective, the legislation of a crime of colonialism could help prevent and thus act as a "deterrent" for prospective economic, political, and military "foreign domination."[73] These statements contest the placing of colonialism, as a discourse and practice, in a closed and untouchable past by demonstrating the continued relevance of colonial domination, as a legal concept, to the present and future.

However, just as with opposition to the crime of colonial domination, these statements in support of it still rely on a dominant conceptualization of the past, present, and future as distinct and discrete states. There is a commitment to acknowledging that colonial domination—a crime witnessed in the past—could be repeated in the present and future. But what is missing from even these statements of support for the crime of colonial domination is a more committed recognition of the enduring significance of the colonial *past* for contemporary international criminal justice. The crime of colonialism is placed as an event in *either* the past, present *or* future, but there is no fulsome acknowledgment of the way in which past colonial harm complicates these very temporal categories and their delineation from each other, as a historical event that inaugurated socially, politically, economically, and legally configured injustices that persist into the present day, demanding both recognition and redress.

There are some, but few, traces of such a more fulsome recognition of the transtemporal nature of colonial harm that (pertinently for our argument in the concluding section of this chapter) surface in relation to a consideration of the power of law as an authoritative social discourse. The chairman of the ILC, for example, argued for the inclusion of the crime of colonial domination in the Draft Code on the basis that even if it was a harm of "historical importance," "[i]t had nevertheless been committed for more than two centuries and its victims had numbered in the millions."[74] Unlike in the debates above, here colonialism is portrayed as both a past act and one that has an enduring hold on the field of international criminal justice due to its temporal scope and human impact. Another member voiced similar sentiments, claiming that opponents of the inclusion of this crime within the Draft Code "missed the point that there had been hardly any other acts in the history of mankind which had caused so much misery to millions of underprivileged people and which were almost universally acknowledged to be crimes."[75] From these kind of perspectives, there is "symbolic" importance in recognizing the historically significant crime of colonial domination in a Code that is a "symbolic instrument," an expression of global sentiment, as much as a technical one.[76] Thus, such approaches to the recognition of colonial harm, although not prevalent in the debates, consider colonialism not only as a past act but one with continuing implications for a contemporary sphere of international criminal justice. They also highlight, as we discuss further below, the significance of law as a dominant sociopolitical discourse as well as a practical apparatus for making claims.

Of course, the recognition of colonial harm in the ILC debates is also limited by their ultimate outcome, namely the removal of the crime of colonial domination from the Code on the basis of state opposition (voiced, interestingly, most strongly by former colonial and settler colonial countries, such as the United Kingdom, Australia, and the Netherlands, as well as others). This outcome mirrors the broader reluctance of settler colonial states to consent to contemporary international law mechanisms, such as the United Nations Declaration on the Rights of Indigenous Peoples, that would necessitate an acknowledgment of the enduring justice issues inherent in their colonial experiences (as will be discussed further in the next chapter).

One other ground of opposition is worth mentioning, because it demonstrates an ongoing reluctance of international law to face up to its own socially, culturally, and historically particular nature. It is a reluctance that compromises its ability to appreciate its own implication in colonial injustice and the way in which it remains complicit in maintaining structurally unequal global arrangements. That is, another key argument against the proposal for a crime of colonial domination was that it was political and thus not a proper focus for law. Certain states critiqued the special rapporteur's Draft Code on the basis that it "often adopts political terms that have no accepted legal definition and wraps them with a legal cloak,"[77] while other states denounce the crime of colonial domination as a "political slogan" that does "not possess the requisite legal content necessary for inclusion" and has "no foundation in international criminal law."[78] Such a criticism is even extended by some to the related crime of apartheid, in the assertion regarding both crimes that "[a] more neutral . . . form of language on both points would help depoliticize matters."[79]

Such arguments are problematic because they rely on a conventional opposition between law and politics that serves to occlude law's own context. Just as law denies its own history by representing itself as timeless,[80] here law refuses to acknowledge its historically, socially, politically, and culturally situated nature.[81]

Yet it is precisely the political nature of international criminal law that is also signified by the eventual excision of Article 18 from the Draft Code. The special rapporteur elects to remove this provision on the basis that it is preferable to propose a Draft Code that is most likely to be accepted by all states.[82] This approach, therefore, situates politics and state interests at the heart of international criminal law, rather than outside its proper scope, and places the ILC—in the words of one Commission member—as "a codifier of the political will of States."[83]

The purpose in highlighting this irony is not to denounce this politicized character of law but to open up to a more wide-ranging consideration of the possibilities inherent in its recognition, which are currently shut down through dominant representations of law as apolitical. What potentials for a more comprehensive recognition of the colonial past and its enduring implications inhere in an acknowledgment of the politically (as well as socially, culturally, and historically) situated nature of international criminal justice? How might an appreciation of the contextual and contingent nature of international criminal law help to see and thereby address the current biases, limits, and structural inequities of this field? Could it assist in both acknowledging Clarke's arguments, discussed above, regarding the inbuilt cultural bias of international criminal law and working to address it? It is relevant in this respect that there are references in the ILC archives to the selectivity of which country's views appeared within the Commission's texts and were considered, with multiple Commission members, including the special rapporteur, observing that "no African or Asian country"[84] had submitted comments on the Code and it was unclear how to interpret such "silence" and its import regarding what crimes should be included in the Code, including that of colonial domination.[85]

A recognition, rather than disavowal, of the politically, culturally, and historically configured nature of international criminal justice might be what is crucial to the field's ability to account for both the colonial past and the implications of this past for the present structures of international criminal law. It may enable, for example, a more active engagement with what Antony Anghie refers to as the "colonial origins of international law," a body of law which—like colonialism—is premised on the visualization of cultural difference and the hierarchical portrayal of certain cultures as somehow lacking and others as somehow universal and representative of a global standard to be attained.[86] In this way, international law thus becomes simultaneously *grounded* in cultural difference as well as *directed* toward somehow remedying it, through bringing non-Western countries into the fold of the so-called universal (read "Western") international law. This means, Anghie argues, that the colonial project was "central to the development of international law," demonstrating the social, historical, and political situation of international law even at its emergence. Moreover, like us, Anghie emphasizes the structural legacies of these "colonial origins," which continue to inform how international institutions and international law operates in the present in relation to non-Western countries.[87]

In this respect, it is notable that claims of renewed colonialism are still leveled at contemporary international justice institutions, such as the first permanent International Criminal Court. Despite the support of African states for the establishment of the Court and their own referrals of certain matters from their countries to the Court, there has been significant critique of the Court from political leaders and academics on the basis of its culturally biased and potentially colonial character.[88] This is partly because of the extreme cultural bias of its operation—since it commenced operations in 2002, the vast majority of its activities have focused on prosecuting African defendants for crimes committed in African countries, sometimes with local and national political resistance. Moreover, it is also in relation to African countries specifically—namely Sudan and Libya—that the United Nations Security Council has invoked its so-called exceptional power to refer matters to the Court without national consent. The Court's operations are thus framed as again compromising the full sovereignty of African governments over their own people and have led to the withdrawal and threatened withdrawal from the Court of multiple African states, alongside a focus on pursuing African-based accountability processes in certain cases.[89]

While claims of the colonialism of the International Criminal Court are sometimes discredited as self-interested attempts by indicted African heads of state to avoid accountability, and the relationship between specific African leaders and specific African communities and the Court is more complicated,[90] such claims testify to the continued salience of the global colonial project and the need for it to be engaged with in a more reflective and considered way. That colonialism is a resonant framework for political leaders from places such as Kenya and the Darfur region of Sudan to use to denounce their prosecution by an international criminal court itself demonstrates the continuing significance of colonialism.[91] And responses to such criticism that simply affirm the nonpolitical character of international justice institutions unhelpfully downplay the inherently political and partial nature of the International Criminal Court's work, mandate, and structure—which enshrines dominant global political inequalities, currently only applies (in theory and practice) to certain countries and certain crimes, and importantly neglects to substantively engage with structural injustices and responsibility for them.[92] As such, a grappling with colonialism (alongside other forms of global and local structural injustice) is arguably a precondition, although not a guarantee, of a more collaborative and substantive international justice enterprise and one that moves beyond a conception of the past, present, and future as distinct and distinguishable. It is these possibilities for a greater *recognition* by international criminal justice of the colonial past, its unjust character, and its continuities in the present *as a practice of structural justice* that we consider in the next section.

BEARING WITNESS TO COLONIALISM AS AN ENDURING INJUSTICE: LAW AS DISCOURSE

How else might colonial harm appear in the texts and practices of law? And how might alternative modes of recognition prioritize a nonlinear and more sophisticated approach to the relation between the colonial past, the postcolonial present, and the possibilities for the future?

Homi Bhabha writes of the importance of postcolonial theory "bearing witness" to the "unequal and uneven forces of cultural representation" implicated in colonial injustice and inequality.[93] Such a "bearing witness" is an intervention in its own right, rather than just a precursor to other actions.[94] In other fields, the notion of "bearing witness" to atrocity is now a popularized form of response to the experience of being exposed to or enduring suffering.[95] It is conceptualized as a potentially ethical and committed act, whereby those who have undergone traumatic experiences, or witnessed those of others, testify to both its occurrence and its broader significance.[96] It thus stands counter to the injustice inherent in not only past episodes of harm but also their nonrecognition.[97] It is a form of response to suffering and trauma that has been often discussed in relation to the Holocaust, although it is used more widely now in connection with media portrayals of events of mass harm, as well as academic and practitioner accounts of them.[98] The existing focus of this literature, however, is largely on individual testimonies and texts. Here we are interested in the capacity of a body and practice of law to "bear witness" to colonialism as a gesture of *structurally* oriented justice.

International criminal justice might more ethically and carefully "bear witness" to the colonial past and its difficult relation to the present and future by more reflexively acknowledging, first, its harmful, criminal, and unjust nature, and, second, its broader and enduring significance. Even if jurisdictionally international criminal law confined itself to engaging with contemporary episodes of harm, it could still—through its judgments, self-representation through websites, outreach, and other official publications and the words and actions of its spokespeople—openly and candidly recognize both colonial practice and its devastating character and effects. This could be as straightforward as framing colonial harm in affectively resonant terms and as an earlier example of a crime against "humanity," or as extensive as more comprehensively admitting the significance of and seeking to engage with contemporary claims regarding the colonial nature of international criminal tribunals. "Bearing witness" to the colonial past could involve a more thoroughgoing acknowledgment that the world in which international criminal justice operates, and the discourse of a global humanity that it employs, is one with a complex colonial past that continues to resonate today; to recognize, as postcolonial theorists have implored, that the world—as both a geographical space and sphere of social relation—is still shaped and structured by the colonial past.[99] Such acts of "bearing witness" would thus testify, at a structural level, to the continued relevance of the past in the present and hence to the connection between the past, the present, and the very possibility of a just and progressive global future.

Moreover, enhancing the appreciability of colonial harm within the sphere of international criminal justice could also—to borrow Michael Rothberg's words in another context—enable "new lines of sight."[100] In particular, a deeper and more sustained engagement with colonial harm and its present and future implications could shed light on the way in which international criminal law itself draws on and hence legitimates the continued rationality of colonial cognitive frameworks—in the case of the ICTR—or is shaped by colonial and postcolonial power dynamics—in the case of the crafting of the jurisdiction and remit of contemporary international tribunals. It may enable a more thorough recognition, therefore, of what is disavowed in the ILC deliberations—namely, the socially, historically, politically, and culturally located nature of international criminal law. In turn, such an acknowledgment of the situated and contingent nature of current doctrines and structures of international criminal justice could facilitate a more reflective disposition on how a field of law that seeks to represent and speak in the name of the *international* may itself be more temporally expansive and culturally diverse.

In this way, the act of "bearing witness" to colonialism, its structurally unjust nature, and its enduring consequences may act as a catalyst for international criminal justice to change, shift, and reform. A recognition of the culturally particular nature of international criminal justice as a legal field could prompt a greater openness to non-Western and alternative understandings of law and justice. This would respond, for example, to the call of postcolonial critics such as Clarke and Mamdani for international criminal justice to be more receptive to definitions and processes of justice that may have more purchase and meaning in the actual contexts with which international criminal law currently engages.[101] An ability and willingness to shift and change its own orientations and approaches in this way might be crucial for building the global legitimacy of a mode of legal understanding and practice that frames itself as international and inclusive and yet has been denounced for its selectivity and, more pointedly, its colonial character. Moreover, as will be taken up more fully in the next chapter, a greater openness to grappling with past colonial injustice might position law, and in this case international criminal law, to more generally adequately acknowledge and address structural harm—of which colonialism is a key component—that has, to date, remained outside the scope of its discourse and practice.

Our purpose, therefore, is to further here, in a different way, our commitment to think more expansively about the possible ways forward, despite the endurance of structural colonial injustice. Here, in focusing on the potential for law to "bear witness" to the colonial past, the law is engaged as more than a technical apparatus for determining guilt and innocence. Rather, law is approached as an influential societal discourse and practice regarding the recognition of harm and the importance of justice. Law here is a socially meaningful framework that accords significance and acknowledgment to suffering as a harm and emphasizes the need for its naming, denunciation, and redress. It is this linking between law and justice and the potentialities that lie within it that is further considered in the next chapter, which discusses more closely the limits but also the possibilities of substantive and structural reform that might emerge from bringing together a contemporary socio-legal framework, transitional justice, with an emphasis on acknowledging and redressing structural injustice.

Chapter 5

TRANSITIONAL JUSTICE AND SETTLER COLONIALISM

Toward Structural Change

> [C]onsensus on the moral meaning of the past often comes at the expense of cutting off future claims that would normally seem to follow from it. To put the point crudely, the cost of achieving a moral consensus that the past was evil is to reach a political consensus that the evil is past.[1]

> Our fundamental problem is the nature of our relationship with Canada. Structural change in laws and policies is essential.[2]

What are the present possibilities of justice for colonial harm? What are the potentials for substantive and structural change, particularly in settler colonial contexts? We have emphasized the harmful nature of colonial practices and called for their more comprehensive recognition. Moreover, we have underscored the structural nature of colonial injury, which complicates the relation between the past, present, and future and which endures—shaping and constraining the life circumstances and opportunities of Indigenous peoples and communities—to this day. From this perspective, it is striking that much dominant contemporary social, political, and legal discourse regarding the colonial past and the settler colonial present does not center around questions of justice and structural change.

Instead, official responses to colonial injustice in settler colonial states have often been ad hoc in nature and circumscribed in scope.[3] For example, key Canadian and Australian initiatives, such as the Canadian Truth and Reconciliation Commission and the governmental apologies in both countries, have only addressed specific instances of human rights violations, namely the state removal of Indigenous children from their families and communities. There has been no apology, for example, for colonization per se, nor a thorough engagement with the historical and contemporary impact of the full extent of settler colonial governance, repression, and exploitation of such Indigenous communities since colonization.[4] Such limited approaches to engaging with the past are problematic in the sense that they can function to obscure other colonial harms and the structural nature of such harm, which is often continuing. Thus, in Canada, Courtney Jung shows how a restrictive focus (on only the experiences of certain residential school claimants) was used by the government to shift attention from the question of group-based and socioeconomic rights for all Indigenous Canadians.[5] In Australia, government reconciliation initiatives can be understood as a case of reconciliation without justice, particularly in the context of a continuing colonial framework.[6] In other contexts, symbolic acknowledgments of past injustice, such as apologies, truth commissions, and commissions of inquiry, have generally been used in lieu of rather than in combination with other initiatives to redress the past, such as reparations.

In this chapter, we explore the potentiality of a more wide-ranging, systematic, and substantive justice agenda regarding colonial structural injustice, as a key move toward a more structurally just situation. Following our discussion of the importance of the *recognition* of the colonial past and its harms (in chapters 3 and 4), this chapter turns to consider the necessity and difficulties of *structural change and reform*. To do so, we turn to the contemporary framework of transitional justice, which is itself premised on the importance of justice, accountability, and social, political, and legal transformation in the wake of mass harm. We critically appraise its potential relevance as a framework for understanding and addressing colonial harm, specifically the foundational and ongoing colonial injustice that characterizes settler colonial societies—such as Australia and Canada—where the settlers came to stay.[7] In so doing, we are not as focused on the question of what transitional justice mechanisms may be best suited for addressing colonial injustice, as much as on the potentiality of transitional justice to provide a new heuristic device through which to appraise Indigenous experiences of colonial injustice and begin to more holistically respond to them.

As such, in considering the utility of a transitional justice approach, we also seek to extend and revise current transitional justice frameworks by connecting them with different contexts and traditions. We draw upon settler colonial theory to respond to more general critiques of the failure of many transitional justice models to acknowledge and respond to structural and socioeconomic harm, in postcolonial and other contexts. We hope that this reconceptualization may offer new possibilities for understanding structural injury and responding to the structural and historical injustices that exist in settler colonial states, including through opening up to Indigenous worldviews and jurisprudences rather than simply continuing to privilege Western frameworks, such as ameliorative transitional justice approaches.[8] In so doing, we build on the work of other scholars who have also sought to extend transitional justice frameworks and expand its approach to "justice" as transformative and distributive.[9] As such, we are not advocating a mechanistic and top-down application of global transitional justice frameworks in postcolonial and settler colonial societies. Rather, reflecting the relational methodology of our book—which brings together different peoples, traditions, temporalities, and perspectives—here we bring transitional justice and settler colonial theory and experiences into relation to explore what new ways of responding to and redressing structural colonial harm might result.

Our focus in this chapter is thus the encounter between transitional justice, settler colonial theory, and experiences of colonialism, and the ways forward—potentially regarding structural reform—that might emerge from it. The chapter begins by outlining the mainstream transitional justice framework and its relative inattention to Indigenous harm, before proceeding to consider the potential benefits of employing transitional justice as a new perspective for addressing colonial and settler colonial harms, particularly given its emphasis on holistic redress and the importance of broad societal engagement with the past and its legacy. We then consider the conceptual potentials of drawing on settler colonial theory to reconsider and revise transitional justice as a field. Continuing our emphasis in this book on the distinctively structural nature of colonial injustice, we propose here that settler colonial theory can be used to underscore the importance of substantive engagement with questions of structural injustice and structural change, by demonstrating the significance of colonial history and its enduring effects and by providing the intellectual tools to challenge the current use of transitional justice as a nation-building practice. We conclude by observing how an integrated conceptual approach to colonial harm, based on transitional justice and settler colonialism, can raise new possibilities for thinking about what an enhanced justice model, which emphasizes the importance of *structural* justice, might require.

TRANSITIONAL JUSTICE AND COLONIAL HARM

Described by Rosemary Nagy as a "global project,"[10] transitional justice is a dominant international framework for conceptualizing and pursuing redress for systematic violations of human rights, including military rule and civil war, genocide, and widespread oppression. It emerged as a discrete field in the late 1980s as a study of the role of law in times of political transition, prompted by the use of legal and quasi-judicial responses to the end of military rule in societies in South and Central America and the collapse of Communism in East and Central Europe.[11] Reflecting these broader academic and practitioner conversations,[12] the term itself was popularized by Ruti Teitel, who observed the particular role that law can play in periods of "transition," namely one of "transitional justice."[13] Teitel argued that law functions differently in times of political upheaval: "In its ordinary social function, law provides order and stability, but in extraordinary periods of political upheaval, law maintains order even as it enables transformation."[14] This function of law in enabling transformation has become the cornerstone of studies of transitional justice,[15] and the framework is now widely employed as an approach to the use of law and justice in the immediate aftermath of mass harm.

Conceptually, the notion of transitional justice envisages a formal shift from authoritarian to democratic rule that is guided by legal and quasi-legal processes. Practically, it is concerned with designing justice approaches to facilitate both individual and broader societal redress for past violence and injustices through a range of mechanisms such as criminal trials, truth commissions, reparations measures, lustration programs, and reconciliation initiatives. Prosecution is only one aspect of transitional justice, which is exemplified by the increasing use of the model of the truth commission as a quasi-judicial institution.

The overall approach therefore sets out to achieve accountability for past wrongs as well as to engender a broader societal transition from "the past" through facilitating reconciliation and wider reconstruction. In the case of South Africa, for example, the process was dominated by a truth commission that was intended not only to establish an authoritative account of—and in this manner establish accountability for—the apartheid past, but also to reconcile a divided nation through drawing on the African concept of *ubuntu*, as well as Christian forgiveness.[16] In East Timor, there was a combination of limited criminal trials and a truth commission process, which in using the local custom of *nahe biti* attempted to encourage reconciliation and ensure accountability for past wrongs through truthful retelling.[17] The transitional justice model has thus proven flexible enough to increasingly accommodate both conventional prosecutions and local customary practices whose responsiveness to particular circumstances is seen as more conducive to achieving just outcomes across time and place.

Interestingly, however, the colonial injustices experienced in settler colonial states have generally remained beyond the purview of transitional justice. Reflecting a broader trend of conceptualizing the West as the locus and agent of justice and human rights that needs to respond to the conflict and abuses occurring in non-Western states,[18] transitional justice has not—until recently—been used as a framework to consider the injustices that have occurred in Western, liberal democratic countries. Liberal democratic societies have been positioned as the desired end points of transitional justice, and transitional justice "has tended to ignore the extent to which liberal democracies themselves might be considered in need of 'postconflict' reconciliation and restorative justice."[19] Indigenous individuals and collectivities have of course been active, throughout time, in drawing attention to the injustices arising from colonialism.[20] While their activism has produced groundbreaking commitments in international human rights law through the United Nations Declaration on the Rights of Indigenous Peoples and the United Nations Permanent Forum on Indigenous Issues, the extensive and enduring harms caused by settler colonial practices and policies, in countries such as Australia, New Zealand, Canada, and the United States of America, have not constituted the traditional focus of transitional justice discourse and practice.[21] Instead, Western countries continue to appear as the actors that can best support transitional justice processes in other postconflict countries such as East Timor, Rwanda, and Libya, rather than the subjects of transitional justice that might need to reckon with their own problematic pasts.

In recent times, however, there has been a greater interest in connecting transitional justice and the historical experiences of Indigenous people in settler colonial states. Arguably this relates, in part, to the recent use in these states of political-legal processes that could be deemed to be "transitional justice mechanisms," such as truth commissions, reparations, apologies, and legal prosecutions.[22] Centered around goals such as acknowledgment and reconciliation, in the case of the former, and accountability, in the case of legal prosecutions, these initiatives have been positioned by governments—implicitly, rather than explicitly—in line with transitional justice rhetoric, as ways of addressing the injustices of the past in order to provide the conditions for a more just societal future. They include initiatives such as the Truth and Reconciliation Commission of Canada (inquiring into the system of residential schools for Aboriginal people that existed in Canada until 1996) and the Australian National Inquiry into the Separation of Aboriginal and Torres Strait Islander Children from Their Families, the governmental apologies delivered in Canada and Australia regarding certain policies in these nations' colonial histories,[23] the reparations funds established in select Australian jurisdictions (such as Tasmania) for distinct colonial injustices,[24] and broader state reconciliation initiatives such as the Australian Council for Aboriginal Reconciliation, which was a key recommendation of the 1991 Royal Commission into Aboriginal Deaths in Custody.[25] In turn, academics and practitioners have shown growing interest in the significance of transitional justice initiatives and approaches for addressing settler colonial harms.[26] Focused on particular country case studies, existing scholarship has critically evaluated the relevance and application of transitional justice approaches to settler colonial injustices.

In the main, however, the spheres of transitional justice and settler colonial scholarship have remained separate: settler colonial theory has traditionally been associated with historical scholarship, whereas transitional justice has, until recently, adopted a legalistic paradigm that is only now being displaced. Further, the "transitional justice"–like measures referred to above have been undertaken as ad hoc and partial initiatives rather than as components of a systemic, comprehensive, and collaborative attempt by settler societies to grapple with their complex and foundational structural injustices. Existing efforts at reform can thus be largely characterized as piecemeal rather than holistic, as welfare rather than justice oriented, and as shying away from a thorough reimagining of sovereign relations between Indigenous peoples and the state.[27] Thus, if decolonization—in Michael Humphrey's words—can be seen "from the transitional justice perspective" as "an instance of transition where there was no accountability, in other words, where impunity prevailed,"[28] the continuance of settler colonialism can only constitute an ongoing injustice that has neither ceased nor been adequately acknowledged or addressed.

TRANSITIONAL JUSTICE: SOME POSSIBILITIES

What possibilities might arise by conceptually approaching colonial harm through a transitional justice framework? As we have begun to suggest, transitional justice may, first, offer the opportunity for a more thorough and multifaceted approach to settler colonial injustice than is assumed. That is, despite some of its temporal limits that we will discuss below, transitional justice nevertheless advocates a holistic ameliorative framework that aims to respond to mass harm systematically and pluralistically. Through varied initiatives, from trials to truth commissions to social and political reconstruction, transitional justice aims to ensure a thorough reckoning with the past, which provides postconflict societies with the necessary foundations to "move on." Indeed this "comprehensive" and "holistic" character of transitional justice, emphasized in early discussions of its role in postconflict societies, has also been highlighted by the United Nations as a key capacity that should be built upon and enhanced.[29] The Secretary-General's seminal report on transitional justice makes it clear that "[w]here transitional justice is required, strategies must be holistic, incorporating integrated attention to individual prosecutions, reparations, truth-seeking, institutional reform, vetting and dismissals, or an appropriately conceived combination thereof."[30]

The use of such a holistic and multifaceted framework to conceptualize and address settler colonial injustice could function as a useful counter to the highly politicized, and often piecemeal, top-down governmental responses that have been offered to date. That is, as flagged above, while certain mechanisms common to transitional justice have been applied to varying degrees in settler states, it has been more difficult to achieve substantial legal or political commitment to acknowledging the collective impacts of colonialism in terms of mass harm, or to moving forward collectively, systematically, and pluralistically from that point to redress them. Initiatives designed to address the past have been undertaken as discrete initiatives, unconnected to a broader and substantive justice agenda through which Indigenous and non-Indigenous peoples in settler colonial states collectively seek to acknowledge and grapple with the devastating effects of colonialism and its ongoing impact and manifestations. This is particularly apparent in the case of Australia, where no treaties were accorded to Indigenous peoples and where public discussions about the past have been particularly damaging and divisive.[31]

Such initiatives have therefore been implemented without sufficiently unsettling the reluctance of settler states to embrace the full impact of their histories, evident more forcefully, perhaps, in their prolonged opposition to endorsing the United Nations Declaration on the Rights of Indigenous Peoples.[32] As Michelle Bonner and Matt James point out, in their comparison of transitional justice processes in Canada and Argentina, the goal of accountability, as legal, political, and social accountability, "while central for justice seekers in Argentina, is in many ways eerily absent in the Canadian case."[33] As such, it becomes clear how the processes of dispossession, including the comprehensive regimes of management and control that followed the overt violence of the frontier, continue to circumscribe the scope for reform in the present: without a commitment to thoroughgoing structural or constitutional change, the process of settler colonization has no formal point of conclusion.[34] In such circumstances, the emphasis in transitional justice on a full reckoning with the injustices of the past potentially offers a more comprehensive and robust agenda for the tasks that face settler colonial societies.

Second, transitional justice approaches also seek to address and engage a broader constituency. From the South African Truth and Reconciliation Commission to the Rwandan *gacaca* trials to the Sierra Leone Truth and Reconciliation Commission, transitional justice mechanisms seek to provide a public account of the past.[35] This public account constitutes an official and authoritative recognition of past harm that can also serve to educate the broader community who witnessed (or failed to witness) these violations at the time.[36] As such, on a practical level, such transitional justice mechanisms are often participatory in nature, involving public hearings of people's testimonies. This social orientation of transitional justice processes may therefore also explain why they are so important to undertake even if, as Bonner and James point out, what happened during periods of injustice and repression is already widely acknowledged by victim communities.[37]

From this perspective, coming to terms with injustice is framed as a shared and societal task: the responsibility not just of perpetrators and victims but also of the broader national community. In settler colonial societies, in which past exploitation of Indigenous peoples may have been systematically ignored, and explicitly denied (as discussed in earlier chapters), such socially oriented transitional justice processes may serve an important pedagogical function. They may facilitate recognition of colonial harm itself, as well as its enduring significance in the present. As Tony Barta has noted, "most Australians have never seriously been confronted by the idea that the society in which they live is founded on genocide."[38] Moreover, in the presence of claims that current socioeconomic inequalities experienced in Indigenous communities are a function of personal choice and agency rather than historical and structural factors, an emphasis on a community-wide engagement with the past and its legacy may foster increased awareness of the impact of the past on the conditions of the present.[39] It might prompt what we have called for earlier in this book: for settler colonial societies to accept responsibility for their history and its impact and ongoing implications, for the past to be understood as central to our present.

Third, responding to our emphasis, in the last chapter specifically, on the significance of whether and how colonial harm is rendered appreciable, transitional justice approaches may also provide a new way of understanding settler colonial harms and their unjust character. Bonner and James write of the opportunity that transitional justice approaches provide to "reframe" past injustices.[40] They give the example of how state actions previously legitimized as "anti-subversive" may be reappraised as distinctly genocidal through the operation of transitional justice processes.[41] In turn, the use of transitional justice frameworks to appraise the injustices experienced in settler colonial states also provides a new mode of speaking and thinking about them. By using transitional justice discourses to discuss the significance of governmental policies and actions in settler colonial states and by placing Indigenous experiences of injustice in relation to more readily acknowledged contemporary human rights violations, the egregious nature of such policies, actions, and injustices may become more appreciable. Put simply, framing settler colonial harms through transitional justice discourse and as comparable to (although different from) other mass harms that have gained more academic and public attention may enable non-Indigenous citizens in settler colonial contexts to recognize injustices in their nations that otherwise may be hard to discern due to dominant official narratives. In naming these injustices using transitional justice frameworks they can then become issues of justice, not welfare.

Moreover, understanding Indigenous experiences in relation to other post-conflict situations, using a transitional justice framework, may also offer new vantage points from which to consider the ongoing challenges that exist in settler colonial societies. It is often observed, for example, that a key problematic in the wake of the Rwandan genocide was that—unlike with the aftermath of the

Holocaust—victims and perpetrators were expected to continue living alongside each other after the genocide had ended.[42] The fact that settler colonial societies also demand this feat of Indigenous and non-Indigenous communities without any comprehensive attempt—as in Rwanda—to holistically acknowledge or address the colonial dispossession of Indigenous peoples that constitutes the precondition for such coexistence is not often discussed in the same way. Transitional justice therefore not only sheds light on the need for comprehensive redress but also on the challenges of dealing with the past that exist in all postconflict contexts. New possibilities for understanding the significance of colonization and its ongoing impact may emerge using transitional justice languages, frameworks, and case studies to conceptualize Indigenous experiences in settler colonial and postcolonial states.

Finally, although we are about to turn to discuss some of the current limits of transitional justice in addressing structural harm, these approaches nevertheless offer an approach to societal change that can be built upon. Transitional justice has conventionally been located in a moment of political change, to enable and shape a political transition—in part—through legal measures, and it thus acts as an existing model for the use of law in enabling sociopolitical transformation.[43] Transitional justice approaches demonstrate the role that law can play in political change, alongside other social and political initiatives. They also demonstrate the potentiality of law, as highlighted by Ruti Teitel, to be both responsive and progressive; to, in the words of Adam Czarnota, "respond at the same time both to the need for radical change and the need for substantial continuity."[44] This use of law as a tool both for the addressing of harm and for institutional and social change can be a strength in tackling long-term structural injustice. This further demonstrates the complexity of the potential relation between law, colonialism, and structural injustice—in which law acts as both a collaborator to structural injustice (as discussed in the previous chapters) and as a potential tool in its dismantling.

TRANSITIONAL JUSTICE AND STRUCTURAL INJUSTICE: SOME LIMITS

As transitional justice has consolidated as an academic field and mode of practical intervention, it has increasingly been subject to critical attention.[45] Commentators have illustrated the contradictory imperatives that characterize transitional justice approaches[46] and have sought to broaden the mandate and scope of transitional justice beyond the provision of once-off justice measures focused often on individual accountability and the protection of civil and political rights. They demonstrate how transitional justice is a particular frame for conceptualizing and addressing societal harm, which—for example—has historically focused unduly on legal approaches to crimes of the past and may fail to adequately adapt to and consider the local contexts in which it is applied.[47]

A growing critique, which is of particular significance to our consideration of the potential relevance of transitional justice to settler colonial injustices, focuses on the inadequate attention of transitional justice to the deeper socioeconomic and structural causes and consequences of conflict.[48] Transitional justice has still mostly operated in accordance with an individualistic legal framework that has not worked to facilitate a deep engagement with such systemic and structural injustices and the types of interventions needed to address them. As a temporal response to political transition, transitional justice has engaged little with broader long-term structural inequities and harms, particularly those that lie outside the conventional transitional justice model of transition from an authoritarian to a democratic regime. Based on a liberal, individualistic model of accountability (traditionally pursued through criminal prosecutions), transitional justice approaches have not fully engaged with the structural and societal arrangements that enable or facilitate human rights violations—what Ratna Kapur refers to as "the institutional arrangements and structures [that] may be deeply implicated in the production of the violation or the harm in the first place."[49] Instead, scholars have argued that transitional justice emphasizes seemingly "exceptional" violations, rather than the more routine and hence "invisible" damage stemming from unjust societal arrangements that do exist in liberal democratic collectivities.[50] While there have been some transitional justice models that have sought to recognize and address the broader systemic causes of injustice, such as the Truth and Reconciliation Commission of South Africa, the Truth and Reconciliation Commission of Peru, the Truth and Justice Commission of Mauritius, and the Commission on Historical Clarification of Guatemala,[51] these have been isolated examples that have functioned more to *recognize* the structural bases of contemporary injustice than provide the necessary means to effectively *confront* and *redress* them.[52]

Importantly, many transitional justice programs have failed to engage with the enduring effects of structural and historical injustice. Lia Kent has considered this in light of the transitional justice approach implemented by the United Nations in East Timor, illustrating the way in which transitional justice mechanisms were inherently ill-equipped to address the legacy of structural violence in that country, including, for example, poverty, poor health, limited education, and lack of economic opportunities for survivors.[53] As we discussed in our introduction, and Rama Mani has explicated in the transitional justice field, such broader social and structural "inequalities" are not easily reduced to questions of individual responsibility and accountability and hence are not adequately addressed through existing transitional justice approaches.[54] Lisa Laplante, in arguing that truth commissions should be more focused on pursuing social justice through an emphasis on economic, social, and cultural rights, has highlighted the current privileging of individualistic civil and political rights.[55] Indeed, Robert Meister frames this downplaying of distributive justice questions as constitutive of the mode of justice offered through transitional justice frameworks. Premised on a demarcation of individual perpetrators who are responsible for the wrongs of the past from the broader population of beneficiaries who were not directly involved in any atrocities but benefitted and can continue to benefit from the unjust societal arrangements that enabled them, transitional justice functions to place issues of social and distributive justice outside its scope.[56]

To some extent, this relative marginalization of structural issues can be explained with reference to various conceptual constraints that inform conventional transitional justice paradigms. Paige Arthur demonstrates how some of the biases and assumptions that characterize transitional justice are traceable to the fact that the field was developed and defined in relation to a distinct set of historical circumstances.[57] Empirically grounded in the social, political, and historical conditions that shaped South and Central American and Eastern and Central European transitions to democracy and the prevailing academic and practitioner approaches to conceptualizing them, transitional justice is based on certain experiences of social and political reform and certain understandings of what might constitute justice. This helps to explain, for example, why transitional justice is structured around the pursuit of legal accountability and institutional reform designed to establish the foundations for a new and legitimate liberal democratic form of governance. Moreover, it explicates why transitional justice is concerned with guaranteeing the broad enjoyment of civil and political rights as the basis of such a democratic society,[58] which in turn leads to its comparative inattention to economic and social justice reforms.[59] These examples demonstrate that current transitional justice models are historically, socially, culturally, and politically particular and are most tailored to certain instances of mass harm.

We would also highlight, further, that the ability of transitional justice to successfully account for colonial injustice and result in structural change can be stymied by its reliance on a certain temporal framework. Transitional justice is premised on the idea of a "point of rupture": a specific point of change from violence and oppression to a "new dawn."[60] The model assumes a moment of political change and upheaval, an overt change of regime, from authoritarianism to democracy (due to its conceptual roots in postcommunist regime change). This, in turn, leads to a certain understanding—one now familiar across our case studies in this book—of the past, present, and future as discrete and sequential. Transitional justice assumes too a linear notion of time as progress,[61] in which the past and the future are seen as separable and successive instead of intertwined and co-implicated. This makes it difficult for transitional justice to acknowledge, and hence redress, the enduring structural arrangements that may have resulted in past as well as present injustice and the ongoing effects of past inequities on present and future generations.

Moreover, when viewed within the broader context of modern European expansion, which had such dramatic consequences for precolonial societies, the field of transitional justice seems presentist in its concerns. With mandates for truth commissions and trials that cover short time frames, the complex impacts of colonial pasts are effectively elided. Instead, transitional justice predominantly engages with contemporary episodes of injustice and their recent histories. For example, transitional justice processes in East Timor focused on the harms perpetrated by Indonesia following their invasion in 1975—their mandates did not stretch back to those of the colonial Portuguese period. As Lia Kent has shown, however, it was during the colonial period that land was taken, shaping later structural injustice.[62] Similarly, the transitional justice process in South Africa focused on harms perpetrated after the rise to power of the National Party in 1948, yet did not examine the complex history of Dutch and British colonial exploitation that established the initial lines of separation. Meanwhile, in Rwanda, despite recognition that a Belgian colonial past had contributed to the genocide in 1994[63] and apologies from Belgian Prime Minister Guy Verhofstadt, this did not feature in legal processes either nationally or, as discussed in the previous chapter, internationally. This failure to appreciate the global and local historical causes of current injustices constitutes a blindness to the role of European colonialism in perpetrating, facilitating, or perpetuating mass harm. Such Eurocentrism complicates the potential of transitional justice to address more comprehensively the kinds of mass harms suffered by recognized "post-conflict" populations as well as by Indigenous peoples in settler societies.

Finally, it is also worth acknowledging that the capacity of transitional justice to account for and address structural injustice is hampered by a further conceptual constraint, namely its current focus on strengthening, rather than challenging, the state.[64] Given its historical foundations and its current association with broader rule of law reform programs, transitional justice is oriented toward laying the foundations for a legitimized, or relegitimized, democratic nation-state. In its positive conceptions, this involves using transitional justice theories and processes to establish both a reformed government infrastructure that gains authority from its willingness to acknowledge the injustice of and depart from previous state practice and a reconstituted social body that is committed to learning from past inequities and ensuring they do not happen again. In its negative conceptions, however, such state-building exercises involve the appropriation of the event and testimonies of the suffering of victims as an opportunity to pursue broader governmental and societal goals.[65] In order to establish a reconstituted national polity, based on the acknowledgment of the past as a basis for "moving forward" into the future, victims are asked to testify to injustice but also leave it in the past, relinquishing, as Robert Meister suggests, any claim to more substantive redress than they may be provided.[66] In this way, transitional justice processes can be utilized as a form of governance and nation-building, rather than of justice for victims. This raises particular problems in relation to settler colonial contexts in which, as we explicate in chapters 2 and 3, the foundations of the nation-state are themselves based on enduring structural inequity.

MOVING TOWARD AN INTEGRATED FRAMEWORK

An acknowledgment of the social, cultural, historical, and political particularity of transitional justice models, and a commitment to ensuring their utility in addressing structural colonial harm, involves their reshaping and renegotiation by affected communities and offers a conceptual space to think about both the limits and possibilities of transitional justice frameworks regarding colonial injury. In exploring, at a conceptual level, what possibilities could emerge from bringing these currently separate spheres into relation, we contend that it is productive to consider how settler colonial theory—which has been so integral to our own appreciation of colonial structural injustice—may enrich dominant transitional justice models.

By unsettling any clear distinction between the past and the present, postcolonial and settler colonial theories can be used to highlight and challenge the artificiality of the temporal framework that currently shapes transitional justice theory and practice and stymies its ability to recognize and redress long-term harm. By underscoring the significance of colonial history, as well as its enduring implications and effects, critical theories such as these serve to counter the current failure of transitional justice to "look backwards" to causes and histories, as well as to look forward to possible broader, more structural solutions. In so doing, these perspectives raise the possibility of understandings of justice that are not limited to identifiable justiciable harms, but as entailing processes that aim to both identify and redress long-standing structural inequities. Settler colonial theory also provides conceptual tools to question the current conceptualization and mobilization of transitional justice as a state-building enterprise. This interrogation is particularly important if transitional justice is to have any relevance in settler societies. As Courtney Jung highlights, transitional justice will be a blunt tool if it simply serves to consolidate the sovereignty and authority of the settler state, when that is the very unjust societal structure that most needs to be challenged.[67]

In this respect, settler colonial theory usefully historicizes Western notions of sovereignty, thereby unseating their status as the inevitable frameworks within which justice questions between Indigenous and non-Indigenous communities are confronted and addressed. Settler colonial theory, that is, is interested in the operations of sovereignty as a concept whose powerful capacity to transcend its social origins supports its apparent neutrality as a key organizing principle of Western political and legal theory and practice. The insights of postcolonial, critical legal, and historical scholars have informed this aspect of settler colonial scholarship by identifying the correlation between the emergence of sovereignty discourse and modern Europe's quest for expansion to the so-called New World.[68] Throughout this period, theologians and jurists strove to rationalize the violence and discrimination that characterized Europe's imperial incursions against its self-representation as uniquely endowed with universal, civilized, and Christian values.[69]

Through tracing the genealogy of what we now know as international law, this interdisciplinary work has identified the discrimination that inheres in the notion and practice of sovereignty and which was made particularly manifest in the "doctrine of discovery." In seeking to adjudicate European rivalries relating to the lands of others, this legal precept was gradually consolidated from the sixteenth century and remained consistent in its understanding of who would qualify as sovereign: whichever European colonizer claimed first discovery would be accorded dominion, but no matter which native peoples were colonized they would never be accorded more than the right of occupation. In constructing Europeans as bearers of so-called universal rights and values, sovereignty discourse accordingly withheld its attributes from those whom it deemed to deviate from these norms. For centuries, Indigenous peoples have been caught up in sovereignty's normative thrall, which has accommodated many disqualifying characteristics, ranging from different religious and cultural practices to inadequate modes of land use.[70]

In thereby demonstrating the responsiveness of sovereignty discourse to European expansion from 1492, as well as to events internal to Europe post-Westphalia more than a century later, this scholarship highlights the ideological (and, of course, legal) force of sovereignty's seeming neutrality in the present. The approach helps explain sovereignty's fortress status both in domestic law and as the basis for membership in the international order. The question of the colonial history of sovereignty discourse therefore goes to the heart of considerations about structural injustice—the subordination of Indigenous peoples and cultures through the process of European expansion is embodied in the very concept that underpins both nation-states and the international order they constitute.[71] Consequently, identifying the interests that have informed sovereignty discourse, in both the past and the present, points to the importance of recognizing the limits to reforms that continue to be conceived and shaped within Western worldviews and jurisprudences alone.

Settler colonial theories and experiences can help to explicate the nature of structural harms, as practically and ideologically manifest. In so doing, they underscore the absolute necessity of engaging with structural and historical harm in any purportedly comprehensive justice program.[72] As one Assembly of First Nations leader, Ovide Mercredi, in Canada explains in the quote we used to open this Chapter: "Our fundamental problem is the nature of our relationship with Canada. Structural change in laws and policies is essential."[73] In this vein, critical historico-legal approaches to settler colonial theory highlight the constitutive violence of law, particularly during the so-called frontier period in settler colonies. As gestured to in chapter 2, in the case of Australia, for example, the expansion of settlement was commonly accompanied by settler calls to make certain repressive laws apply to Aboriginal people alone. Ranging from exemplary executions, to the refusal of testimony, to summary justice provisions, to racialized legislation designed to break up families and communities, through to the extremes of martial law in times of apparent crisis, such suspensions of the rule of law not only contradicted British claims to peaceful settlement. In facilitating dispossession in the face of Indigenous peoples' resistance, the resort to exceptional procedures in domestic law also helped secure the territorial basis for sovereignty: Indigenous peoples' resistance had shown that the discursive claims of international law over who should or should not be sovereign were far from self-evident on the ground.[74]

TRANSITIONAL JUSTICE AS A MEANS OF STRUCTURAL JUSTICE

What emerges from this discussion is a proposal for an enhanced transitional justice model, which draws on the strength of transitional justice as a program of legal and non-legal processes enabling social and political change, while also focusing on structural and historical harm. An enhanced transitional justice model would be characterized by its foregrounding of the importance of structural justice, which opens the state and its foundations up to question rather than simply reaffirming them, and acknowledges the contiguity between the past and present, in terms of the continued resonance of past harms in the present, and indeed their failure to be really characterized as past at all. It would be attentive to the complex nature of structural injustice, which is politically, socioeconomically, legally, and ideologically located, and ingrained in both practical societal arrangements and institutions, but also in dominant societal discourses. Such a justice model may be one way to approach the necessity of substantive and structural reform in moving toward a more structurally just situation in settler colonial and postcolonial contexts.

In current academic work on transitional justice in settler colonial contexts, there have been some hesitations expressed about the potential disjunctures between transitional justice approaches and settler colonial realities. One concern that has been raised is whether it is misleading to talk about transitional justice in settler colonial states given the clear lack of transition that characterizes them. Rosemary Nagy—for example—notes that "while it is important to acknowledge and address systemic human rights abuse, it is also rather awkward to affix the label 'transitional' to justice long denied in liberal democracies."[75] It may be, however, that we need to think about transition differently—as not solely transition from an authoritarian to a democratic regime, as initially understood in the transitional justice paradigm and reflected in the wake of military dictatorships in South America and East-Central European postcommunist regime change, but as transition from unjust relations to just relations[76]—that is, as the transforming of the social, political, economic, and legal frameworks that underlie settler colonialism. This includes recognizing and addressing the ongoing denial of Indigenous sovereignty and the potential to place Indigenous peoples outside the rule of law in governance. It is these structural injustices that continue to inform enduring injustice in the present.

Transitional justice offers the possibility of a more thorough and comprehensive response to settler colonial harm. That is, in addition to being a form of justice defined by its temporality (a *transitional* justice), transitional justice is also a *justice model*. Transitional justice, as a field and practice, is concerned with the importance and mechanics of recognizing and redressing widespread and state-sanctioned harm through the use of political-legal initiatives such as trials, truth commissions, apologies, and reparations to achieve political and social goals that include accountability, reconciliation, and reconstruction. It is in this sense that the United Nations has emphasized the pluralistic capacity of transitional justice.[77] While transitional justice initiatives may not always be so comprehensive in practice, transitional justice—as a justice model oriented toward providing a political-legal framework for change—can offer practical and conceptual tools to place responses to Indigenous injustice within a broader "justice agenda," and to rethink underlying unjust relations, through which both Indigenous and non-Indigenous communities in settler colonial states may more collectively and holistically address the past and its ongoing effects.

Recent scholarship on the concept of "structural injustice" recognizes the need for a more comprehensive mode of accounting for mass harms than approaches that focus on predominantly state-based actions or individual culpability, or both. The work of political philosopher Catherine Lu, developing Young's concept of structural injustice and mentioned in our introduction, is pertinent to our concern to highlight the long-term historical injustices arising from colonialism.[78] Lu notes that injustices such as colonialism are facilitated and legitimated through complex local and global societal networks whose redress requires expansive rather than narrow analytical frameworks.[79] On this view, a structural justice model would involve a shift from individualistic and state-focused modes of redress toward a more thoroughgoing evaluation of the structural vestiges of "past" harms and an openness to deep and wide-ranging reforms, including Indigenous jurisprudences, that would transform the social, political, legal, and economic arrangements that enabled them. A structural justice model would pay attention to both the causes and legacies of the initial harms perpetrated.

A transitional justice framework enhanced by the notion of structural justice may also provide the theoretical resources to rethink the relation between justice, injustice, and transition, and to reconsider what it means to pursue just outcomes as a society. It may indeed prompt consideration of how justice measures could themselves *facilitate* a process of transition rather than simply respond to it. Jung writes of the "transformational capacity" of transitional justice measures;[80] Wendy Lambourne and others have discussed how transitional justice may be understood as a "transformative justice."[81] On this view, transitional justice—reconceived as a discourse and practice that enables as well as accompanies transition—could be more proactive in orientation. Rather than pursuing redress for past injustice as a singular goal, transitional justice may be directed toward ensuring substantive justice through prompting societal, political, and economic change that addresses the structural underpinnings of harm and injustice in societies.

A more robust transitional justice model may also be better placed to identify and analyze the range of different harms that might constitute the focus of transitional and other justice measures. A focus on a broader spectrum of events of injustice may further a recognition of the different types of harm that may require redress—from the traditional focus of transitional justice on physical harms to an acknowledgment of the significance of socioeconomic, "cultural," and "intergenerational" injuries.[82] Recognizing these different state-based injustices will enable a more comprehensive approach to redress that acknowledges different forms of harm and differing modes of redress, but with all having a place within a "justice agenda."

Unsettling the presentist and linear temporal focus of transitional justice can also facilitate the elaboration of a justice framework premised on a complex and nuanced approach to "past" harms. The recognition of the ongoing resonance of past harms (enabled by postcolonial and settler colonial perspectives) could pave the way for a theorization of the nature of historic harms. Building on existing acknowledgments of the intergenerational transmission of past trauma and injury in affected families and communities, there is scope to inquire further into the character and attributes of historic injustices that remain unaddressed. Do such injustices simply endure, manifesting as they did when inflicted; do such injustices become compounded over time, their effects exacerbated and inflamed; or, indeed, does the character of such injustices change with the passage of time, and are they altered by either their longevity or the societal failure to effectively acknowledge and address them?

A more inclusive approach to the types of harms relevant to transitional justice could result in new practical interventions. That is, if transitional justice processes are extended to account for and address expansive histories of past oppression, their scope may also need to be temporally broad. Rather than focusing on the establishment of institutions, such as tribunals and truth commissions that operate for a defined period, the emphasis may shift to ongoing and long-term interventions designed to comprehensively address structural injustices and their enduring legacy.[83] Such approaches may be particularly relevant in settler colonial societies in which injustices have been so enduring. Meanwhile, as Jung notes, stand-alone initiatives, such as apologies and truth commissions, must be situated within broader programs designed to fully redress the past.[84]

What remains critical, however, as we discussed in chapter 3, is that any such justice initiatives are not simply conceived within Western frameworks but are also informed by Indigenous worldviews, and that they seek to transform existing inequitable institutional frameworks that have been largely unquestioned.[85] In settler colonial states, where questions of historical and structural injustice risk being downplayed and discredited, the imperative to explore new ways of thinking and responding to the harms inflicted on Indigenous peoples and communities remains strong. A robust "justice agenda," based on the insights gained through *bringing together* transitional justice frameworks and settler colonial theories and experiences, may facilitate the structural reform and change that is crucial to moving toward a situation of structural justice. Such a "justice agenda" would again recognize the role of law, plurally conceived, regarding the pursuit of more just relations in settler colonial and postcolonial contexts. It is in a similar vein that the following chapter considers the power of the historic claims made on law by Indigenous peoples, claims that are recorded in the legal archive and are capable of reactivation to pursue societal and legal change in the present.

Chapter 6

CLAIMING THE RECORD OF LAW

Reimagining Law as a Site of Justice

> We are Kenyans in our 70s and 80s who have travelled to London from our rural villages to tell the world of the torture and trauma we lived through at the hands of the British colonial regime. With the support of the Kenyan Human Rights Commission, we have come to London to issue our legal claims. This is the first time that we have left Kenya and so, for us, this is a defining moment in our lives.[1]

> So we are being destroyed while white Australia is calling for reconciliation, they are still taking the land away. . . . This is not a political stunt. This is a cry for someone to listen to what is happening.[2]

The claim to law remains powerful. Despite the use of law as a core instrument in the subjugation and destruction of Indigenous peoples under colonialism, the institution of law continues to be turned to in the pursuit of justice. The power of the claim is embodied in Gejoworrung man Martin Simpson declaring to the 1881 Coranderrk Inquiry, "We came to see that the blacks get justice."[3] It is present in Kikuyu woman Jane Muthoni Mara stating to the British High Court of Justice, "I want the British Government to compensate me for the suffering I have been caused as a result of the abuse I was subjected to in the camps. . . . I want the British citizens of today to know what their forefathers did to me and to so many others."[4] And it is Gungalidda elder Wadjularbinna Nulyarimma telling the Supreme Court in Australia that "[t]he genocide, the acts of genocide are continuing in every law and legislation white Australia makes for us and every time they take more of our land,"[5] and fellow Embassy claimant Wiradjuri elder Isobell Coe saying "[w]e need you to know the truth and we hope that you give us time."[6]

By engaging specifically with the claims made on law by Indigenous peoples and communities, this final substantive chapter continues to deepen our consideration of the role of law, despite its implication in the structural injustice of colonialism, to act as a site of justice. We suggest that the claims made on and through law for the recognition and redress of colonial injustice, even if they fail to generate legally "successful" outcomes, nevertheless create a space of possibility in which colonial injury, along with possibilities for justice, can be heard in the past, present, and future. Such claims create an official record of colonial harm and invite colonial and postcolonial bodies of law to hear and witness evidence of their own constitutive and historical violence and its structural character. That this record endures means that it is capable of reactivation in the present and future to pursue transformative social and political goals. It is in this way that the 1881 Coranderrk Inquiry gathered and preserved the testimonies of the Coranderrk residents, enabling the Minutes of Evidence project to reactivate them in a dramatic performance as a means of sparking new and present public conversations about historical and structural injustice. In the past and present, claims for redress can thus create "meeting points" within and alongside law and demonstrate the possibility of just relations within the unjust structure of colonialism.

In this chapter, we explore this dynamic further by discussing two encounters between Indigenous claimants and colonial law: first, the 1998 genocide hearings in the Supreme Court of the Australian Capital Territory (ACT) in Canberra, Australia, that were initiated by members of the self-declared Aboriginal Tent Embassy, and second, claims made by Kenyans to the British colonial administration during the "Kenyan Emergency" (1952–60), and their later use in a case seeking redress from the British state in the High Court of Justice. In each, we can observe how these encounters, through the contestation of colonial law and the assertion of justice claims, serve to create a legal record of structural injustice that remains—and point to new means of creating just relations. Both put on record a means of structural justice. The hearings initiated by the Aboriginal Tent Embassy put on record the assertion of sovereignty by the claimants that articulate lawful relations, along with the recognition by the Court that genocide occurred as part of the colonization of Australia. In relation to the Kenyans who experienced state-orchestrated harm during colonialism, these historical records of harm, which assert sovereignty and a means of lawful relations, have informed more contemporary cases against the British state. As legal records, they form the basis of the possibility of future just relations.

While the colonial structure still frames the operation of law in postcolonial contexts—influencing whether such claims are upheld—these encounters between law and colonialism raise possibilities for just relations, by demonstrating the enduring sovereignty of claimants and placing just alternatives to colonial injustice on record. Claims of injustice may be unable to be heard while law is complicit in or silenced by the violence. Yet it is the record made in law that has the capacity to constitute a normative space for a future structural justice, one that may necessarily happen outside yet with reference to law. As discussed in chapter 3, this can transform an encounter between different peoples and laws into a potential meeting point. The record can make visible both the structures of injustice that continue and the possibilities of justice that can be held.

As such, we consider the archive of law as being alive to possibility—of enhancing the appreciability of structural colonial injustice, of grounding present and future claims to justice, and of non-Indigenous engagements with their own law and their own responsibility for it (as discussed in chapters 2 and 3). In this chapter, we introduce our approach to law's record, before considering our two case studies, the record created, and this record's ongoing significance.

THE RECORD OF LAW

In our focus here on the record created through the claims made on law and their dynamism in shaping the colonial legal spaces in which they are advanced, we understand law's record as fluid, capable of being positioned in the past, present, and future, and continually reshaped through its reactivation. Law's record exists in the present, yet speaks to both the past and the future. It embodies the interrelationship of space and time, what Mariana Valverde has explained through use of the term "chronotope": that space and time are interwoven and help us understand the governance and governing of law.[7] The reactivation of this record—which reveals both injustice and alternative ways forward—allows for it to be a dynamic and continuing source of justice that can be built upon and referred to.

This record can be understood as an archive, and there is much scholarship around the use and role of law as archive. It has been suggested that the archive of law has a defining role in relation to memory and authority, that its self-generation is implicit in its constitutive and continuing violence, and that its record is colonially circumscribed and determined.[8] This is alongside work that critiques the archive as partial and powerful.[9] The conceptualization of the record of law that we put forward draws on this body of work in terms of the location of the record of law, as within the colonial construct, yet proposes a different understanding to the archive of law as top-down, monolithic, and intractable.

In understanding the record of law as one of possibilities, tied to past, present, and future, we see it as a potential site of generation of further sites of justice. We consider the record not only as a file-able archive but also as a generative and claimable space. This is not to discount its constraints—who is heard in legal commissions or courts, how harms are understood, what legal concepts are used to arbitrate the harm, what Emilios Christodoulidis has termed the "vocabulary" of law that can determine value.[10] The archive embodies what is claimed of law, despite its constrictions—and how these can be subverted as a tool of resistance and of possibility. Ratna Kapur identifies the law as "a site of discursive struggle," complementing the work of critical race theorists on the potentials of legal storytelling, through which the voices of lived experience disrupt dominant narratives and reveal structures of oppression.[11]

This use of law draws too on the radical feminist project of using resistance to legal discourse to generate alternate accounts and possibilities. Carol Smart has argued, for example, that in providing a forum for "articulating alternative visions and accounts" and as a "focal point" for these resistant discourses to be heard, "law remains a site of struggle."[12] Yet we suggest that this struggle is waged both within and outside of law, through the creation of alternate spaces of contestation inside law that have the possibility to be taken up outside of law. This recognizes the silencing violence of state law, yet asks that we understand law as pluralist—that its record contains multiple spaces and has the possibility, through its reactivation, to generate further normative spaces.

Through understanding state law as one form of normative order, we allow for possibilities of change through generating different meeting points outside of law, while still using this (pluralist) record of law. This follows an understanding of the law as a "multiple network of legal orders," what Boaventura de Sousa Santos has spoken of as "interlegality"[13] and early legal sociologists

Eugen Ehrlich and Leon Petrażycki referred to as "living law"[14] and "intuitive law,"[15] respectively, and which was built upon in the work of Adam Podgórecki.[16] State law can be a reference for, but not necessarily the sole site of, justice—particularly in settler colonial and postcolonial contexts (see chapter 3). These different sites of law of necessity work together—it is in this potential of collaboration that we may find the generation of sites of justice.

Furthering our recognition of the plurality of law in colonial contexts, here we also bring a legal pluralist approach to the conceptualization of the legal archive, emphasizing that even state law itself is not a monolithic construct, but contains multiple normative spaces that coexist and contend with the multiple sites of law outside the structure of state law. In drawing on a legal pluralist understanding of law, in terms of understanding law as both including but not being limited to state law, we locate ourselves as making a contribution to legal pluralism that goes beyond the linear distinction drawn between "classic" legal pluralism that the colonizer will always dominate the colonized and their law[17] and "new" legal pluralism as multiple systems of ordering.[18] This is shown through observing the carving out of a space within state law that creates a space of both encounter and meeting place, and which is then referred to in the constitution of a normative space of social and political change outside of state law.

State law is sought after for its norm-affirming properties, as a space of enforcement—yet as a space too where norms can be contested. It is what Mari Matsuda spoke of when she related the story of Frederick Douglass, who escaped from slavery and went on to play a key role in the antislavery movement in the United States: "He chose to believe in the Constitution, but at the same time, refused to accept a racist Constitution."[19]

The *remains* of this contestation, as the record of law, can be continued and reactivated in consideration of what a structural justice may require and the shape it must take. In the following section, we consider two different colonial encounters that have resulted in the creation of a record made in law capable of reactivation toward just ends.

TRACING THE CLAIMS MADE IN LAW

The Aboriginal Tent Embassy Claims, Australia, 1998

On 17 July 1998 in Australia's capital of Canberra, Wadjularbinna Nulyarimma of the Gungallida, Isobell Coe of the Wiradjuri, Billy Craigie of the Gamilaraay, and Robbie Thorpe of the Gunnai, together from the Aboriginal Tent Embassy, brought a "writ of mandamus" to compel the registrar of the Magistrates Court to issue warrants for the arrest of the Prime Minister John Howard, Deputy Prime Minister Tim Fischer, and two members of Parliament, Brian Harradine and Pauline Hanson, on charges of genocide. They had earlier gone to the Canberra police station and to the Magistrates Court to ask that the arrests be made. These arrests were refused by the police sergeant, who said "he had never heard of such an offence,"[20] and by the registrar, who responded that "the offences alleged . . . are unknown to the law of the ACT."[21] As a consequence of the writ, a hearing to determine the claims made was held in the Supreme Court of the Australian Capital Territory before Justice Ken Crispin.[22]

The Aboriginal Tent Embassy had been established on the grounds of Parliament House in 1972 as an action of political protest and an assertion of sovereignty in response to the denial of land rights legislation. What began with the staking of a beach umbrella in the ground is now a permanent presence outside the now Old Parliament House, having weathered forced removals and become a focal point for debate and protest. In her foreword to the book that celebrated its fortieth anniversary, Larissa Behrendt wrote that "the notions of the Tent Embassy, of Aboriginal community control, of equal access but distinct identity keep the conversation from compromise and assimilation."[23] One of the central claimants, Isobell Coe, was to demonstrate to the court the role of the Embassy as a site of protest:

> I am one of the people that have been fighting for 26 years because my elders sent me to the Aboriginal Tent Embassy in 1972 and I have not given up. They may be dead and gone, but the spirit that they sent me there with in 1972 still lives on within me today.[24]

When the Aboriginal Tent Embassy claimants approached the Magistrates Court, new legislation was at that moment being debated in the Australian Parliament that would further curtail Aboriginal access to land. The Native Title Amendment Bill 1997 was the latest iteration of the legislative regime established in 1993 to regulate Aboriginal land claims.[25] This was part of a long history of colonial dispossession and demonstrates the significance, which we noted in our introduction and chapter 2, of *land* in settler colonial arrangements.[26] The claim made by the Embassy was that the imminent introduction of the revised Native Title Act put Aboriginal peoples at even greater risk of destruction and was part of a long history of genocidal practices.[27] It was put to the court that the native title legislation demonstrated "intent to destroy" as required by the 1948 United Nations Convention on the Prevention and Punishment of the Crime of Genocide that Australia had signed, although not implemented. It is in this context that Wadjularbinna Nulyarimma, who initiated the legal actions, uttered the words that we drew upon to frame this chapter: "So we are being destroyed while white Australia is calling for reconciliation, they are still taking the land away. . . . This is not a political stunt. This is a cry for someone to listen to what is happening."[28]

Significantly, in relation to our repeated emphasis on the *enduring* nature of colonial structural injustice, this hearing opened a space in which the concept of continuing, not only past, harm was put on record. The claimants asked that John Howard and Tim Fischer (as prime minister and deputy prime minister) be charged with attempted genocide and conspiracy and complicity in genocide in their formulation of the amendments to the Native Title Act and enactment into legislation; that Brian Harradine (independent member of the Senate) be charged with complicity in genocide in his agreeing to the Native Title Amendment Bill; and that Pauline Hanson (MP and leader of the racist One Nation party) be charged with public incitement to commit genocide. All members of the Australian Parliament were charged with complicity in genocide through failing to enact the United Nations Genocide Convention:

> It is our submission that those persons named in the motion have been complicit in enacting this [Native Title] legislation, which is intended to bring about the destruction of Aboriginal Peoples of Australia. And are crimes against our Aboriginal humanity. The effect of these laws will be to perpetuate our colonized state of being, and the denial of our inherent right to become as we were prior to the invasion fully self-determining and independent peoples.[29]

Affidavits were gathered from around the country to demonstrate the ongoing destruction. Testimony was given in relation to the continuation of child removal and its impact, the state of health of Aboriginal people and their institutional experiences, and the traumatic and ongoing effects of dispossession. Wadjularbinna told the court, "The genocide, the acts of genocide are continuing in every law and legislation white Australia makes for us and every time they take more of our land.[30] The claimants demonstrated that past and current practices of removal from land constitute destruction, what Damien Short has termed "continuing genocidal relations,"[31] and Larissa Behrendt has shown is inherent to the process of colonization.[32] The hearing created a space in which the harm perpetrated and suffered could be understood differently from that of the dominant narratives of current Aboriginal disadvantage as an issue of welfare not of structural injustice (see chapter 2) and of genocide as past not present.[33] The connection between the past and the present, and the inherently structural nature of settler colonialism, could be seen and appreciated.

The testimony of lived realities as *dispossessed peoples* put on record the connection between colonial practices of dispossession and present day harm. It sought to make appreciable these ongoing harms. Critically, it sought to move from a state of knowledge of dispossession to acknowledgment of its impact.[34] As Wadjularbinna stated in her affidavit to the court, "You know we're not making it up—your own government statistics and departments tell you what is happening to us."[35] She is referring here to the mass of empirical data on high Aboriginal mortality rates, on the disproportionate level of incarceration of Aboriginal peoples in Australia, and on the myriad ways in which the life opportunities of Aboriginal peoples are so gravely different from that of the rest of the Australian population.[36] The testimony by those living this structural injustice was designed to foster recognition: as Isobell Coe put to the court, "Now, you people do not know what has happened in this country. You will never know until Aboriginal people stand up and tell you."[37]

The hearing initiated by the Aboriginal Embassy created an official record of the enduring structural injustice of settler colonialism in Australia. Its transcript and affidavits constitute an accounting of the continuation of colonialism. Yet these claims and testimony in the ACT Supreme Court also turned the legal encounter—between Indigenous and non-Indigenous holders of law—into a meeting point. We now turn to the Aboriginal Embassy hearing as a practical example of Western law adapting to providing a meeting place of law, to consider just ways forward, and to bring these laws into relation.

The hearings were held over seven days from July to September 1998. This included a morning at the Aboriginal Embassy, in the grounds outside Old Parliament House. The claimants asked Justice Ken Crispin whether the court could convene at the Embassy itself, to which he agreed, and the formal legal hearing was transplanted to the Embassy site. The Supreme Court of the ACT convened around the permanent campfire at the Aboriginal Embassy at the request of the claimants on the morning of 23 July 1998, bringing Aboriginal law into relation with settler law.

The hearing was conducted by the Embassy claimants as an assertion of lawful relations, as discussed in chapter 2. Ceremonial spears were used to demonstrate the different systems of law and the confrontations and possible ways forward—"the two laws are clashing, your law and our law"— with Kevin Buzzacott welcoming people to "our old court"[38] and using the spears to illustrate the ways forward to "clear the blockage," to "heal this country right throughout."

This was sovereign to sovereign. As Isobell Coe said to the Court at the Embassy, "We have never relinquished sovereignty to our country in any way, in any shape and form."[39] From this space of sovereignty a meeting place was sought, in order, to use the words of Wadjularbinna in her affidavit, that "the genocide against our people and all Aboriginal peoples be stopped and prevented."[40] The Embassy claimants showed a way forward, utilizing both Aboriginal law and "white man's" law—the power of European law to issue arrest warrants, but also the power of Aboriginal law to "clear the blockage."[41] Kevin Buzzacott concluded:

> But I want to help you. I am here to help you. These people, we can support you, we can show you a way that nobody has ever known.[42]

This moment around the fire at the Embassy enabled Indigenous and non-Indigenous holders of law to come into proximity and create a space for consideration of how lawful relations between them might unfold. In showing how the two laws could be brought together, the claimants created a space in which just alternatives were put on record. After telling the hearing of the lived realities for many Aboriginal people, Wadjularbinna called on Justice Crispin:

> There must be no doubt in your mind because there is none in ours, and the people we have left behind, the people we see go to mental institutions are men who have left us, are men who cannot live as men any more on their land, the mothers and the grandmothers and the women who have to live as they do, the young women who are raped daily by the police, by the system that you say is just, it is not just. Now, it is your opportunity to find any possible thing that you can to assist us as peoples of this country to make it better for the future of all

> people in the future. Our children, our grandchildren will not have a change if you cannot do this today, and I beg you that you see in your heart and in your learned books that you can make this change, thank you.[43]

The Supreme Court judgment ultimately did not find for the claimants. Justice Crispin ruled that charges of genocide could not be brought against members of Parliament who engage in the making of legislation and no "intent" to perpetrate genocide could be found in the Native Title Amendment Bill. Yet he did find that genocide had been committed during the colonization of Australia, and that there existed no domestic genocide legislation to cover the charges, supporting two key claims brought. Significantly, he held that "[t]here is ample evidence to satisfy me that acts of genocide were committed during the colonization of Australia."[44] This had never been recognized so clearly in Australian law.[45] His judgment also included much of the testimony of the claimants, in particular that of Wadjularbinna, the central claimant who had told her and her family's story of dispossession to the court. Her testimony thus made up much of the remaining legal record.

The claimants from the Aboriginal Tent Embassy seized this moment to create a space in which they asserted themselves as holders of law and as sovereigns. Settler law used this opportunity to come into relation with Aboriginal laws. Together they established a meeting place, where evidence of the effects of dispossession and genocide could be placed on record, and just alternatives considered. In creating a meeting place between two laws—and in showing how settler law could respond—they turned an encounter into a possible way forward.

Claims against the British Colonial State, Kenya 1952–60

This assertion of sovereign relations can also be observed in another time and space: in the British colonial state of Kenya. Kenyans subject to harsh colonial rule continued to assert their sovereignty as Kenyans and their status as British subject and citizens. They made these claims through, and in relation to law, a record that remains.

During the period of colonial rule in Kenya, in particular during the "State of Emergency" declared by the British colonial administration and in operation in the years 1952 to 1960, the Kenyan people made many claims on British law to acknowledge and respond to their situation. The suspension of "ordinary" law through the State of Emergency meant that in this *absence* of law Kenyans sought to create a means of lawful recognition of their situation by the colonial authorities both in Kenya and in Britain. The assertion of a state and sovereign relations were central to many of the claims. The claimants sought to bring the colonial administration and the British state into proximity with themselves as citizens and subjects.

The emergency legislation came with the commitment of British army troops and was in response to the perceived threat by the activities of the insurgent group known as the "Mau Mau." A system of detention and torture camps was established by the colonial administration, and it is estimated that 150,000 Kenyans were detained in detention camps and "screening centres" without trial—an estimated one in four Kikuyu males between 1952 and 1958, with many women also detained and subject to horrific torture.[46] In the face of systematic abuse of members and alleged members of the Mau Mau (most who suffered abuse were not in fact Mau Mau), many claims for redress and recognition were made to law and alongside law. These claims survive and form the basis of a later court hearing brought to the British High Court of Justice by surviving detainees, the record of which informs this discussion.

These earlier claims were directed both to the British colonial administration and to the British sovereign. Over the years of the "Emergency" hundreds of letters were sent by detainees outlining the abuse that they endured, including terrible assaults and torture by members of the security forces. These complaints were all recorded in the Minutes of the Chief Secretary's Complaints Coordinating Committee (the Minutes of the CSCCC) that had been set up by the Executive Council to "receive complaints of ill-treatment by members of the Security Forces and to direct such complaints to the appropriate authorities."[47] The allegations of systematic abuse were further corroborated and brought to the attention of the colonial administrators and the secretary of state for the colonies by the detainees themselves, with letters written by detainees seeking justice to British members of Parliament as well as to the Complaints Coordinating Committee.

As such, similarly to the Aboriginal Tent Embassy case, the structural injustice of colonial rule is made clear to colonial officials and put on record. Written to the secretary of state for the colonies, and sent by detainees at Manyani Special Detention Camp, grievances are detailed under headings that include "Detainees' Legal Rights," "Brutality of Officers," and "Representative and Political Rights." The section on "Detainees' Legal Rights" commences with "[a]dministration in special camps is something beyond human understanding," and begins its conclusion with "[t]he mention of justice to these poor men who have been made destitute through the Govts carelessness, and a deaf ear to practical claims is a ghostly dream."[48]

The assertion of citizenship and of sovereignty is central to many of the claims. The claims outline both the terrible privations suffered and a political claim for equality and representation. Women imprisoned with their children at Kamiti Camp wrote to the chairman of the Commonwealth Parliamentary Association "to lay before you grievances in this camp and misery," detailing the abuses suffered, and finishing:

> We place before you all the above for your consideration with the other Commonwealth delegates and also seek the cry over to the mother parliament for their final decision to eliminate them and please let the Queen see them herself. We shall be glad indeed when we see all the troubles are eliminated by your kind deed.[49]

Here we see the assertion of citizenship: a statement by claimants that as British citizens and as Kenyans you need to treat us justly.[50] A petition from detainees at Manyani Special Detention Camp to the governor of Kenya is premised on the enduring sovereignty of the Kenyan people. Outlining among other grievances the process of land consolidation and forced labor, the petition protests the new constitution and writes that they "endorse the demand of African Elected Members for 15 more seats in the Legislative Council."[51] A further petition from Manyani to the governor has "Freedom" as its first subheading: "We are extremely hungry and thirsty of freedom and nothing can satisfy our hunger and thirst save entire liberation of our country."[52]

These claims, recorded in the Minutes, constitute both enduring testimonies to colonial injustice and significant assertions of the importance of striving for lawful and sovereign relations. Through the claims made on and documented in law, a space is created where both the injustice is recorded along with its alternate possibility, that of political emancipation and partnership as equal sovereign citizens. The claims assert a space of contestation that can transform a legal encounter into a meeting place, demonstrating new ways forward. Whether this is heard, however, is dependent on the broader structures in which state law is situated.

LAW'S SITUATEDNESS

Dominant social and political orders can cancel out any effect of legal decisions and silence the injustices documented. Law, as legal sociologists have shown, does not always "steer."[53] This is particularly marked in colonial and postcolonial situations. As we set out in our introduction, the Coranderrk Inquiry was successful in agreeing with the residents that the station was not well run, yet its impact was stymied by subsequent political developments. The Aboriginal Tent Embassy case stated that genocide occurred during the colonization of Australia, yet this failed to be heard and felt outside the courtroom. The claims made by Kenyan detainees were put on record, yet they had no hearing in the colonial state. In the context of enduring colonial relations—which are inherently structurally located—isolated legal findings cannot always be implemented and claims cannot necessarily be more widely heard. The colonial social, political, and legal structure frames law's possibilities and the uses to which law and inquiries are put. And inquiries can be used as a means of confirming, rather than altering, colonial arrangements.

During the "Emergency" period in Kenya, there were a plethora of legal responses, commissions, and cases. Five different legal inquiries were established, alongside a number of criminal cases. Yet the harm continued. Ways were found to circumvent the rule of law yet remain within the structure of "legality." Strategic studies scholar Huw Bennett, an expert witness in the later British High Court of Justice hearings, has shown how the British army, despite its claims that it does not "do war crimes," was complicit in establishing a legal framework that allowed systematic atrocities to be carried out.[54] Historian David Anderson, also an expert witness in these hearings, remarked that on looking through the historical evidence "[a] strong impression is given that the avoidance of legal consequence is a foremost issue in administrative discussions."[55]

These views help to contextualize how, while in the British-Kenyan colonial relation there existed a system of legal review, this did not result in any systemic change. The inquiries remained within a colonial framework and mind-set and were, in fact, designed to limit legal and political recognition of the broader structural inequities. Seen this way, the various inquiries can be understood as a means of "moving on," with no systemic recognition and response to the testimonies of injustice that they enabled to be spoken.[56] The flagrant awareness by the colonial state that this is the purpose of these inquiries is exposed with the suppression of a section of the report of the Holmes Inquiry that arose from criticisms of police by the judges of the Court of Appeals for Eastern Africa. At the conclusion of the inquiry, the president of the court wrote to the governor to ask that part 1 not to be published on the grounds that "[t]his report as it stands will give the impression to the casual reader in Kenya that the criticisms of the judge in criminal case No. 240 of 1954 (Regina v Muiri & Others) have been answered, when in fact they have not; and will not satisfy the trained critic in London who will detect at a glance that no really searching inquiry has been made."[57] That the secretary of state for the colonies agreed not to publish it demonstrates their agreement with this finding.

The Minutes of the CSCCC to which detainees could bring their claims outline the way claims were used as a means of supporting the governance of the colonial state. Claims of abuse were systematically refuted and discounted. In the report of the *Incidents in Thuita and Kahuti Village* in which women were subject to mass beatings and suspected Kiama Kia Muingi (grown out of a wing of the Mau Mau movement) members were arrested and beaten, one of whom died, the claims made by the Kenyan people were refuted largely on the grounds of supposedly objective medical evidence or failure to report at the time of the incident, with one finding that "[d]eceased person had a skull which was extremely thin." In another set of claims, *Abuse of 15 Detainees in the Aguthi and Kandongo Camps*, the investigators discredited the claimants by stating that their complaints were "the result of hysterics and not ill treatment." In another report, the Minutes record that "[t]he two persons named as being removed to hospital as the result of being beaten were proved in a medical statement to have been suffering from typhoid and pleurisy respectively, and an examination of each at the time of the complaint . . . had shown no signs of beating."[58]

Anderson notes that many of these cases were never prosecuted and thus provide significant new evidence in the present as to the nature and integrity of investigations and prosecutions, in particular: "All of the evidence of interference suggests that the CCC [Chief Secretary's Complaints Coordinating Committee] were involved with the extrajudicial management of cases so as to have the charges struck out or reduced, or to alter the presentation of evidence to be brought before a court."[59] A letter from detainees at the Athi River Detention Camp observes that "[t]his act of avoiding proper proceedings of a trial in court makes us suspicious of the Committee of ever exercising the traditional British justice."[60] These Minutes are critical in establishing that officials in London were aware of the full extent of complaints of abuse against colonial officials and security personnel in Kenya, and yet, as Anderson notes, they demonstrate "a regular pattern of institutional resistance to accountability for abuses"[61]—a high number of prosecutions discussed before the Chief Secretary's Complaints Coordinating Committee were acquitted.

Criminal cases were also often a charade, both against alleged members of the Mau Mau and other Kenyans and against members of the colonial forces. In the case against Jomo Kenyatta, the leader of the Kenyan independence movement, historian Caroline Elkins, the first expert witness in the eventual British High Court of Justice hearing, narrates the political nature of the trial, with the judge calling for a bribe.[62] Attempts to prosecute systematic abuses within interrogation centers were stymied. In 1954, Assistant Police Commissioner D. G. MacPherson, the head of Kenya's Criminal Investigation Department, under the instruction of Commissioner of Police Arthur Young, investigated sixteen cases of abuse. His attempts to bring perpetrators to court were, according to Anderson, "obstructed by a combination of non-co-operation from administrative officers and interference by the Executive," which included "the production of false reports, testimonies and evidence by Chiefs and Home Guards, as well as the deliberate falsification of evidence by European Colonial Administrators."[63] Only four of the cases proceeded, and only one went to trial. In the magisterial inquiry into the *Summary Execution of ex-Mau Mau in Dagorette*, the fifteen-year-old half brother of the deceased (Kamau) gave testimony that he had seen two European guards murder Kamau in cold blood. The court discounted the half brother, opining that he was "a glib precocious untruthful boy" and that the two men had been shot lawfully while fleeing custody.[64]

While there is some reflection on the structure of abuse at the time, with certain judges and police questioning the way that it is made acceptable, this is ignored and there is no systemic change. The Special Emergency Assize Courts were established to hear Mau Mau cases and ran with modified rules of evidence. As Anderson notes, "There was no respite in abuse and torture cases being brought before the courts over 1953 and 1954,"[65] which prompted a response from some judges, as he narrates:

> Several judges wrote despairingly of their irritation at being compelled, as they saw it, toward what was an obvious sleight of hand. Some wrote letters of complaint to the Chief Justice. Among them was Justice Law, who, on 15 January

1955, wrote a candid note in which he lamented the endemic practice of every element of the security forces and prison service to beat every prisoner as a matter of course.[66]

There are few official findings of abuse. Those that do make clear claims of abuse are not heard, whether African or European. In June 1954, European settler-farmer Jack Hopcraft submitted to the attorney general "a significant and substantive document alleging abuses committed against his African labourers in screening camps in the Nakuru District."[67] While the likely veracity of these complaints was acknowledged by senior colonial administration officials, as Anderson outlines, no action was taken due to the colonial government's fear of the potentially "shattering" impacts of an investigation.[68] In light of increasing criticism of the torture technique of "screening," particularly by the East African Appeal Court, Vincent Glenday was appointed to "undertake a special, internal inquiry into abuses taking place in screening camps and interrogation centers."[69] The manner in which this inquiry was conducted, visiting only selected camps and focusing on "screening" when detainees arrived, meant that the findings were limited. However, Glenday did find that "considerable and often undesirable pressure was applied in some camps,"[70] yet his report was subsequently cited frequently by the Kenya administration as giving authority to its continued use of "screening."[71] In this manner, law provided continuing authority for the perpetration of harm.

The Holmes Inquiry arose from criticisms of police by the judges in Her Majesty's Court of Appeals for Eastern Africa in Mombasa in August 1954. The appeal judges concluded in their judgment in *R v Njuguna s/o Kamani and Three Others*:

> It is a matter of grave concern when criminals go unpunished: It is a matter of equally great concern that the Court should administer justice according to law. The implications of this case are indeed grave, suggesting as they do the danger that police force in Kenya is tending to become a law unto itself, the Courts will fail in their duty if they ignore or pretend not to see the danger when it is apparent on the evidence before them.[72]

Yet the inquiry was led by the commissioner of police, together with Justice Holmes, who had discounted the allegations of abuse by the four Kikuyu men in the first trial and had found them guilty of the murder of two Europeans. A later commission, the Fairn Commission, initiated after eleven detainees at the Hola detention center were beaten to death, had an intentionally narrow mandate: to "make recommendations on the future of the camps only, and that it was not to investigate past practices."[73] This followed the initial internal inquiry by Senior Resident Magistrate William Henry Goudie who found that "[i]n each case death was found to have been caused by shock and haemorrhage *due to multiple bruising caused by violence*" (emphasis in original),[74] yet he went on to hold that there was insufficient evidence to hold anyone accountable for the murders.[75] Despite the limited scope of the Fairn Commission's terms of reference, the commission did refer to past "abuses, including the use of 'shock treatment' in the camps as a way of forcing detainees to confess; it also directed that "in no circumstances should ['shock treatment'] be employed in the future."[76]

Due to these findings, the administration tried to restrict the impact of the public release of the report. On 27 August 1959, the secretary of state sent a telegram to the governor requesting that the report be published during President Dwight Eisenhower's visit to ensure that it received "no undue publicity."[77] While the Fairn Commission resulted in "the dismissal of two officers, the retirement of another and the resignation of a fourth," as the judge in the later British High Court of Justice judgment was to note, "the impression I have is that the process of enquiry and reporting was regarded by both governments in Nairobi and London as one of damage limitation rather than full investigation."[78]

Even these limited findings are buried, and as Elkins has observed in the case of the Fairn Commission, they can be an "attempt to massage the facts."[79] The findings by judges in the case of *R v Njuguna s/o Kamani and Three Others*, in which they expressed concerns there was a danger that the police were at risk of becoming a law unto themselves, ended up not being heard. So too the concerns of Assistant Police Commissioner Duncan MacPherson, who despite initiating investigations into consistent brutality in interrogation centers came up against obstructions in the colonial administration, writing to one member of Parliament that "I thought that I could have had much more co-operation or even an appreciation of what I was trying to do. I thought that the spirit was lacking and I cannot recollect any occasion when I enjoyed what I was entitled to."[80] These examples of the British colonial efforts to ensure the continued inattention to Kenyan injury, despite recognition of the abuse, reveal the way that state law is located within a colonial structure that limits its possibilities.

While the findings by the Supreme Court in relation to the genocide claims made by the Aboriginal Embassy were significant, they too had little impact at the time. The lawyer assisting the Embassy claimants had pushed for an early decision, arguing that this had the potential to influence the upcoming Australian federal elections, and would assist in removing Prime Minister John Howard, who had pushed through the amendments to the Native Title legislation. Yet the judgment received little to no media coverage and came up against the prevailing discourse in Australia that was unwilling and unable to accept genocide as part of the foundation of the state. The affirmation in law that genocide had occurred during colonization in Australia did not at that time succeed in establishing a new space for discussion of structural injustice and of genocide in Australia.

Law's capacity to respond to justice claims is socially and politically determined, as is its ability to be a broader normative force. We can observe how in the colonial state, as in other situations of state crime, law is companion and collaborator that makes "allowable" the harm perpetrated.[81] Yet in the making of the record of colonial structural injustice, in the endurance of this record, and in its future reactivation, the possibility of justice remains.

REACTIVATING THE LEGAL RECORD

In 2009, a British legal firm, Leigh Day & Co, brought a claim in the British courts on behalf of five Kenyan survivors—Paulo Nzili, Wambugo Wa Nyingi, Jane Muthoni Mara, Susan Ngondi, and Ndiki Mutua—against the Foreign and Commonwealth Office. By the time of the second hearing in the High Court of Justice, Susan Ngondi had died and Ndiki Mutua decided to withdraw his claim. However, it is the original written claim that five applicants submitted to the British Prime Minister Gordon Brown that we used to introduce this chapter.

The voices of Kenyans who had been subject to torture and detention under British colonial rule had struggled to be heard during the time of the colonial administration. For years following Kenyan independence, their voices continued to be silenced. In 2003, alongside the formation of the Mau Mau War Veterans Association in Kenya, the Kenyan government enacted legislation that determined that the Mau Mau were no longer a criminal organization, a provision that had remained active since the colonial "State of Emergency." This enabled the Kenyan Human Rights Commission to gather individual testimonies of the atrocities perpetrated when Kenya was under British colonial rule. Prior to this, three academics, Caroline Elkins, David Anderson, and Huw Bennett, had separately been working on a record of the atrocities through the historical archives in Kenya and the United Kingdom, as well as through speaking with individuals and communities in Kenya.[82] The uncovering and invocation of this historical record, which countered the prevailing narrative of Britain as a benign colonial power, proved to be key to the success of contemporary legal hearings about this past harm. Justice Richard McCombe, presiding over the two High Court of Justice hearings in 2011 and 2012,[83] was to term this evidence the "principal trigger for the initiation of the claims."[84]

In the proceedings, the Kenyan applicants claimed that the current British Foreign and Commonwealth Office

> is liable to them . . . by causing and/or permitting, and/or failing to take adequate measures to prevent, their torture and/or inhuman and degrading treatment and false imprisonment by employees and agents of the [British] Colonial Administration [in Kenya between 1952 and 1961].[85]

In the first High Court of Justice hearing (7–14 April 2011) before Justice McCombe, the court was asked to determine "whether a claim can properly be brought now against Her Majesty's Government in the United Kingdom"[86] on the basis that

> [t]hey [the claimants] submit that the evidence discloses, at the very least, an arguable case that the UK Government, through the Colonial Office and the Army (under General Erskine), played a material part in the creation and maintenance of a system for the suppression of the rebellion, in part by means of torture and other mistreatment of detainees. For this, they submit, they have a properly arguable case that the UK Government as such has a direct and joint liability with the Colonial Administration for what occurred.[87]

This first hearing found that there was a case to answer for the liability of the British government. A second hearing (16–20 and 23–25 July 2012) then focused on whether there would be an issue of limitations as the events to be investigated occurred from 1952 on, sixty years prior to the probable contemporary trial dates.[88] The judgment for this hearing allowed the entry into argument of the principle of vicarious liability, opening the door to the British government being potentially liable for the abuses perpetrated by members of the British army and colonial security forces engaged in guarding prisons and camps. It was also held that, despite the passage of time, a case should proceed for the remaining three claimants.

The claims brought to the High Court of Justice regarding the abuse experienced by alleged members of the Mau Mau during the Kenyan colonial administration relied heavily on the record of law. They were based on the Minutes of the CSCCC, discussed earlier in this chapter, that contain the claims made and the responses given; records of legal cases, inquiries, and commissions; and letters written by detainees documenting the abuse, together with the broader documentary evidence including Executive Council and War Council records. The judgment of the first hearing also includes in its appendices a selection of documents circulated between the colonial administration and the British government around a proposed new regulation to allow greater force against some detainees. It was these detailed records that provided contemporary evidence of the past systematic abuse and detention of alleged Mau Mau insurgents and supporters and of the complicity of the British government in this harm, and which Justice McCombe draws on in his two judgments. The expert witness statements of Elkins, Anderson, and Bennett catalog this evidence and were also central to the court proceedings and judgments.[89]

Importantly, the veracity of this documentary evidence was not refuted during the hearing. In his opening paragraph of the judgment, Justice McCombe stated: "Suffice it to say that if the allegations are true (and no doubt has been cast upon them by any evidence before the court), the treatment of these claimants was utterly appalling."[90] He was later to conclude in his judgment to the second hearing:

> Turning to the factual issues arising, it seems to me that these can be fairly and cogently resolved largely by reference to the documents. The relationship between the perpetrators and the UK government does not depend upon oral evidence and liability would not be dependent upon knowledge of the defendant or an intention on its part to commit torture. . . . The answers to those questions, to my mind, turn principally on documents not the evidence of witnesses.[91]

In this way, Justice McCombe stays within the preference of law for documents, not oral evidence—a preference that has in practice disadvantaged Indigenous claims to justice[92] and prioritized the records of the administration,[93] but, perhaps with paradoxical effect, in this case it also ensured the enduring significance of the archive of the claims made against this administration.[94] Notably, in these archives, much of the evidence provided consists of the claims of Kenyans themselves, in their own words, alongside the responses of the colonial administration.

The record of law is made central in these hearings and the two judgments. Justice McCombe, for example, refers to two criminal cases whose judgments outline and protest the torture of detainees.[95] In doing so, he places the inadequacy of police investigations at the time on contemporary judicial record. The substance of the letter written by the Commissioner of Police Sir Arthur Young in 1954, who had resigned after less than a year, to the governor regarding the failure to sufficiently investigate abuses was recited, disclosing that "[a]n African who is unfortunate enough to suffer from the brutalities which are clearly evident has no one to whom he can complain and no one to regard his interests."[96] The following paragraph records the outcome of the Holmes Inquiry:

> The Holmes report into the matters covered by the judgment of Cram J in R v Muiri & Ors. (Criminal Case No, 240 of 1954) was criticized by the President of the East African Court of Appeal in a letter to the Governor in March 1955, on the basis that "no really searching inquiry" had been made and as a result the relevant part of the report was not published.[97]

Moreover, with reference to the Minutes of the CSCCC, Justice McCombe notes in his judgment that they "seem to reveal a continuing pattern of abusive conduct being reported to the Committee"; they document "another example of the type of violent sexual abuse such as that now accepted to have been perpetrated on Mrs. Mara"; and, that "[t]he selection of these papers . . . tend to support Professor Anderson's conclusion that:

> [i]n summary, the CCC cases show repeatedly that initial criminal investigations by police are suspended by the Attorney-General who then orders a Preliminary Investigation, after which the charge is altered in the records of the CCC without explanation and a conviction on that lesser charge then rapidly achieved.[98]

Utilized in these recent cases are the archival records of the sanctioning of torture[99] and the lack of repercussion of the conviction for the death of a detainee,[100] together with the lead up to one key inquiry, the Fairn Commission, including the caution from the governor to the colonial secretary: "As you know, I have in the past advised you to resist demands for a judicial enquiry."[101] The 1959 telegram sent by the secretary of state to the governor in the wake of the inquiry, with its findings that violence and torture were routinely used in the detention camps, is also referred to, disclosing that:

> [m]inisters are anxious that if possible Report of your views should be published during President Eisenhower's visit to ensure it receives no undue publicity. Visit ends next Wednesday September 2nd.[102]

McCombe concludes that "the impression that I have is that the process of enquiry and reporting was regarded by both governments in Nairobi and London as one of damage limitation rather than full investigation."[103] He concludes his outline of attempts to address the abuses through judicial means at the time: "For present purposes . . . I consider that there is good evidence of attempts by both governments, throughout the emergency, to limit enquiries and investigations into abuses committed in the camps."[104] Reading both of his judgments gives a strong sense of the extent of the abuses, and their systemic nature, acting as contemporary testimony to their veracity and enduring significance.

Ultimately, the court found there was a strong case to hear the claim: "There is ample evidence even in the few papers that I have seen suggesting that there may have been systematic torture of detainees during the Emergency."[105] With respect to the archive, he also notes that:

> [t]he materials evidencing the continuing abuses in the detention camps in subsequent years are substantial, as is the evidence of the knowledge of both governments that they were happening and of the failure to take effective action to stop them.[106]

As such, these contemporary hearings allowed for the reactivation of the legal record that had been negated and dismissed at the time, and subsequently buried. During the case, further evidence came to light—the British government was forced to disclose documents it had been hiding in what became known as the Hanslope Archives. The release of these documents led Justice McCombe in the second hearing to state:

> Looking at those claimants' evidence, I think that it will be quite possible to determine sufficiently clearly where and when they suffered their injuries and the official status of those responsible for inflicting them. It will also be possible, on the documents arranged and collated chronologically, together with the other evidence, to determine whether the injuries occurred because of a breach of duty on the part of the United Kingdom government.[107]

This contemporary reinvoking of the historical record not only allowed these claims and experiences of colonial injustice to be heard again. It also underscored the structural nature of colonial harm. The contemporary claims explicitly sought to show that the abuse at issue was not the actions of a few rogue individuals, but the nature and effect of the structure established by the colonial administration and its relationship to the United Kingdom government as the colonial power. As the applicants stated, "This claim is not premised on liability for the individual assaults and batteries inflicted on the Claimants per se but rather it is averred that liability arises because of the Defendant's role in the creation of the system under which those assaults were committed."[108] Here, the court echoed concerns expressed by members of Parliament at the time.[109]

The High Court's hearing of this claim, as well as its own attentiveness to the pervasive institutional obstruction of claims to justice throughout the colonial administration, thus stands as evidence of the capacity of law to engage with structure, not only individuals.[110] We can see here how the use of the record of law, both the claims made on law during the "Emergency" as well as law's response, helped to instantiate the colonial harms suffered as not an aberration, or a matter of individual deviance, but as outcomes of a broader structure of locally and externally directed colonial oppression and exploitation. And through these proceedings, both contemporary and historical, there is also now an official record that the harms experienced by the complainants were the product of a broader structure of perpetration established by the colonial power in conjunction with the colonial administration:

> The present evidence suggests to me that the Colonial Administration would have followed insistent instructions from the British government in London

> and the security forces would have followed such instructions from General Erskine, without any need to revoke the constitutional arrangements or even to threaten to do so. London was apparently paramount and "what London said, went." The idea that torture of the type alleged could have been perpetrated as widely as it appears to have been if the British government or General Erskine had genuinely wanted it to stop seems, at least arguably, unlikely.[111]
>
> . . .
>
> In the present case, the evidence so far available suggests that this colonial power played a distinctly "hands on" role in the management of the Emergency. It was not standing aloof, merely offering advice and assistance when the local government asked for it.[112]

This recognition of the institutional and structural nature of colonial harm was crucial given the British government's response to the contemporary case. On one hand, in the second 2012 hearing, to the great surprise of the court, before the cross-examination of the first witness, the government barrister began with a statement of recognition of the harm experienced by the witnesses. Mr. Mansfield QC asked the interpreter to:

> [p]lease explain this to the witness, what I am going to say to you? The defendant, the British government, does not dispute that Mr Nzili suffered torture and other ill-treatment at the hands of the Colonial Administration. It is accepted that he personally suffered bad injuries but I have to ask him a few questions about other matters.[113]

This statement was made to all three claimants. As Justice McCombe recorded in judgment to this hearing, "There remains, therefore, no outstanding issue as to the fact of those claimants' injuries and the manner of their infliction."

Yet, on the other hand, despite recognizing Kenyan injury, at trial, the British government also denied its responsibility for it, maintaining that the colonial administration in Kenya was a separate and independent entity to Britain. Thus, Justice McCombe continues that "legal responsibility on the part of Her Majesty's Government in the United Kingdom remains hotly contested."[114] In the end, the government also did not leave the matter to go to trial. It negotiated a settlement agreement just before the full trial was scheduled to begin. This settlement included monetary reparations to those claimants who brought the initial claim, and to a further 5,228 Kenyans whose claims had been gathered by Leigh Day; a memorial built in Nairobi to victims in Kenya; and an apology given in the British Parliament. This recognition was to be tremendously important to Kenyan survivors, as evidenced by the local reception to the erection of the memorial in Nairobi. Yet the settlement was framed as part of a "process of reconciliation," of creating closer "commercial, security and personal links that benefit both our countries" with a focus on tourism, terrorism, and trade.[115] In contrast to the response of the High Court of Justice, it failed to acknowledge the colonial structural relationship between Kenya and Britain. The government continued to deny responsibility, and to only offer regret,[116] despite the court stating in judgment that a full and fair trial was possible and desirable given the weight of evidence presented thus far.[117]

Using the legal and documentary record as their basis, these hearings provided a space for appreciation of the harms and created a further record of the colonial abuses and their structural character. The hearings and the response in judgment demonstrated the extent of the historical injustices perpetrated, their continuation into the present in the way they continued to affect the lives of the claimants, and of the structure of the colonial relationship between Britain and Kenya that framed the systematic perpetration of abuse.

The settlement of the contemporary cases, focused on individual harms and the political necessities of settlement rather than exposure, meant that a structural justice was not found in law. What the reactivation of the record of law has done, however, in putting the structural abuses on record, is provide an opportunity for a far broader discussion outside of law of Britain's role in colonial era abuses as central to the claims of empire.[118] The creation of this space of possibility for activation of a structural justice draws on the record of law and the claims made to law. In making visible the harms perpetrated, it has also made visible the relations that were sought to be established within the unjust structure of colonialism. The formulation of the claims also reveals a desire to establish just relations. These hearings have enabled a means of bringing *into relation* the British Empire and its colonial survivors. That the record remains, and is a record both of injustice and of possibility, means that we can move outside of a binary of justice and injustice to create spaces outside of law, using the record of law, to consider what a structural justice may demand.

REACTIVATING THE RECORD OF LAW AS A STRUCTURAL JUSTICE

What is significant for our consideration of structural colonial injustice and the possibility of structural justice is that the record of law remains. It can be returned to and reactivated. Revisiting these records allows us to hear these justice claims and bring their possibilities of just relations into the present. These "hidden" stories can be made public, through their revival in legal courts, in parliamentary statements, and in public fora such as a theatrical performance or in the school curriculum. As such they bring the past—with its record both of injustice and of just possibilities—into the present.

The reactivation of the record can render structural injustice starkly appreciable. In the "minutes of evidence," which comprises the transcript of the 1881 Coranderrk Inquiry, the testimonies, together with the responses by commissioners, reveal the discriminations and injustices experienced by Indigenous peoples and communities. The statements of many of the European witnesses testify to the racist discourse that prevailed at the time and informed colonial policies—and has continued to do so. The Mau Mau judgments of the British High Court of Justice, in putting on record the correspondence between the Kenyan colonial administration and the British government, expose the deliberate decisions of the time not to use legal accountability to address the abuses perpetrated.

Both the creation and revival of the record demonstrates the failures of law, which we see increasingly highlighted in the transitional justice literature discussed in the previous chapter (which emphasized the limits and occlusions generated through law's presentist and ahistorical approach).[119] This curtails a recognition of both historical harm and its structural and enduring nature. As such, Justice Crispin in the Aboriginal Tent Embassy hearing could recognize past, but not present, genocide, which meant little recognition of a continuing structural injustice and the connection between present and past harms that claimants spoke of. Yet the creation by the Embassy claimants of this record of harms—despite the inability of law to fully recognize it at present—means that we have a record that can be used. The openness of settler law to providing a space for this record also demonstrates the possibilities of just relations in the present and future.

The record is thus one of injustice as well as possible ways forward. The reactivation of the record reveals not only the structural injustice, but the just alternatives put forward and put on record *within* law. The creation of a space of claims and contestations within law is part of the record of law that remains. Speaking as sovereign and self-determining peoples and political participants, the Aboriginal Tent Embassy claimants, the Coranderrk residents, and the Kenyan detainees show another way to proceed. The Kenyans' claim to citizenship and political agency demonstrates how they can be partners in the Kenyan state and British subjects. The Coranderrk residents show how they can work the land together and live together justly. The Aboriginal Embassy claimants outline how settler law and Aboriginal law each have a part to play in "unblocking" the state in which Australia now finds itself. The collaboration evidenced through these claims, and the alternate ways forward put on record, is central to this record of law that contains possibilities of just ways forward.

The record and its reactivation is not enough, however, to establish a structural justice. The British High Court of Justice hearings and the subsequent settlement and apology by Britain do not in themselves constitute a structural justice. The apology was framed as a gesture of "reconciliation" and of better relations between countries, rather than an acknowledgment of the structure of colonization and its ongoing resonance. Instead, what may begin the process of a structural justice is recognition of the colonial frameworks established by Britain, their brutal impact, and their legacy. The record of law may play a part in this—both the record from the time and its use in the High Court hearings. This may not change the dominant political narrative of the glory of the British colonial enterprise—indeed, it remains, as Priyamvada Gopal points out.[120] Yet what we can hope for out of the hearings, besides the critical recognition that they offer those bringing the claims, is that they may assist in the creation of a space of appreciability, toward a normative shift from the previous dominant narrative of the Mau Mau as terrorist and the British colonial state as savior. In their reactivation of the legal record, the High Court hearings provide a reference point in the creation of a new public narrative of recognizability of the extent and nature of the harms perpetrated, from which we can start to consider what just redress and reform in relation to the British colonial legacy may look like. In putting on record the voices from the time, and their articulation of a broader justice, the legal record and claims can provide an indication of a way forward, one that is located in political enfranchisement, race relations, and sovereignty.

Law's capacity to provide justice is socially and politically constituted—in different moments in time, injustice can be heard—the Coranderrk claims were heard (in part) in the Inquiry, but not more broadly at the time, and the abuses perpetrated in Kenya could only be heard once the Mau Mau movement became a legitimate partner in the postcolonial Kenyan state. We know law can silence. As an authoritative and normative state voice, it has the power to name or fail to name harms (as we discussed in chapter 4). Yet we cannot discount the power of the claims made to and within law, their ability to bring into relation and reframe dominant understandings, to create spaces in and alongside law that reveal injustice and pursue justice.

Importantly, law's ability to create change is predicated on the structure in which it is embedded. If, following Patrick Wolfe, as discussed in our introduction, we understand colonialism as "a structure rather than an event,"[121] we are more able to appreciate the limitations of individual legal moments within the broader structure of colonialism. Despite this, the record that is created *through the claims made on it* contains the possibility of change, through its ability to remain and be reconstituted both in and outside of law.

It is in looking to the past—for possibilities of collaboration and change—that we may have a sense of a future justice. In this way, the record of law can be used to *reactivate* claims, and to hold law and governance to account. The record and its reactivation may create a space where structural justice and injustice may be reflected on and made appreciable. It is in relation to law, but not solely through law, that a process of structural justice may be initiated. The past is thus not simply the site of injustice but also the space and the experience through which present and future just relations can emerge.

Chapter 7

CONCLUSION—STRUCTURAL JUSTICE

A Method of "Meeting Points"

> Remember that the future is not somewhere we are going, it is something we are creating. Every day, we do things that make some futures more probable and others less likely.[1]

This book has examined the possibility of just relations within the unjust structure of colonialism. We have done this through an analysis of encounters between law and colonialism, encounters that we argue raise for consideration new ways of understanding structural colonial harm and moving toward a more just present and future. And as articulated in our introduction, this book is itself an encounter, or what we would refer to as a "meeting point," that brings together a criminological concern with hidden and structural harm, an historical studies commitment to acknowledging the importance and complexity of the past, and a socio-legal focus on further understanding the intricate connection between law, structural inequality, and the question of justice. In bringing diverse disciplinary fields on the question of law and colonialism into relation, we develop a new conceptual and methodological framework for understanding and pursuing structural justice. Possibilities for structural justice, we suggest, emerge through being *in relation* and actively engaging with the ethics, politics, and equity of broader structures in which our thoughts and actions are embedded.

MOVING FORWARD: PAST, PRESENT, FUTURE

The task of coming into relation as a means of pursuing structural justice cannot be an ahistorical one. Our present is shaped by our past. The colonial past remains present, alerting us to the continuities of injustice that remain and also to the means of articulating a more just present and future. The productive encounters of the past, of which the Coranderrk Inquiry is one, contain pathways for us today. An emphasis on the interrelationship between the past, present, and future has been key to our central argument regarding the nature of colonial injustice and the possibilities for justice that remain. The past, we have shown, is not just the site of colonial injustice, but also the basis upon which to make sense of the present and to move collectively and collaboratively toward a more just future.

Like Iris Marion Young, we see the task of theorizing structural injustices as intimately linked to questions of responsibility. Young rejects as inappropriate a "liability model" of responsibility that relies principally on legal notions of guilt or blame and proposes in its stead a "social connection model" within which "all agents who contribute by their actions to the structural processes that produce injustice have responsibilities to work to remedy these injustices."[2] This model of responsibility is importantly informed by the past but primarily "forward-looking":

> The point is not to blame, punish, or seek redress from those who did it, but to enjoin those who participate by their actions in the process of collective action to change it.[3]

Throughout this book, we have repeatedly sought to bring the past, the present, and the future into relation to illustrate how this co-constitutive relationship is not simply a source of injustice but also the grounds upon which just futures and a structural justice may be founded. Like Berber Bevernage, we contend that it is possible to "find utopian potential in what is commonly considered to be the future, the present, and the past."[4] It is through a more committed recognition of the past and its enduring significance in the present that the beginning of just relations might be found.

In particular, we have shown how an engagement with the past enables a more fulsome recognition by non-Indigenous polities of the inherent and enduring relationality between different societies and laws created through the colonial encounter. It allows for a broader acknowledgment by non-Indigenous peoples of the continuing power of Indigenous structures of knowledge and law. It thereby lays the groundwork for a commitment in the present to approaching colonial-Indigenous encounters as lawful encounters, involving the productive collision and intersection of different systems of law.

Through a process of bringing into relation the past, the present, and the future, it also becomes possible for non-Indigenous communities to embark on a process of contextualizing what they understand as law and opening up to a more ethical "meeting" of Indigenous and non-Indigenous laws. Such a process can serve to challenge, in Eve Darian-Smith's words, the self-presentation of Western law as "ahistorical" and "float[ing] above the melee of human experience and historical specificity."[5] Instead, Western law can be more accurately perceived as particular, relational, historically located, and the product of lived human experience, enabling the historical denial of law's particularity that facilitated its forceful colonial imposition on other places and peoples to be unsettled. This is a necessary precondition to the form of "lawful relations" articulated by critical legal scholars in Australia whose groundbreaking work on enduring engagements between Indigenous and non-Indigenous ways of knowing, including ways of knowing law, has helped inform our own understandings.[6]

Coming into relation, as a method of pursuing structural justice, is thus an ethical point as well as a methodological one. As an ethical point, it cannot be abstracted—we must practice it, through coming into relation and being exposed to new vantage points.[7] This can be challenging and uncomfortable but can also be a method through which it becomes possible to see that there is the capacity to interact justly still. Moreover, we posit that coming more consciously and meaningfully into relation is an ethical responsibility in settler colonial and postcolonial contexts—one that emerges from a more committed recognition, by non-Indigenous peoples in particular, of the interrelation between the past, the present, and the future.[8]

KEEPING HOLD OF JUSTICE

Our analysis in this book has highlighted the nature of colonialism as inaugurating and sustaining enduring structural inequality in global and local contexts.

The discussion has emphasized, moreover, the continuing complicity of Western legal systems in the colonial enterprise wherever they fail to acknowledge the full significance of colonialism's hold in the present and persistently seek to reassert their primacy over other ways of knowing and being in the world. While drawing attention to certain histories of ongoing oppression, our interdisciplinary approach has nevertheless also interrogated the capacity of different laws and legal systems to better acknowledge and redress the structural injustices of colonialism, to explore alternative ways forward both within and beyond law. We have positioned such possibilities as existing *despite* the seeming intractability of structural injustice and as potential steps in a commitment by postcolonial and settler colonial communities to move toward a practice of structural justice. Keeping hold of justice, for us, means holding the lived reality of structural injustices along with the responsibility to continue to work in new and expansive ways *within* continuing colonial orders in order to acknowledge, challenge, and diminish them.

To this end, this book presents alternative ways forward including through greater recognition of the lived experience of past colonial harm and its ongoing implications in the present (chapters 2, 4) together with more informed consideration of non-Indigenous peoples' relationship to, and responsibility for, their own law and its practices (chapters 2, 3). Such acts may in turn enable non-Indigenous peoples and societies to engage lawfully with the legal systems and ways of knowing of others and facilitate an opening up to alternative ontologies of law (chapter 3). They could also give rise to crucial structural reforms and modes of legal redress that better reflect the relationality between Indigenous and non-Indigenous societies and laws and address the injustice of the imposition of Western frameworks on Indigenous communities in denial of their sovereignty (chapters 3, 5, 6).

Opportunities for meaningful change may be found within and through law. We have shown how the past record of Western and colonial law can be reactivated to pursue just ends in the present (chapter 6). Further, we have shown how the legal encounter can be transformed into a meeting point, between Indigenous and non-Indigenous holders of law, and between different legal orders, in which just alternatives can be spoken and heard (chapters 3, 6). Such opportunities may also reside in the potential of law to be part of a more wide-ranging, systemic, and substantive "justice agenda," which is attentive to the structural character of colonial harm and opens up the state and its foundations to question; one which recognizes, in Ovide Mecredi's words (chapter 5), that "structural change in laws and policies is essential."[9] It is in this way that we have argued that law (plurally conceived) may be understood both as centrally implicated in the injustice of the colonial past and as having a critical role in realizing a more just future.

The purpose of our discussion, therefore, has been to pursue a collaborative argument, grounded in deeply engaging with different historically, geographically, and jurisdictionally situated encounters between law and colonialism, from a shared framework concerned with colonial structural injustice and the need to find more constructive ways forward. Our aim was collectively to substantiate and elaborate the structurally unjust nature of colonial harm and to explore the possibilities for justice and just relations that *continue to exist*. As such, our conceptualization of structural justice is one that arises from our joint reflections on the insights that emerged from bringing together these different encounters across time and space. For us, the act of keeping hold of justice is therefore not an isolated one, but a practice and orientation, one that is premised in a specific methodology of bringing peoples, encounters, laws, temporalities, and perspectives into dynamic relation.

Indeed, it is this methodology of establishing productive meeting points—between different historical experiences, temporalities, forms of law, and, significantly, ontologies of law—that can spark new modes of identifying, understanding, acknowledging, and redressing colonial structural injustice that we put forward as a key contribution of our work. Our method in this book is one that seeks to bring disciplines, peoples, encounters, and temporalities "into relation" to make visible both the structures of past injustice that continue into the present and the possibilities of future justice that nevertheless remain. As such, rather than offer a prescriptive or generalized argument about what practices of structural justice should look like in particular times and places, it is instead this method that we hope might resonate with others grappling with problems of structural injustice in different places and contexts. It is a method produced through the conceptual framework and collaborative relations of the Minutes of Evidence project and its innovative and expansive modes of engaging with colonial harm, to which we now return as a way to conclude our discussion.

MINUTES OF EVIDENCE AND A METHOD OF "MEETING POINTS"

> [H]ow as scholars, practitioners and bearers of law we can move beyond relatively detached engagements with structural injustice to establish meeting points that foster collaborative relationships between Indigenous and non-Indigenous people that have the capacity to bring a whole range of shared and distinctive experiences, understandings, knowledges and laws to bear on the question of how to live together justly in settler societies?[10]

These are some of the driving questions that motivated our work together on the Minutes of Evidence project, an Australian Victoria-based collaboration between Indigenous and non-Indigenous researchers, performing artists, educators, and community and government agencies interested in promoting new ways of engaging with structural injustice in Australia and elsewhere. To enhance broader community understanding of the inequities arising from intransigent and often hidden colonial harms, the project sought to create public spaces within which to explore, share, and interrogate Victoria's colonial past and present in new and engaging ways.

To this end, the three dimensions of the project—research, education, and performance—were underpinned by a commitment to create "meeting points" in schools, on Country, in theaters, between scholars and practitioners, between the past and the present, between the broader community and experiences of colonial injustice, and between different systems of Indigenous and settler law. In so doing, these "meeting points" fostered proximity, creating spaces for awareness of structural injustice and consideration of what a structural justice may demand. It enabled the exploration of new forms of relational engagement. As Lilly Brown, one of our co-researchers on the project, explained, "meeting points" constituted "really amazing opportunities to think about complexity and the idea of structural justice which does not let you get away with anything. You have to think about the past, the present and the implications for the future but at the same time acknowledge that we are in this moment creating the future in that way."[11]

The specific history of the Coranderrk Inquiry provided a central "meeting point" for all partners on the project and was used as a means of realizing shared ambitions to make structural and historical harm visible and appreciable in the present. This history was reenacted through performance, research, and education.

Coranderrk: We Will Show the Country brought this history to contemporary audiences in the form of a verbatim theater play based on the original "minutes of evidence" of the 1881 Coranderrk Inquiry, along with letters, newspaper articles, and petitions from the time. The play was performed on Country before descendants of the original Coranderrk community—including at the original site where witnesses had delivered their testimonies over 130 years earlier—enjoyed multiple sold-out seasons at theater and community venues in Melbourne and Sydney, and toured metropolitan and regional schools in Victoria. Performances brought together descendants of the Coranderrk story, settler and Aboriginal, with question and answer sessions providing a means for public audiences, project members, and actors to explore issues relating to structural and historical injustice.

Education was designed as a way to further extend the project's field of engagement. Through consultation and collaboration, the project enabled the development of new modules in the state secondary school curriculum, providing teachers and students a means of engaging with this history to make sense of our present, embedding the theater production through its testimony, the Coranderrk history, and Koori perspectives in Australian education, and developing protocols for engagement with Indigenous communities around these resources. The project collaboratively designed a dynamic public website and facilitated the digitization of the original "minutes of evidence" and a DVD of the individual testimonies from the performance that is being used to generate further public conversations in diverse locations.

It was only through collaboration that these unique project outputs were enabled. Through collaboration, project partners were able to produce something wholly new, which transcended each of their individual expertise. Using this relational method generated new insights and new relationships, leading to the elaboration of our collective understanding and portrayal of structural colonial injustice and the possibility of structural justice. For partner organization La Mama Theatre, the project provided "the opportunity to think and approach work differently, sustain partnerships, [and] access to research that contextualizes the work in a broad and meaningful way."[12] For partner organization the Department of Education and Training Victoria, "The Coranderrk story is at the heart of the [curriculum] resource, but it also links to issues like justice, activism, sovereignty, self-determination, maintenance of culture and other themes."[13] For partner organization VicHealth, the project's "impact on community, student and teachers' understanding of racism and racial, ethnic and cultural diversity has been considerable."[14] For partner organization Koorie Heritage Trust, "The ongoing performances of the Coranderrk play, the curriculum development component and the research outcomes have a life beyond the Project, which will continue to have an impact on both the Indigenous and non-Indigenous Community for many years to come."[15] Together, project partners provided the opportunity for new public conversations about structural injustice and structural justice in the present and for the future.

KEEPING HOLD OF STRUCTURAL JUSTICE

Our methodology in this book has been to bring different historical experiences, academic and personal perspectives, temporalities, and laws (and ways of knowing law) into relation to spark new ways of understanding colonial harm, the role of law, and the potentiality of justice. It is through bringing together different disciplines and diverse encounters between law and colonialism that we have been able to develop an argument about the injustice of structural colonial harm and yet the possibilities for just relations within it. It is through such productive encounters that we have deepened our understanding of colonial injustice and developed our concept of structural justice. It is through our engagement with lived and specific experiences of colonial harm across time and space that we come to conceptualize structural justice as being based on an historical consciousness and a recognition of the enduring significance of the past; discursively and practically manifest, premised on making colonial injustice appreciable as well as pursuing its practical redress; and as still implicating laws (plurally conceived), as a partner to *both* structural inequity and the possibility of a more just and respectful future.

Thus, for us, the possibility of such a structural justice is found in the productive nature of encounters—in the interrelation between peoples and laws, different legal orders, different disciplinary frameworks, and, importantly, the

Figure 3. Uncle Jack Charles (playing William Barak) reading the petition in *Coranderrk: We Will Show the Country*, a dramatic reenactment of the testimony at the 1881 Parliamentary Inquiry into the Coranderrk Aboriginal Reserve, Victoria, Australia. A 2011 production by the Ilbijerri Theatre Company at La Mama Courthouse Theatre in Carlton, Victoria: Isaac Drandic (director), Rachel Maza (dramaturgy), Giordano Nanni and Andrea James (script), with actors Syd Brisbane, Uncle Jack Charles, Jim Daly, Peter Finlay, Greg Fryer, Liz Jones, Tom Long, Melodie Reynolds, and Glenn Shea. Photograph: Steven Rhall.

past, present, and future. It is by holding together sometimes seemingly contradictory or diverse goals, perspectives, ways of being, and temporal states that the possibilities for justice can be found. This also means for us that structural justice—as it emerges and is pursued inside and outside the law—is a fundamentally relational phenomenon, grounded in openness and engagement. It entails a respectful and collaborative commitment to acknowledging the continuing effects of colonial harms and to supporting and sustaining meaningful social, legal, and political change. It is a form of justice that emerges from relations between one another and actively engages with the ethics, politics, and equity of broader structures.

Acknowledging the interrelation between the past, present, and future as a potentially "forward-looking" practice of responsibility reinvests individuals and communities with agency and room to move. It may raise complicated questions for non-Indigenous peoples about their relation to their own law and its unjust practices, but it also provides a basis upon which to respectfully engage with the laws of others and collaboratively work together inside and outside law to redress all manifestations of colonial injustice as they are expressed politically, economically, socially, and legally. It enables the present to be conceptualized as not only a place of injustice, but of possibility, responsibility, and relationality. It compels a recognition that there are possibilities to interact justly still.

NOTES

Chapter 1

1. The original source is the "Report of the Board Appointed to Enquire into, and Report upon, the Present Condition and Management of the Coranderrk Aboriginal Station, Together with the Minutes of Evidence" (Melbourne: Government Printer, 1882), 132, available at http://www.minutesofevidence.com.au/research/#archival-sources. Quoted in Giordano Nanni and Andrea James, *Coranderrk: We Will Show the Country* (Canberra, ACT: Aboriginal Studies Press, 2013), 169. Settlers and officials commonly described different Indigenous peoples and countries throughout colonial Australia as "Aboriginal." In this book, we use "Indigenous peoples" when referring to settler societies as a specific type of colonial formation, or to Aboriginal and Torres Strait Islander peoples collectively; to "Aboriginal peoples" in the context of mainland Australia/Tasmania; and to "Koori peoples" when speaking specifically of Victoria. At times, we also consider the localized circumstances of distinctive peoples or nations within these colonial boundaries, including, for example, the Wiradjuri nation of south-central New South Wales, and the Wurundjeri and other peoples of the Kulin nation (Boonwurrung; Dja Dja Wurrung; Taungurong; Wathaurong) of central Victoria.

2. In 1835, the explorer John Batman claimed to have negotiated a transfer of land with Wurundjeri people of the Kulin nation in the newly established Port Phillip district (later to become the colony of Victoria), but Governor Richard Bourke of New South Wales quickly declared that only the Crown could exercise such powers and disallowed the so-called treaty. See Richard Broome, *Aboriginal Victorians: A History since 1800*, 4th ed. (Crows Nest, NSW: Allen and Unwin, 2005); Bain Attwood and Helen Doyle, *Possession: Batman's Treaty and the Matter of History* (Carlton, VIC: Miegunyah Press, 2009); Gary Presland, *First People: The Eastern Kulin of Melbourne, Port Phillip & Central Victoria* (Melbourne: Museum Victoria Publishing, 2010).

3. In certain places, some legal pluralism was still evident until the 1840s. See Lisa Ford, *Settler Sovereignty: Jurisdiction and Indigenous Peoples in America and Australia, 1788–1836* (Cambridge: Harvard University Press, 2010); Damen Ward, "A Means and Measure of Civilisation: Colonial Authorities and Indigenous Law in Australasia," *History Compass* 1, no. 1 (2003): 1–24.

4. See Broome, *Aboriginal Australians*; Leigh Boucher and Lynette Russell, eds., *Settler Colonial Governance in Nineteenth Century Victoria* (Canberra: ANU Press and Aboriginal History Inc., 2015), particularly 1–26, and 63–94.

5. See also the related work of partner investigators on the Minutes of Evidence project, Zoë Laidlaw and Alan Lester, eds., *Indigenous Communities and Settler Colonialism: Land Holding, Loss and Survival in an Interconnected World* (Houndmills, Basingstoke: Palgrave Macmillan, 2015).

6. The Minutes of Evidence Project: Promoting New and Collaborative Ways of Understanding Australia's Past and Engaging with Structural Justice was funded by the Australian Research Council, LP110200054 (http://minutesofevidence.com.au). Partner organizations include the University of Melbourne, VicHealth, Department of Education and Early Childhood Development, Victorian Aboriginal Education Association Incorporated, Koorie Heritage Trust, Arts Victoria, Ilbijerri Theatre Company, La Mama Theatre, State Library of Victoria, Regional Arts Victoria, Deakin University, University of Sussex, and Royal Holloway University of London.

7. The script was co-written by a senior research fellow on the project, non-Indigenous writer/historian Giordano Nanni, and Yorta Yorta/Kurnai playwright/theatre maker Andrea James. An annotated script was published as Nanni and James, *Coranderrk: We Will Show the Country*. The performance history for *Coranderrk: We Will Show the Country* is published on the Minutes of Evidence website: http://www.minutesofevidence.com.au/performance/coranderrk-we-will-show-the-country-performance-history-credits/. This consisted of an initial pilot and workshop, 13–15 August 2010 (La Mama Courthouse Theatre, Melbourne); community consultation readings, 6 May 2011 (Melba Hall, University of Melbourne) and 7 May 2011 (Sanctuary House, Healesville); public premiere season, 16–27 November 2011 (La Mama Courthouse Theatre, Melbourne); second season, 11–12 February 2012 (Indigenous Arts Festival, BMW Edge, Federation Square, Melbourne); third season, 28 June–1 July 2012 (Playhouse Theatre, Sydney Opera House, Sydney). In 2013, the Minutes of Evidence project together with Ilbijerri Theatre Company developed a new version of the play, entitled *CORANDERRK*, targeted specifically at school audiences. Pilot readings of this performance were staged on 15–16 August at the Memorial Hall, Healesville, and at the Open Stage Theatre, University of Melbourne. *Coranderrk: We Will Show the Country*, fourth season, 12–23 August 2015 (La Mama Courthouse Theatre, Melbourne); regional tour, 11–20 September 2015; On Country Performance, 21 February 2016; Melbourne Town Hall, 31 May 2016; fifth season, 26–27 July 2016 (Harold Michell Performance Space, Institute of Koorie Education, Deakin University, Geelong); Wurundejeri Land Council in participation with Telstra, 28 July 2016; La Mama Courthouse Theatre, Melbourne, 3–7 August 2016. See also Penelope Edmonds, "Theatre of Evidence," *History Australia* 9, no. 2 (2012): 205–7.

8. See Jennifer Balint et al., "The 'Minutes of Evidence' Project: Creating Collabora-

tive Fields of Engagement with the Past, Present and Future," in *Settler Colonial Governance in Nineteenth-Century Victoria*, ed. Leigh Boucher and Lynette Russell (Canberra, ACT: ANU Press and Aboriginal History Inc., 2015), 203–24.

9. Our reference to proximity here draws on the work of cultural geographer Gearóid Ó Tuathail, *Critical Geopolitics: The Politics of Writing Global Space* (Minneapolis: University of Minnesota Press, 1996), 220–21.

10. For an overview of the range of other academic outputs from the project, see http://minutesofevidence.com.au

11. See also Mariana Valverde, "From Persons and Their Acts to Webs of Relationships: Some Theoretical Resources for Environmental Justice," *Crime, Law and Social Change* 68, no. 5 (2017): 547–62.

12. See the collection from Austin Sarat and Thomas R. Kearns, eds., *Justice and Injustice in Law and Legal Theory* (Ann Arbor: University of Michigan Press, 1996). In particular, see the editors' introduction contextualizing past and present engagements between law and justice: Thomas R. Kearns and Austin Sarat, "Legal Justice and Injustice: Toward a Situated Perspective," in *Justice and Injustice in Law and Legal Theory*, ed. Austin Sarat and Thomas R. Kearns (Ann Arbor: University of Michigan Press, 1996), 1–18.

13. The literature on this topic is significant, encompassing both generalized critiques of law and those which demonstrate its unjust outcomes for particular groups. See, for example, Aileen Moreton-Robinson, ed., *Sovereign Subjects: Indigenous Sovereignty Matters* (Crows Nest, NSW: Allen and Unwin, 2007), pt. 1; Roberto Mangabeira Unger, *The Critical Legal Studies Movement* (Cambridge: Harvard University Press, 1986); Patricia Williams, "The Obliging Shell: An Informal Essay on Formal Equal Opportunity," *Michigan Law Review* 87, no. 8 (1989): 2128–51; Derrick A. Bell, "Who's Afraid of Critical Race Theory?," *University of Illinois Law Review* 1, no. 4 (1995): 893–910; Joan Hoff, *Law, Gender, and Injustice: A Legal History of U.S. Women* (New York: New York University Press, 1991); Leslie Moran, *The Homosexual(ity) of Law* (London: Routledge, 1996).

14. See, among many other possible examples, Margaret Thornton, "Feminism and the Contradictions of Law Reform," *International Journal of the Sociology of Law* 19 (1991): 453–74; Maria Giannacopoulos, "Offshore Hospitality: Law, Asylum and Colonisation," *Law Text Culture* 17 (2013): 163–83; Carl Stychin and Didi Herman, eds., *Sexuality in the Legal Arena* (London: Athlone, 2000); Mari Matsuda, "When the First Quail Calls: Multiple Consciousness as Jurisprudential Method," *Women's Rights Law Reporter* 11 (1989): 7–10; Marc Galanter, "Why the 'Haves' Come Out Ahead: Speculations on the Limits of Legal Change," *Law & Society Review* 9, no. 1 (1974): 95–160.

15. Carol Smart, *Feminism and the Power of Law* (London: Routledge, 1989); Wendy Lambourne, "Transitional Justice and Peacebuilding after Mass Violence," *International Journal of Transitional Justice* 3 (2009): 28–48; Rama Mani, *Beyond Retribution: Seeking Justice in the Shadows of War* (Cambridge: Polity Press, 2002). See also chapter 5.

16. From a vast literature, see Edward W. Said, *Orientalism* (New York: Pantheon

Books, 1978); Samir Amin, *Eurocentrism*, trans. Russell Moore (New York: Monthly Review Press, 1989); Robert Young, *White Mythologies: Writing History and the West* (New York: Routledge, 1990); Ratna Kapur, *Erotic Justice: Law and the New Politics of Colonialism* (London: Glasshouse Press, 2005). For critical review and analysis, see Patrick Wolfe, "History and Imperialism: A Century of Theory, from Marx to Postcolonialism," *American Historical Review* 102, no. 2 (1997): 388–420; Dane Kennedy, "Imperial History and Post-Colonial Theory," *Journal of Imperial and Commonwealth History* 24, no. 3 (1996): 345–63; Ella Shohat, "Notes on the 'Post-Colonial,'" *Social Text*, nos. 31–32 (1992): 99–113; Ann Laura Stoler, "Imperial Debris: Reflections on Ruins and Ruination," *Cultural Anthropology* 23, no. 2 (2008): 191–219.

17. Shaunnagh Dorsett and Shaun McVeigh, *Jurisdiction* (Abingdon, Oxon: Routledge, 2012). See also Christine Black, *The Land Is the Source of the Law: A Dialogic Encounter with Indigenous Jurisprudence* (New York: Routledge, 2011); Ann Genovese, "On Australian Feminist Tradition: Three Notes on Conduct, Inheritance and the Relations of Historiography and Jurisprudence," *Journal of Australian Studies* 38, no. 4 (2014): 430–44; Mark McMillan and Martin Clark, "Making Sense of Indigeneity, Aboriginality and Identity: Race as a Constitutional Conundrum since 1983," *Griffith Law Review* 24, no. 1 (2015): 106–26; Nicole Watson, "Justice in Whose Eyes? Why Lawyers Should Read Black Australian Literature," *Griffith Law Review* 23, no. 1 (2014): 44–60; Larissa Behrendt, Chris Cunneen, and Terri Libesman, *Indigenous Legal Relations in Australia* (South Melbourne, VIC: Oxford University Press, 2009); Aileen Moreton-Robinson, *The White Possessive: Property, Power, and Indigenous Sovereignty* (Minneapolis: University of Minnesota Press, 2015). More generally, see among others, Robert A. Williams, *The American Indian in Western Legal Thought: The Discourses of Conquest* (New York: Oxford University Press, 1990); Robert J. Miller et al., *Discovering Indigenous Lands: The Doctrine of Discovery in the English Colonies* (Oxford: Oxford University Press, 2010); Glen Sean Coulthard, *Red Skin, White Masks: Rejecting the Colonial Politics of Recognition* (Minneapolis: University of Minnesota Press, 2014); Mariana Valverde, "Jurisdiction and Scale: Legal 'Technicalities' as Resources for Theory," *Social and Legal Studies* 18, no. 2 (2009): 139–57.

18. Judith Butler, *Precarious Life: The Powers of Mourning and Violence* (London: Verso, 2004), xx; Judith Butler, *Frames of War: When Is Life Grievable?* (New York: Verso, 2009), chap. 1; Paddy Hillyard and Steve Tombs, eds., *Beyond Criminology: Taking Harm Seriously* (London: Pluto Press, 2004). Criminology as a field of study is centrally focused on what harm is criminalized and how this shapes social and political and legal responses to it.

19. Peter Goodrich, *Languages of Law: From Logics of Memory to Nomadic Masks* (London: Weidenfeld and Nicolson, 1990); Eugen Ehrlich, *Fundamental Principles of the Sociology of Law*, trans. Walter L Moll (Cambridge: Harvard University Press, 1936); David Nelken, "Eugen Ehrlich, Living Law, and Plural Legalities," *Theoretical Inquiries in Law* 9, no. 2 (2008): 443–71; Leon Petrażycki, *Law and Morality* (Cambridge: Harvard

University Press, 1955); Andrzej Kojder, "Leon Petrażycki's Socio-Legal Ideas and Their Contemporary Continuation," *Journal of Classical Sociology* 6, no. 3 (2006): 333–58.

20. Dorsett and McVeigh, *Jurisdiction*; Genovese, "On Australian Feminist Tradition"; Ann Genovese, "Critical Decision, 1982: Remembering *Koowarta v Bjelke-Petersen*," *Griffith Law Review* 23, no. 1 (2014): 1–15; Ann Genovese, "Critical Decision 1983: Remembering *Commonwealth v Tasmania*," *Griffith Law Review* 24, no. 1 (2015): 1–15.

21. Boaventura de Sousa Santos, "Law: A Map of Misreading. Toward a Postmodern Conception of Law," *Journal of Law and Society* 14, no. 3 (1987): 279–302; Sally Engle Merry, "Legal Pluralism," *Law & Society Review* 22, no. 5 (1988): 869–96; Stoler, "Imperial Debris"; Renisa Mawani, *Colonial Proximities: Crossracial Encounters and Juridical Truths in British Columbia, 1871–1921* (Vancouver: UBC Press, 2009).

22. Kamari Clarke, *Fictions of Justice: The International Criminal Court and the Challenge of Legal Pluralism in Sub-Saharan Africa* (New York: Cambridge University Press, 2009); Mahmood Mamdani, "The New Humanitarian Order," *New Nation*, September 2008; Antony Anghie, *Imperialism, Sovereignty and the Making of International Law* (Cambridge: Cambridge University Press, 2005).

23. Nanni and James, *Coranderrk: We Will Show the Country*, 5–32; Diane Barwick, *Rebellion at Coranderrk*, ed. Laura E. Barwick and Richard E. Barwick (Canberra, ACT: Aboriginal History Inc., 1998); Broome, *Aboriginal Australians: A History since 1788*, 74–80.

24. "Report of the Board Appointed to Enquire into, and Report upon, the Present Condition and Management of the Coranderrk Aboriginal Station, Together with the Minutes of Evidence," 67–68.

25. Ibid., 68.

26. The Aborigines Protection Act 1886 (Vic), known as the Half Caste Act, was an amendment to the Aboriginal Protection Act 1869 (Vic): "An Act to provide for the Protection and Management of the Aboriginal Natives of Victoria." For analysis, see Broome, *Aboriginal Victorians: A History since 1800*; Tony Birch, "Archive Box—Series One: Matters in Relation to Aborigines Act (1886)," *Law Text Culture* 7 (2003): 142–47.

27. Patrick Wolfe, "Nation and MiscegeNation: Discursive Continuity in the Post-Mabo Era," *Social Analysis* 36 (1994): 99–152; Broome, *Aboriginal Australians: A History since 1788*.

28. Zoë Laidlaw, "Breaking Britannia's Bounds? Law, Settlers, and Space in Britain's Imperial Historiography," *Historical Journal* 55, no. 3 (2012): 821; Alan Lester and Fae Dussart, *Colonization and the Origins of Humanitarian Governance: Protecting Aborigines across the Nineteenth-Century British Empire* (Cambridge: Cambridge University Press, 2014).

29. Laidlaw, "Breaking Britannia's Bounds?," 824; Elizabeth Kolsky, *Colonial Justice in British India: White Violence and the Rule of Law* (New York: Cambridge University Press, 2011), 35.

30. Anghie, *Imperialism, Sovereignty and the Making of International Law*; Williams, *American Indian in Western Legal Thought.*

31. Ratna Kapur, "Precarious Desires and Ungrievable Lives: Human Rights and Postcolonial Critiques of Legal Justice," *London Review of International Law* 3, no. 2 (2015): 268.

32. Jennifer Balint, *Genocide, State Crime, and the Law: In the Name of the State* (New York: Routledge, 2012); Kapur, *Erotic Justice.*

33. Iris Marion Young, "Responsibility and Global Justice: A Social Connection Model," *Social Philosophy and Policy* 23, no. 1 (2006): 114.

34. Ibid.

35. Johan Galtung, "Violence, Peace, and Peace Research," *Journal of Peace Research* 6, no. 3 (1969): 171. Recent important critical engagements with structural violence include, for example, Marxist philosopher and cultural theorist Slavoj Žižek's formulation of subjective, objective, and systemic violence in *Violence: Six Sideways Reflections* (New York: Picador, 2008).

36. Nancy Scheper-Hughes and Philippe Bourgois, "Introduction: Making Sense of Violence," in *Violence in War and Peace: An Anthology*, ed. Nancy Scheper-Hughes and Philippe Bourgois (Malden, MA: Blackwell Publishing, 2004), 1.

37. Bamfield was also known as Michie: Nanni and James, *Coranderrk: We Will Show the Country*, 73.

38. "Report of the Board Appointed to Enquire into, and Report upon, the Present Condition and Management of the Coranderrk Aboriginal Station, Together with the Minutes of Evidence," 9.

39. Catherine Lu, "Colonialism as Structural Injustice: Historical Responsibility and Contemporary Redress," *Journal of Political Philosophy* 19, no. 3 (2011): 262.

40. For further reading, see Wolfe, "Nation and MiscegeNation"; Patrick Wolfe, "Land, Labor, and Difference: Elementary Structures of Race," *American Historical Review* 106, no. 3 (2001): 866–905; Patrick Wolfe, *Traces of History: Elementary Structures of Race* (London: Verso, 2016). For related analyses, see Lorenzo Veracini, *Settler Colonialism: A Theoretical Overview* (Basingstoke: Palgrave Macmillan, 2010); Daiva Stasiulis and Nira Yuval-Davis, eds., *Unsettling Settler Societies: Articulations of Gender, Race, Ethnicity and Class* (London: SAGE Publications, 1995); Donald Denoon, *Settler Capitalism: The Dynamics of Dependent Development in the Southern Hemisphere* (New York: Oxford University Press, 1983).

41. Wolfe, "Nation and MiscegeNation," 96.

42. *Mabo and Others v Queensland* (No. 2), 1992 HCA 23, 175 CLR 1 (hereafter "*Mabo*"). For analysis, see Gerry Simpson, "Mabo, International Law, Terra Nullius and the Stories of Settlement: An Unresolved Jurisprudence," *Melbourne University Law Review* 19 (1993): 195–210; Stewart Motha, "The Failure of Postcolonial Sovereignty in Australia," *Australian Feminist Law Journal* 22 (2005): 107–26; Wolfe, "Nation and Mis-

cegeNation"; Peter Rush, "An Altered Jurisdiction: Corporeal Traces of Law," *Griffith Law Review* 6 (1997): 144–68; Wayne Atkinson, "'Not One Iota' of Land Justice: Reflections on the Yorta Yorta Native Title Claim, 1994–2001," *Indigenous Law Bulletin* 5, no. 6 (2001): 19–23; Ann Curthoys, Ann Genovese, and Alexander Reilly, *Rights and Redemption: History, Law and Indigenous People* (Sydney, NSW: University of New South Wales Press, 2008).

43. Anghie, *Imperialism, Sovereignty and the Making of International Law*; Williams, *American Indian in Western Legal Thought.*

44. Marcia Langton, "Dominion and Dishonour: A Treaty between Our Nations?," *Postcolonial Studies* 4, no. 1 (2001): 13–26; Noel Pearson, "Mabo Lecture: Where We've Come From and Where We're at with the Opportunity That Is Koiki Mabo's Legacy to Australia," in *Dialogue about Land Justice: Papers from the National Native Title Conferences* (Arrernte Country: Aboriginal Studies Press, 2003), 33–51; Shaunnagh Dorsett and Shaun McVeigh, "Conduct of Laws: Native Title, Responsibility, and Some Limits of Jurisdictional Thinking," *Melbourne University Law Review* 36 (2012): 470–93.

45. Iris Marion Young, *Responsibility for Justice* (New York: Oxford University Press, 2011), 55.

46. See, for example, Thomas Pogge, "Priorities of Global Justice," *Metaphilosophy* 32, nos. 1–2 (2001): 6–24; Butler, *Precarious Life*; Žižek, *Violence*, 8–33.

47. Butler, *Precarious Life*, xx; Butler, *Frames of War*, chap. 1.

48. Taken from Tony Birch's filmed address to the audience on Minutes of Evidence website: http://www.minutesofevidence.com.au/performance/. See also Tony Birch, "'The Invisible Fire': Indigenous Sovereignty, History and Responsibility," in *Sovereign Subjects: Indigenous Sovereignty Matters*, ed. Aileen Moreton-Robinson (Crows Nest, NSW: Allen and Unwin, 2007), 105–17.

49. Edward Curr also claimed that Aboriginal people should be regarded as children (except in matters of criminal law) and that Coranderrk residents should be removed and the reserve made available to settlers. See Samuel Furphy, *Edward M. Curr and the Tide of History* (Canberra: ANU Press, 2013). Curr's testimony is available in "Report of the Board Appointed to Enquire into, and Report upon, the Present Condition and Management of the Coranderrk Aboriginal Station, Together with the Minutes of Evidence," 120–27; Nanni and James, *Coranderrk: We Will Show the Country*, 62–72. See *Members of the Yorta Yorta Aboriginal Community v Victoria & Ors* (1998) FCA 1606; *Members of the Yorta Yorta Aboriginal Community v Victoria* (2002) HCA 58, 214 CLR 422.

50. Aileen Moreton-Robinson, "Imagining the Good Indigenous Citizen: Race War and the Pathology of Patriarchal White Sovereignty," *Cultural Studies Review* 15, no. 2 (2009): 61–79; Aileen Moreton-Robinson, "Writing Off Indigenous Sovereignty: The Discourse of Security and Patriarchal White Sovereignty," in *Sovereign Subjects: Indigenous Sovereignty Matters* (Crows Nest, NSW: Allen and Unwin, 2007), 86–102; Jon

C. Altman and Melinda Hinkson, eds., *Coercive Reconciliation: Stabilise, Normalise, Exit Aboriginal Australia* (North Carlton, VIC: Arena Publications Association, 2007); Nicole Watson, "The Northern Territory Emergency Response—Has It Really Improved the Lives of Aboriginal Women and Children?," *Australian Feminist Law Journal* 35, no. 1 (2011): 147–63.

51. Kapur, *Erotic Justice*, 23.

52. Berber Bevernage, "The Past Is Evil/Evil Is Past: On Retrospective Politics, Philosophy of History and Temporal Manichaeism," *History and Theory* 53, no. 3 (2015): 350–52. For an overview of predominantly historical studies of law and colonialism, see Laidlaw, "Breaking Britannia's Bounds?"

53. Stewart Motha, *Archiving Sovereignty: Law, History, Violence* (Ann Arbor: University of Michigan Press, 2018), 20.

54. "Report of the Board Appointed to Enquire into, and Report upon, the Present Condition and Management of the Coranderrk Aboriginal Station, Together with the Minutes of Evidence," 9–10; Nanni and James, *Coranderrk: We Will Show the Country*, 90.

55. "Report of the Board Appointed to Enquire into, and Report upon, the Present Condition and Management of the Coranderrk Aboriginal Station, Together with the Minutes of Evidence," 135–36; Nanni and James, *Coranderrk: We Will Show the Country*, 167.

56. Wolfe, "Land, Labor, and Difference."

57. Dorsett and McVeigh, *Jurisdiction*, 6.

Chapter 2

1. Dorsett and McVeigh, *Jurisdiction*, 128.

2. Tony Birch, "'I Could Feel It in My Body': War on a History War," *Transforming Cultures EJournal* 1, no. 1 (2006): 23.

3. John Borrows, *Drawing Out Law: A Spirit's Guide* (Toronto: Toronto University Press, 2010), 44.

4. Goodrich, *Languages of Law*, 214; see also Motha, *Archiving Sovereignty*.

5. Goodrich, *Languages of Law*, 5.

6. Borrows, *Drawing Out Law*, 66.

7. Ibid.

8. Dorsett and McVeigh, *Jurisdiction*, 128.

9. Ibid.

10. *Mabo and Others v Queensland* (No. 2), 1992 HCA 23, 175 CLR 1.

11. For instances of legal pluralism, and the complex process of establishing exclusive territorial sovereignty in settler colonies, see Dorsett and McVeigh, *Jurisdiction*, 24–41, 100–101; Ford, *Settler Sovereignty*; Ward, "Means and Measure of Civilisation"; Paul G.

McHugh, *Aboriginal Societies and the Common Law: A History of Sovereignty, Status, and Self-Determination* (New York: Oxford University Press, 2004).

12. As discussed in the introduction. See further Young, *Responsibility for Justice*; Lu, "Colonialism as Structural Injustice."

13. The significance of how the relationship between the past, present, and future is perceived is a consistent focus of our inquiry. Individual chapters identify and consider the implications of these different understandings for promoting structural justice in various contexts, but for initial reading, see Berber Bevernage, "Writing the Past Out of the Present: History and the Politics of Time in Transitional Justice," *History Workshop Journal* 69, no. 1 (2010): 111–31; Black, *Land Is the Source of the Law.*

14. Wolfe elaborated this governing logic in "Nation and MiscegeNation." See also Patrick Wolfe, *Settler Colonialism and the Transformation of Anthropology: The Politics and Poetics of an Ethnographic Event* (London: Cassell, 1999); Veracini, *Settler Colonialism*. For Wolfe's response to critiques within the field, particularly concerning the relative weight accorded to structures and individual agency in settler colonial contexts, see Patrick Wolfe, "Recuperating Binarism: A Heretical Introduction," *Settler Colonial Studies* 3, no. 3 (2013): 257–79.

15. See Will Kymlicka, *Multicultural Citizenship: A Liberal Theory of Minority Rights* (New York: Oxford University Press, 1995).

16. Among others, the Yarralin people of the North Territory describe this negative "rebound" as inevitable as long as the original injustice is not attended to: see Deborah Rose Bird, *Dingo Makes Us Human: Life and Land in Australian Aboriginal Culture* (Oakleigh, VIC: Cambridge University Press, 2000). See also Chris Healy, *From the Ruins of Colonialism: History as Social Memory* (Cambridge: Cambridge University Press, 1997); Maria Nugent, *Captain Cook Was Here* (Port Melbourne, VIC: Cambridge University Press, 2009); Borrows, *Drawing Out Law.*

17. The state of Victoria is undertaking a treaty process with Koori peoples, see Victorian Government, "Treaty Legislation: Advancing the Treaty Process with Aboriginal Victorians Act 2018," n.d., https://www.vic.gov.au/aboriginalvictoria/treaty/treaty-legislation.html. For information on the national native title determination process and related local land use agreements initiatives across Australia, see National Native Title Tribunal, "Tribunal's Role," n.d., http://www.nntt.gov.au/aboutus/Pages/default.aspx

18. Settler colonial theory accounts for such local variations in different historical contexts: see Wolfe, "Land, Labor, and Difference"; Julie Evans et al., eds., *Sovereignty: Frontiers of Possibility* (Honolulu: University of Hawaii Press, 2013).

19. See Julie Evans, "Where Lawlessness Is Law: The Settler-Colonial Frontier as a Legal Space of Violence," *Australian Feminist Law Journal* 30, no. 1 (2009): 3–22.

20. In 1835, an unofficial attempt by settler John Batman to treat with Aboriginal people in the Port Phillip District of New South Wales (now known as Victoria) was disallowed. For discussion, see Attwood and Doyle, *Possession.*

21. On the significance of law's "will to record," see Peter Goodrich, *Reading the Law: A Critical Introduction to Legal Method and Techniques* (New York: Blackwell, 1986), chap. 5.

22. Ibid., 51.

23. Sydney Cove was named after British secretary of state Thomas Townshend, Lord Sydney. Grace Karskens notes that "[t]he Sydney region was the country of about thirty distinct groups of Aboriginal people whose ancestors had very likely arrived in the region at least 40,000 years earlier": *The Colony: A History of Early Sydney* (Crows Nest, NSW: Allen and Unwin, 2009), 3.

24. "You are to endeavour by every possible means to open an intercourse with the natives, and to conciliate their affections, enjoining all our subjects to live in amity and kindness with them": Governor Phillip's Instructions, 25 April 1787, quoted in Frederick Watson, *Historical Records of Australia* 1, ser. 1 (Sydney: Library Committee of the Commonwealth Parliament, 1917), 13.

25. See Karskens, *Colony*; Alan Atkinson, *The Europeans in Australia: A History* (New York: Oxford University Press, 1997).

26. See Karskens, *Colony*; Henry Reynolds, *The Other Side of the Frontier: Aboriginal Resistance to the European Invasion of Australia* (Ringwood, VIC: Penguin, 1982); Henry Reynolds, *The Forgotten War* (Sydney: NewSouth Publishing, 2013). For discussion of the role of magistrates in managing frontier conflict in Australia, see Amanda Nettelbeck, "'Keep the Magistrates Straight': Magistrates and Aboriginal 'Management' on Australia's North-West Frontiers, 1883–1905," *Aboriginal History* 38 (2014): 19–37; Amanda Nettelbeck and Lyndall Ryan, "Salutary Lessons: Native Police and the 'Civilising' Role of Legalised Violence in Colonial Australia," *Journal of Imperial and Commonwealth History* 46, no. 1 (2018): 47–68.

27. The Blue Mountains are in Darug and Gundungurra Country.

28. Frederick Watson, "Introduction," in *Historical Records of Australia*, vol. 11, ser. 1, vii–xxvi. The Bigge Report precipitated these reforms.

29. The historiography includes Kelly K. Chaves, "'A Solemn Judicial Farce, the Mere Mockery of a Trial': The Acquittal of Lieutenant Lowe, 1827," *Aboriginal History* 31 (2007): 122–40; Bruce Elder, *Blood on the Wattle: Massacres and Maltreatment of Australian Aborigines since 1788* (Frenchs Forest, NSW: Child and Associates, 1988); David Roberts, "Bells Falls Massacre and Bathurst's History of Violence: Local Tradition and Australian Historiography," *Australian Historical Studies* 26, no. 105 (1995): 615–33; T. Salisbury and Percy J. Gresser, *Windrayne of the Wiradjuri: Martial Law at Bathurst in 1824* (Sydney: Wentworth Books, 1971); Mary Coe, *Windradyne, a Wiradjuri Koorie* (Canberra: Aboriginal Studies Press, 1989); John Connor, *The Australian Frontier Wars, 1788–1838* (Sydney: University of New South Wales Press, 2002); Albert Jaime Grassby and Marji Hill, *Six Australian Battlefields: The Black Resistance to Invasion and the White Struggle against Colonial Oppression* (North Ryde, NSW: Angus and Robertson, 1988). See also Stan Grant, "At Poisoned Waterhole Creek I Tell My Son about the Slaughter of Our People," *Guardian*, 12 October 2015.

30. *Sydney Gazette and New South Wales Advertiser*, 8 January 1824, 2, http://nla.gov.au/nla.news-page494770

31. *Sydney Gazette and New South Wales Advertiser*, 10 June 1824, 2, http://trove.nla.gov.au/newspaper/page/494866

32. Brisbane to Bathurst, 18 June 1824: Watson, *Historical Records of Australia* 11, ser. 1, 283.

33. *Sydney Gazette and New South Wales Advertiser*, 22 July 1824, 2, http://nla.gov.au/nla.news-article2183067. Salisbury and Gresser note settler pressure to reduce reports of numbers killed to prevent stockkeepers from abandoning their posts: *Windrayne of the Wiradjuri*, 26.

34. *Sydney Gazette and New South Wales Advertiser*, 29 July 1824, 2, https://trove.nla.gov.au/newspaper/page/494894. The meeting took place 22 July.

35. Trial quotes in this and subsequent paragraphs are from *R v Johnston, Clarke, Nicholson, Castles, and Crear* 1824 NSWSupC 8 (12 August 1824, hereafter "*R v Johnston et al.*"): case reported in "Supreme Court of Criminal Jurisdiction," *Sydney Gazette and New South Wales Advertiser*, 12 August 1824, 2, http://nla.gov.au/nla.news-article2183123, also available at http://www.law.mq.edu.au/research/colonial_case_law/nsw/cases/case_index/1824/supreme_court/r_v_johnston_and_others/

36. "Proclamation by His Excellency Lachlan Macquarie," *Sydney Gazette and New South Wales Advertiser*, 4 May 1816, 1, http://nla.gov.au/nla.news-article2176637

37. "Proclamation By His Excellency Lachlan Macquarie," *Sydney Gazette and New South Wales Advertiser*, 4 May 1816, 1, https://trove.nla.gov.au/newspaper/article/2176637

38. See John Thomas Campbell, "Proclamations &c Black Natives Establishment of Institution for Children Government and General Orders Government House Sydney: 10th December 1814" (Sydney, 1814), http://www.law.mq.edu.au/research/colonial_case_law/nsw/other_features/correspondence/documents/document_5/. Also reported in "Government and General Orders," *Sydney Gazette and New South Wales Advertiser*, 10 December 1814, 1, http://nla.gov.au/nla.news-article629022. Note provision fourteen states "[t]hat no Child after having been admitted into the Institution shall be permitted to leave it, or to be taken away by any person whatever whether parents or other relatives until such time as the Boys shall have attained the age of sixteen years and girls 14 years, at which ages they shall be respectively discharged."

39. "Proclamation by His Excellency Lachlan Macquarie," *Sydney Gazette and New South Wales Advertiser*, 4 May 1816, 1, http://nla.gov.au/nla.news-article2176637

40. Macquarie to Bathurst, 18 March 1816: Watson, *Historical Records of Australia* 9, ser. 1, 54.

41. Instructions Issued to the Three Detachments of the 46th Regiment, 9 April 1816: "Directions were given that all aborigines, men, women, and children, who were met with from Sydney onwards, were to be made prisoners of war; any who 'showed fight' or en-

deavored to run away were to be shot, and their bodies hung from trees in the most conspicuous places near where they fell, so as to strike terror into the hearts of the surviving natives.": ibid., 9:854, note 36.

42. Macquarie to Bathurst, 8 June 1816: ibid., 9:140.

43. "Proclamation By His Excellency Lachlan Macquarie," *Sydney Gazette and New South Wales Advertiser*, 20 July 1816, 1, http://nla.gov.au/nla.news-article2176728; see also "Proclamation By His Excellency Lachlan Macquarie," *Sydney Gazette and New South Wales Advertiser*, 2 November 1816, http://nla.gov.au/nla.news-article2176884

44. Karskens notes that Macquarie's dispatch to Bathurst on 25 May 1816 elaborated on the nature of the "terror" referred to in the Proclamation to the Aborigines: *Colony*, 508.

45. "Proclamation By His Excellency Sir Thomas Brisbane," *Sydney Gazette and New South Wales Advertiser*, 14 August 1824, 1, http://nla.gov.au/nla.news-article2183147

46. The law of martial law was notoriously uncertain and officials' hopes for indemnity unstable. Legal historian Michael Taggart observes that mid-nineteenth century debates about the use of martial law exposed its ambiguities: "There were no generally accepted rules; they were not clear and intelligible but were beset with contradictions; they were not publicly promulgated; and so people could not order their affairs accordingly. In short, there was no certainty": "Ruled by Law?," *Modern Law Review* 69, no. 6 (2006): 1018. For further discussion, see Rande W. Kostal, *A Jurisprudence of Power: Victorian Empire and the Rule of Law* (New York: Oxford University Press, 2005); Julie Evans and Tessa Fluence, "Securing the Settler Polity: Martial Law and the Aboriginal Peoples of Van Diemen's Land," *Journal of Australian Colonial History* 15 (2013): 1–22; S. D. Lendrum, "The 'Coorong Massacre': Martial Law and the Aborigines at First Settlement," *Adelaide Law Review* 6, no. 1 (1977): 26–43. On the justification of settler self-defense, see Sidney L. Harring, "The Killing Time: A History of Aboriginal Resistance in Colonial Australia," *Ottawa Law Review* 26, no. 2 (1994): 385–424.

47. *Sydney Gazette and New South Wales Advertiser*, 19 August 1824, 1, https://trove.nla.gov.au/newspaper/article/2183140. For further discussion of Windrayne/Saturday, including his relationships with certain settlers who spoke in favor of Aboriginal people, see David Roberts, "Windradyne (1800–1829)," *Australian Dictionary of Biography* (Canberra: National Centre of Biography, Australian National University, 2005).

48. Brisbane to Bathurst, No. 13, 3 November 1824, encl. Proclamation: Watson, *Historical Records of Australia*, 1917, 11:409. Even without Brisbane's delay, communications could take months to reach Britain and generally made a mockery of British claims to oversight regarding matters of procedural justice, especially in cases of "emergency."

49. Brisbane to Bathurst, No. 18, 31 December 1824: ibid., 11:430–31.

50. Darling to Bathurst, 6 October 1826, CO 201/173: Watson, *Historical Records of Australia* 17, ser. 1, 609.

51. Darling to Landholders at the Hunter River, 5 September 1826: ibid., 17:576–77.

52. Darling to Bathurst, 6 October 1826, CO 201/173: ibid., 17:609.

53. Bathurst to Darling, 14 July 1825, CO 202/14: ibid., 17:18–21.

54. See also Karskens, *Colony*; Atkinson, *Europeans in Australia*; Heather Goodall, *Invasion to Embassy: Land in Aboriginal Politics in New South Wales* (St. Leonards, NSW: Allen and Unwin, 1996).

55. For fuller discussion, see Evans and Fluence, "Securing the Settler Polity."

56. For further discussion of the South Australian case, see Ford, *Settler Sovereignty*; Julie Evans, "Colonialism and the Rule of Law: The Case of South Australia," in *Crime and Empire, 1840–1940: Criminal Justice in Local and Global Context*, ed. Barry S. Godfrey and Graeme Dunstall (Cullompton, Devon: Willan Publishing, 2005), 57–75; Ward, "Means and Measure of Civilisation."

57. Permanent Under Secretary James Stephen's minute, 19 February 1841, Gawler to S/S, no. 12, 15 August 1840, CO 13/16, National Archives, London.

58. S/S to Grey, "Confidential," 14 December 1841, CO 396/2, National Archives, London.

59. Dorsett and McVeigh, *Jurisdiction*, 7.

60. Wolfe, "Nation and MiscegeNation."

61. For detailed accounts, see, for example, Elizabeth Nelson, Sandra Smith, and Patricia Grimshaw, eds., *Letters from Aboriginal Women of Victoria, 1867–1926* (Melbourne: History Department, University of Melbourne, 2002); Boucher and Russell, *Settler Colonial Governance in Nineteenth Century Victoria*. See also Goodall, *Invasion to Embassy*; Anna Haebich, *Broken Circles: Fragmenting Indigenous Families 1800–2000* (Fremantle, WA: Fremantle Arts Centre Press, 2000); Laidlaw and Lester, *Indigenous Communities and Settler Colonialism*.

62. See, for example, Australian Human Rights and Equal Opportunity Commission, "Bringing Them Home: Report of the National Inquiry into the Separation of Aboriginal and Torres Strait Islander Children from Their Families" (Sydney, NSW, 1997); Elliott Johnston, *National Report of the Royal Commission into Aboriginal Deaths in Custody* (Canberra, 1991).

63. Australian Bureau of Statistics, "4517.0—Prisoners in Australia, 2018: Aboriginal and Torres Strait Islander Prisoner Characteristics" (Canberra, 2018).

64. *Mabo and Others v Queensland (No. 2)* (1992) HCA 23, 175 CLR 1; Aboriginal Land Rights (Northern Territory) Act 1976; Native Title Act 1993 (Cth); Traditional Owner Settlement Act 2010 (Vic).

65. Dorsett and McVeigh (*Jurisdiction*, 99) write that "the contemporary focus on territorial jurisdiction has often rendered Indigenous jurisdictions invisible to common law. For many critics, in such situations it is more appropriate to draw on the resources of a jurisdiction of conscience to enable a meeting place of law. Within such a jurisdiction a meeting place might be imagined, with difficulty, in terms of the acknowledgement of common humanity or of a shared understanding of, or ambition for, just relations."

66. Christine Black, "Maturing Australia through Australian Aboriginal Narrative Law," *South Atlantic Quarterly* 110, no. 2 (2011): 347–62. See also Black, *Land Is the Source of the Law*; Moreton-Robinson, *White Possessive*.

67. Dorsett and McVeigh, *Jurisdiction*, 114.

Chapter 3

1. Moreton-Robinson, *White Possessive*.

2. Australian Electoral Commission, "Electoral Milestones for Indigenous Australians," 2017, https://www.aec.gov.au/indigenous/milestones.htm

3. The referendum allowed Indigenous people to be included in census statistics and the federal government to legislate on matters involving them. See John Chesterman and Brian Galligan, *Citizens without Rights: Aborigines and Australian Citizenship* (Cambridge: Cambridge University Press, 1997).

4. On settlers attending to their practice, their place, and their law, see Dorsett and McVeigh, *Jurisdiction*; Genovese, "On Australian Feminist Tradition"; Genovese, "Critical Decision, 1982"; Genovese, "Critical Decision 1983."

5. Adrian Little and Mark McMillan, "Invisibility and the Politics of Reconciliation in Australia: Keeping the Conflict in View," *Ethnopolitics* 16, no. 5 (2016): 519–37.

6. As noted in our introduction, here and throughout the book, we draw on the discussion of lawful relations articulated in Dorsett and McVeigh, *Jurisdiction*.

7. Aileen Moreton-Robinson, *Talkin' Up to the White Woman: Aboriginal Women and Feminism* (St. Lucia, QLD: University of Queensland Press, 2000).

8. Country, meaning Indigenous nations' territories. All the land mass of the continent was occupied by distinct Indigenous polities that remain linked to the ontological connections.

9. *Mabo* was a landmark 1992 judgment delivered by the High Court of Australia. In *Mabo*, Eddie Mabo, David Passi, and James Rice of the Meriam people sought a declaration of their entitlement to their lands on the Mer Islands. The High Court recognized that at the time of colonization the lands claimed by British settlers were already occupied by Indigenous peoples and governed by Indigenous law. The High Court thus overturned the previous designation by settler law of those lands as *terra nullius* (lands belonging to no-one), which had been used to justify colonial dispossession. For more information, see Australian Institute of Aboriginal and Torres Strait Islander Studies, "Mabo Case," 2015, https://aiatsis.gov.au/explore/articles/mabo-case

10. A degree of legal pluralism was evident in some Australian colonies until the 1840s, see Ford, *Settler Sovereignty*; Ward, "Means and Measure of Civilisation."

11. Australian Institute of Aboriginal and Torres Strait Islander Studies, "Day of Mourning and Protest Aborigines Conference—75th Anniversary: 26th January 1938," 2019, http://aiatsis.gov.au/exhibitions/day-mourning-26th-january-1938

12. Another example is the Aborigines Progressives Association led by Yorta Yorta men Sir Doug Nicholls and Jack Patten that developed a manifesto describing the conditions of Aboriginal peoples: see ibid.

13. Ernst Hartwig Kantorowicz, *The Kings' Two Bodies: A Study in Mediaeval Political Theology* (Princeton: Princeton University Press, 1957).

14. Moreton-Robinson, *White Possessive.*

15. Ibid.

16. Motha, "Failure of Postcolonial Sovereignty in Australia"; Damien Short, "The Social Construction of Indigenous 'Native Title' Land Rights in Australia," *Current Sociology* 55, no. 6 (2007): 857–76; Nicole Watson, "What Do We Want? Not Native Title, That's for Bloody Sure," in *The Aboriginal Tent Embassy: Sovereignty, Black Power, Land Rights and the State*, ed. Gary Foley, Andrew Schaap, and Edwina Howell (New York: Routledge, 2014), 284–98.

17. Joan Gillison, "Bon, Ann Fraser (1838–1936)," *Australian Dictionary of Biography* (Carlton, VIC: Melbourne University Press, 1979).

18. See further, Dorsett and McVeigh, *Jurisdiction*, 31.

19. Petition submitted to the Inquiry, 16 November 1881: "Report of the Board Appointed to Enquire into, and Report upon, the Present Condition and Management of the Coranderrk Aboriginal Station, Together with the Minutes of Evidence," 98; Nanni and James, *Coranderrk: We Will Show the Country*, 32.

20. "Report of the Board Appointed to Enquire into, and Report upon, the Present Condition and Management of the Coranderrk Aboriginal Station, Together with the Minutes of Evidence," 8; Nanni and James, *Coranderrk: We Will Show the Country*, 161–71.

21. "Report of the Board Appointed to Enquire into, and Report upon, the Present Condition and Management of the Coranderrk Aboriginal Station, Together with the Minutes of Evidence," 132; Nanni and James, *Coranderrk: We Will Show the Country*, 169.

22. Brennan J in *Mabo*, para. 42.

23. Ibid., Deane and Gaudron JJ, para. 39.

Chapter 4

1. Judge Silvia Fernández de Gurmendi 2017, *Thank You Remarks for the 2017 Stockholm Human Rights Award*, Stockholm, 20 November 2017. Available: https://www.icc-cpi.int/itemsDocuments/171120-stat-pres.pdf

2. Frantz Fanon, *The Wretched of the Earth*, trans. Constance Farrington (New York: Grove Press, 1966), 96.

3. Rome Statute of the International Criminal Court, preamble, emphasis added.

4. See, for example, ibid.; the statements of the Minister of Justice (Netherlands) and President of the International Criminal Court in M. Cherif Bassiouni, ed., *The Pursuit of International Criminal Justice: A World Study on Conflicts, Victimization, and Post-Conflict Justice* (Antwerp: Intersentia, 2010), 133, 134, 142–44.

5. See Aimé Césaire, *Discourse on Colonialism*, trans. Joan Pinkham (New York: Monthly Review Press, 2000).

6. The purpose in selecting these two encounters, and bringing them into relation with each other, is not to position them as somehow representative, but to reflect on what they reveal about law's—specifically international criminal law's—recognition of colonial injustice and how this might be otherwise.

7. Gayatri Chakravorty Spivak, "Can the Subaltern Speak?," in *Marxism and the Interpretation of Culture*, ed. Cary Nelson and Lawrence Grossberg (London: Macmillan, 1988), 271–312.

8. Said, *Orientalism*; Achille Mbembé, *On the Postcolony* (Berkeley: University of California Press, 2001).

9. Shohat, "Notes on the 'Post-Colonial'"; Dipesh Chakrabarty, *Provincializing Europe: Postcolonial Thought and Historical Difference* (Princeton: Princeton University Press, 2000); Ella Shohat and Robert Stam, *Unthinking Eurocentrism: Multiculturalism and the Media*, 2nd ed. (New York: Routledge, 2014).

10. See, for example, Hillyard and Tombs, *Beyond Criminology*; Joachim J. Savelsberg and Hollie Nyseth, "Collective Representations of Atrocities and National Identity: The Case of Darfur," in *Crossing Borders, Shifting Boundaries: National and Transnational Identities in Europe and Beyond*, ed. Franz Höllinger and Markus Hadler (Frankfurt: Campus Verlag, 2012).

11. Butler, *Frames of War*, chap. 1, introduction; Butler, *Precarious Life*, preface. See also Roxanne Lynn Doty, *Imperial Encounters: The Politics of Representation in North-South Relations* (Minneapolis: University of Minnesota Press, 1996).

12. Butler, *Precarious Life*, xx.

13. See Smart, *Feminism and the Power of Law*; Marc Galanter, "The Radiating Effects of Courts," in *Empirical Theories about Courts*, ed. Keith O. Boyum and Lynn M. Mather (New York: Longman, 1983), 117–42.

14. Statute of the International Criminal Tribunal for the Prosecution of Persons Responsible for Genocide and Other Serious Violations of International Humanitarian Law Committed in the Territory of Rwanda and Rwandan Citizens Responsible for Genocide and Other Such Violations Committed in the Territory of Neighbouring States, between 1 January 1994 and 31 December 1994 (1994), Articles 1 and 7.

15. Alison Des Forges and Timothy Longman, "Legal Responses to Genocide in Rwanda," in *My Neighbor, My Enemy: Justice and Community in the Aftermath of Mass Atrocity*, ed. Eric Stover and Harvey M. Weinstein (New York: Cambridge University Press, 2004), 54–55.

16. Ibid., 55–56; Jean-Marie Kamatali, "The Challenge of Linking International Criminal Justice and National Reconciliation: The Case of the ICTR," *Leiden Journal of International Law* 16 (2003): 120.

17. Although focusing primarily on the judgments of the ICTR, this chapter and discussion also considers materials made available on the Tribunal's website as also constituting official representations of the Tribunal's mandate and work and approach to colonial history. Relevant tribunal judgements were identified through searches on the Tribunal database for judgments referring to colonialism. As such, there may be other judgments that implicitly address colonialism that are not covered by the analysis in this chapter.

18. *The Prosecutor v. Jean-Paul Akayesu (Trial Judgement)* (International Criminal Tribunal for Rwanda, ICTR-96-4-T, 2 September 1998) (hereafter, "*Akayesu*"), paras. 78–111.

19. See *The Prosecutor v. Ferdinand Nahimana, Jean-Bosco Barayagwiza, Hassan Ngeze (Appeal Judgment)* (International Criminal Tribunal for Rwanda, ICTR-99-52-A, 28 November 2007), para. 106 (hereafter "*Nahimana et al.*").

20. See, for example, *The Prosecutor v. Clément Kayishema and Obed Ruzindana (Trial Judgment)* (International Criminal Tribunal for Rwanda, ICTR-95-1-T, 21 May 1999) (hereafter "*Kayishema and Ruzindana*"), paras. 31–54.

21. See, for example, Alison Des Forges, *"Leave None to Tell the Story": Genocide in Rwanda* (New York: Human Rights Watch, 1999), 38; Helen M. Hintjens, "Explaining the 1994 Genocide in Rwanda," *Journal of Modern African Studies* 37, no. 2 (1999): 249–50.

22. *Nahimana et al.*, 108.

23. *Kayishema and Ruzindana*, 35.

24. In other sections of the judgments, for example, there are references to the ways in which the Tutsis, although the preferred class preceding independence, were induced to adopt a religion, namely Christianity, which they had initially resisted to maintain their position of power in Rwandan society: see *Akayesu*, 84. Also relevant here is the judges' acknowledgment of the shifting nature of colonial allegiances and the privileges that flowed from them, as the Catholic Church and colonial administrators began to support the majority Hutu, rather than minority Tutsi, population in the lead up to Rwandan independence: *Kayishema and Ruzindana*, 85–86.

25. United Nations, "The Genocide—Timeline," Legacy Website for the International Criminal Tribunal for Rwanda, accessed 31 January 2019, http://unictr.irmct.org/en/genocide#timeline

26. See Nesam McMillan, *Imagining the International: Crime, Justice, and the Promise of Community* (Stanford: Stanford University Press, 2020).

27. See also Anghie, *Imperialism, Sovereignty and the Making of International Law*. Tracing this testimony to colonialism in the ICTR materials in this way, however, is to adopt a feminist approach as outlined by Anne Orford, citing Threadgold, of reading the Tribunal materials "in ways that such texts were generically and institu-

tionally never meant to be read": *Reading Humanitarian Intervention: Human Rights and the Use of Force in International Law* (Cambridge: Cambridge University Press, 2003), 38.

28. *Kayishema and Ruzindana*, 33.

29. Ibid., 31.

30. Ibid.

31. *Nahimana et al.*, 105, 107.

32. *Kayishema and Ruzindana*, 31; see also *Akayesu*, 78.

33. *Nahimana et al.*, 109.

34. *Akayesu*, 83, 112, 127; United Nations International Criminal Tribunal for Rwanda, "The Genocide," 1994.

35. See Aaron Ohlmann, *20 Years Challenging Impunity* (United Nations International Criminal Tribunal for Rwanda, 2014), http://unictr.irmct.org

36. United Nations, "The Genocide—Timeline."

37. Butler, *Precarious Life*; Butler, *Frames of War*, introduction.

38. Butler, *Precarious Life*, xxi.

39. *Kayishema and Ruzindana*, 523.

40. Ibid., 37.

41. Ibid., 32.

42. *Nahimana et al.*, 109.

43. Stoler, "Imperial Debris," 193–95. The insightful scholarship of Charlotte Mertens brought Stoler's work to our attention. See Charlotte Mertens, "Frames of Empire: Congo and Sexual Violence" (PhD diss., University of Melbourne, 2017).

44. Nancy Rose Hunt, "An Acoustic Register, Tenacious Images, and Congolese Scenes of Rape and Repetition," *Cultural Anthropology* 23, no. 2 (2008): 226–28, 237–39, 243.

45. See Mertens, "Frames of Empire."

46. See, for example, Paul Kagame, "Speech by President Kagame at the 15th Commemoration of the Genocide against the Tutsi at the Nyanza Memorial Site in Kicukiro," 7 April 2009; Paul Kagame, "Speech by President Paul Kagame at the 20th Commemoration of the Genocide against the Tutsi," 7 April 2014.

47. Kamari Clarke, "Rethinking Africa through Its Exclusions: The Politics of Naming Criminal Responsibility," *Anthropological Quarterly* 83, no. 3 (2010): 625–51.

48. Richard Ashby Wilson, "When Humanity Sits in Judgment: Crimes against Humanity and the Conundrum of Race and Ethnicity at the International Criminal Tribunal for Rwanda," in *In the Name of Humanity: The Government of Threat and Care*, ed. Ilana Feldman and Miriam Ticktin (Durham, NC: Duke University Press, 2010), 27–57.

49. Ibid., 31.

50. Mahmood Mamdani, "From Conquest to Consent as the Basis of State Formation: Reflections on Rwanda," *New Left Review* 216 (1996): 6.

51. Pellet in International Law Commission, *Yearbook of the International Law Com-*

mission 1992: Summary Records of the Meetings of the 44th Session, 4 May-24 July 1992, vol. 1 (New York: United Nations, 1994), 17, para 33.

52. International Law Commission, *Yearbook of the International Law Commission, 1984: Report of the Commission to the General Assembly on the Work of Its 36th Session*, vol. 2, part 2 (New York: United Nations, 1985), 7, paras 10–1. This was later known as the Draft Code of Crimes Against the Peace and Security of Mankind.

53. Ibid., 10, para. 27.

54. Ibid., 17, para. 63.

55. Ibid., 11, para. 30.

56. It was originally included as Article 15 and became Article 18 in the 1991 draft that formed the basis of state consultation: International Law Commission, *Yearbook of the International Law Commission, 1991: Report of the Commission to the General Assembly on the Work of Its 43rd Session*, vol. 2, part 2 (New York: United Nations, 1994), 93, para 167. It is also notable that both the later and earlier drafts of the Code also referred to related activities, such as economic and political intervention, annexation, aggression, and apartheid, which can and have constituted part of colonial regimes, in addition to the crime of colonial domination itself.

57. Thiam, "Second Report on the Draft Code of Offences against the Peace and Security of Mankind," extract from the International Law Commission, *Yearbook of the International Law Commission, 1984: Report of the Commission to the General Assembly on the Work of Its 36th Session*, 2, part 2:96, paras 47–48.

58. See, e.g., United Nations General Assembly Resolution 3103 (XXVIII) Basic Principles of Legal Status of the Combatants Struggling against Colonial and Alien Domination and Racist Regimes (12 December 1973), available from http://www.un.org/documents/ga/res/28/ares28.htm

59. Razafindralambo in International Law Commission, *Yearbook of the International Law Commission, 1995: Summary Records of the Meetings of the 47th Session, 2 May-21 July 1995*, vol. 1 (New York: United Nations, 1997), 15, para 4.

60. This description of state crime draws on Richard Vernon's definition of what constitutes a "crime against humanity": "What Is Crime Against Humanity?," *Journal of Political Philosophy* 10, no. 3 (2002): 231–49. See also Balint, *Genocide, State Crime, and the Law*; Penny Green and Tony Ward, *State Crime: Governments, Violence and Corruption* (London: Pluto Press, 2004).

61. Pellet in International Law Commission, *Yearbook of the International Law Commission 1992: Summary Records of the Meetings of the 44th Session, 4 May-24 July 1992*, 1:17, para 33.

62. Jacovides in International Law Commission, *Yearbook of the International Law Commission, 1995: Summary Records of the Meetings of the 47th Session, 2 May-21 July 1995*, 1:20, para 8.

63. Mikulka in ibid., 15, para. 11.

64. Thiam, Bennouna, and Jacovides in ibid., 52, para. 11. See also 11, para. 3; 20, para. 8, respectively.

65. Thiam in ibid., 52, para. 11.

66. Vargas Carreño in ibid., 17, para. 24.

67. International Law Commission, *Yearbook of the International Law Commission, 1993: Documents of the 45th Session*, vol. 2, part 1 (New York: United Nations, 2000), 101, para 23.

68. Rosenstock in International Law Commission, *Yearbook of the International Law Commission 1992: Summary Records of the Meetings of the 44th Session, 4 May-24 July 1992*, 1:38, para 33.

69. Szekely in International Law Commission, *Yearbook of the International Law Commission, 1995: Summary Records of the Meetings of the 47th Session, 2 May-21 July 1995*, 1:18, para 34.

70. Mahiou and Al-Khasawneh in ibid., 14, 37, paras 29, 33, respectively.

71. Razafindralambo in ibid., 15, para. 4.

72. Mahiou in ibid., 14, para. 29.

73. Villagrán Kramer in ibid., 25, para. 51.

74. The chairman in ibid., 32, para. 37.

75. Idris in ibid., 33, para. 5.

76. The chairman in International Law Commission, *Yearbook of the International Law Commission, 1995: Report of the Commission to the General Assembly on the Work of Its 47th Session*, vol. 2, part 2 (New York: United Nations, 1998), 23, para 77. The chairman in International Law Commission, *Yearbook of the International Law Commission, 1995: Summary Records of the Meetings of the 47th Session, 2 May-21 July 1995*, 1:32, para. 37.

77. United States of America in International Law Commission, *Yearbook of the International Law Commission, 1993: Documents of the 45th Session*, 2, part 1:103, para. 5.

78. United Kingdom in ibid., 101, para. 23.

79. Rosenstock in International Law Commission, *Yearbook of the International Law Commission 1992: Summary Records of the Meetings of the 44th Session, 4 May-24 July 1992*, 1:38, para. 33.

80. Goodrich, *Languages of Law*, 214.

81. See Sarah M. H. Nouwen and Wouter G. Werner, "Doing Justice to the Political: The International Criminal Court in Uganda and Sudan," *European Journal of International Law* 21, no. 4 (2010): 941–65. See also further discussion in chapter 2 of this volume.

82. Thiam in International Law Commission, *Yearbook of the International Law Commission, 1995: Summary Records of the Meetings of the 47th Session, 2 May-21 July 1995*, 1:3, para. 1.

83. Tomuschat in ibid., 11, para. 10.

84. See Razafindralambo in ibid., 14, para. 2. See also Thiam, who refers to "third world countries" in ibid., 3, para. 1.

85. Kabatsi in ibid., 18, para. 32.

86. Anghie, *Imperialism, Sovereignty and the Making of International Law*, 2–4.

87. Ibid., 3, 117, 136, 179, and chapter 3 in particular.

88. See, for example, Kenneth Roth, "Africa Attacks the International Criminal Court," *New York Review of Books*, 6 February 2014; Christine Schwöbel-Patel, "International Criminal Court Must Not Ignore Threats of an African Mass Withdrawal," *The Conversation*, 8 February 2017; "Africa Debate — Is the ICC Targeting Africa Inappropriately?," ICC Forum, 2014, http://iccforum.com/africa

89. See, for example, Kamari M. Clarke, Abel S. Knottnerus, and Eefje de Volder, "Africa and the ICC: An Introduction," in *Africa and the ICC: Perceptions of Justice*, ed. Kamari M. Clarke, Abel S. Knottnerus, and Eefje de Volder (Cambridge: Cambridge University Press, 2016), 1–35; Clarke, *Fictions of Justice*; Mahmood Mamdani, "Responsibility to Protect or Right to Punish?," *Journal of Intervention and Statebuilding* 4, no. 1 (2010): 53–67; Mamdani, "New Humanitarian Order."

90. Clarke, Knottnerus, and de Volder, "Africa and the ICC," 4–5; Roth, "Africa Attacks the International Criminal Court."

91. Thierry Cruvellier, "The ICC, Out of Africa," *New York Times*, 6 November 2016.

92. Clarke, Knottnerus, and de Volder, "Africa and the ICC," 1–2, 10–12.

93. Homi K. Bhabha, *The Location of Culture* (London: Routledge, 2004), 245.

94. Ibid.

95. Fuyuki Kurasawa, *The Work of Global Justice: Human Rights as Practices* (New York: Cambridge University Press, 2007), 23–25.

96. See Primo Levi, *The Drowned and the Saved*, trans. Raymond Rosenthal (London: Abacus, 1989); Giorgio Agamben, *Remnants of Auschwitz: The Witness and the Archive*, trans. Daniel Heller-Roazen (New York: Zone Books, 1999). There is a growing and important literature that critically reflects on the ethics and politics of attempts to "bear witness," which interrogates—for example—the modes of relation it makes available and its sociopolitically situated nature: see, for example, Wendy S. Hesford, "Documenting Violations: Rhetorical Witnessing and the Spectacle of Distant Suffering," *Biography* 27, no. 1 (2004): 104–44; Shoshana Felman and Dori Laub, *Testimony: Crises of Witnessing in Literature, Psychoanalysis, and History* (New York: Routledge, 1992); Kurasawa, *Work of Global Justice*; Fiona C. Ross, *Bearing Witness: Women and the Truth and Reconciliation Commission in South Africa* (London: Pluto Press, 2003).

97. For a related discussion, see Jill Stauffer, *Ethical Loneliness: The Injustice of Not Being Heard* (New York: Columbia University Press, 2015).

98. See Denise Leith, *Bearing Witness: The Lives of War Correspondents and Photojournalists* (Milsons Point, NSW: Random House, 2004). See also the accounts of Paul Farmer, *Pathologies of Power: Health, Human Rights, and the New War on the Poor* (Berkeley: University of California Press, 2003); James Dawes, *That the World May Know: Bearing Witness to Atrocity* (Cambridge: Harvard University Press, 2007).

99. See, for example, Shohat, "Notes on the 'Post-Colonial.'"
100. Michael Rothberg, *Multidirectional Memory: Remembering the Holocaust in the Age of Decolonization* (Stanford, CA: Stanford University Press, 2009), 18–19, 3.
101. Clarke, "Rethinking Africa through Its Exclusions," 646–47; Mamdani, "New Humanitarian Order."

Chapter 5

1. Robert Meister, *After Evil: A Politics of Human Rights* (New York: Columbia University Press, 2011), 25.
2. Ovide Mercredi, Assembly of First Nations leader, Canada, cited in Michelle Bonner and Matt James, "The Three R's of Seeking Transitional Justice: Reparation, Responsibility, and Reframing in Canada and Argentina," *International Indigenous Policy Journal* 2, no. 3 (2011): 19.
3. See Courtney Jung, "Canada and the Legacy of the Indian Residential Schools: Transitional Justice for Indigenous People in a Nontransitional Society," in *Identities in Transition: Challenges for Transitional Justice in Divided Societies*, ed. Paige Arthur (Cambridge: Cambridge University Press, 2011), 217–50.
4. See ibid., 230–31; Tony Barta, "Sorry, and Not Sorry, in Australia: How the Apology to the Stolen Generations Buried a History of Genocide," *Journal of Genocide Research* 10, no. 2 (2008): 201–14.
5. Jung, "Canada and the Legacy of the Indian Residential Schools," 226.
6. See Damien Short, *Reconciliation and Colonial Power: Indigenous Rights in Australia* (Aldershot: Ashgate, 2008); Damien Short, "When Sorry Isn't Good Enough: Official Remembrance and Reconciliation in Australia," *Memory Studies* 5, no. 3 (2012): 293–304; Andrea Durbach, "'The Cost of a Wounded Society': Reparations and the Illusion of Reconciliation," *Australian Indigenous Law Review* 12, no. 1 (2008): 22–40.
7. Wolfe, "Nation and MiscegeNation."
8. On the importance of establishing lawful relations in settler societies, see Christine Black, Shaun McVeigh, and Richard Johnstone, "Of the South," *Griffith Law Review* 16, no. 2 (2007): 299–309; Nin Tomas, "Maori Concepts and Practices of Rangatiratanga: 'Sovereignty?,'" in *Sovereignty: Frontiers of Possibility*, ed. Julie Evans et al. (Honolulu: University of Hawaii Press, 2013), 220–49; Taiaiake Alfred, *Wasáse: Indigenous Pathways of Action and Freedom* (Peterborough, UK: Broadview Press, 2005).
9. Rama Mani, "Dilemmas of Expanding Transitional Justice, or Forging the Nexus between Transitional Justice and Development," *International Journal of Transitional Justice* 2 (2008): 253–65; Lisa J. Laplante, "Transitional Justice and Peace Building: Diagnosing and Addressing the Socioeconomic Roots of Violence through a Human Rights Framework," *International Journal of Transitional Justice* 2 (2008): 331–55; Lambourne, "Transi-

tional Justice and Peacebuilding after Mass Violence"; Ismael Muvingi, "Sitting on Powder Kegs: Socioeconomic Rights in Transitional Societies," *International Journal of Transitional Justice* 3 (2009): 163–82; Huw Lloyd Williams, "Wacky Races: Miller, Pogge and Rawls, and Conceptions of Development in the Global Justice Debate," *Journal of International Political Theory* 10, no. 2 (2014): 206–28.

10. Rosemary Nagy, "Transitional Justice as Global Project: Critical Reflections," *Third World Quarterly* 29, no. 2 (2008): 276.

11. For a detailed account of its emergence, see Paige Arthur, "How 'Transitions' Reshaped Human Rights: A Conceptual History of Transitional Justice," *Human Rights Quarterly* 31, no. 2 (2009): 321–67; Bronwyn Leebaw, "The Irreconcilable Goals of Transitional Justice," *Human Rights Quarterly* 95 (2008): 98–106.

12. Arthur, "How 'Transitions' Reshaped Human Rights."

13. Ruti G. Teitel, *Transitional Justice* (New York: Oxford University Press, 2000). For initial work in this area, see also Neil J. Kritz, ed., *Transitional Justice: How Emerging Democracies Reckon with Former Regimes* (Washington, DC: United States Institute of Peace Press, 1995).

14. Teitel, *Transitional Justice*, 6.

15. See Ruti G. Teitel, *Humanity's Law* (New York: Oxford University Press, 2011); Kritz, *Transitional Justice*; Priscilla B. Hayner, *Unspeakable Truths: Facing the Challenge of Truth Commissions* (New York: Routledge, 2002); Luc Huyse, "Justice after Transition: On the Choices Successor Elites Make in Dealing with the Past," *Law & Social Inquiry* 20, no. 1 (1995): 51–78; Martha Minow, *Between Vengeance and Forgiveness: Facing History after Genocide and Mass Violence* (Boston: Beacon Press, 1998); Naomi Roht-Arriaza and Javier Mariecurrena, eds., *Transitional Justice in the Twenty-First Century: Beyond Truth versus Justice* (Cambridge: Cambridge University Press, 2006); Chandra Lekha Sriram, *Confronting Past Human Rights Violations: Justice vs. Peace in Times of Transition* (New York: Frank Cass, 2004); Ramesh Thakur and Peter Macontent, *From Sovereign Impunity to International Accountability: The Search for Justice in a World of States* (Tokyo: United Nations University Press, 2004); Tricia D. Olsen, Leigh A. Payne, and Andrew G. Reiter, *Transitional Justice in Balance: Comparing Processes, Weighing Efficacy* (Washington, DC: US Institute of Peace Press, 2010).

16. For general reading on the South African case, see Lyn S. Graybill, "Pursuit of Truth and Reconciliation in South Africa," *Africa Today* 45, no. 1 (1998): 103–33; Wilson, "When Humanity Sits in Judgment"; David Philips, "Defining 'Reconciliation': A Critical Analysis of the Understanding and Use of the Word in South Africa's Truth and Reconciliation Commission," in *Biennial Conference of the South African Historical Society* (Cape Town: University of Cape Town, 2005); Claire Moon, *Narrating Political Reconciliation: South Africa's Truth and Reconciliation Commission* (Lanham, MD: Lexington Books, 2008).

17. For general reading on the East Timor case, see Elizabeth Stanley, *Torture, Truth*

and Justice: The Case of Timor-Leste (London: Routledge, 2009); Jeffrey Kingston, "Balancing Justice and Reconciliation in East Timor," *Critical Asian Studies* 38, no. 3 (2006): 271–302; Suzanne Katzenstein, "Hybrid Tribunals: Searching for Justice in East Timor," *Harvard Human Rights Journal* 16, no. 6 (2003): 245–78; Lia Kent, *The Dynamics of Transitional Justice: International Models and Local Realities in East Timor* (Abingdon, Oxon: Routledge, 2012).

18. Makau W. Mutua, "Savages, Victims, and Saviors: The Metaphor of Human Rights," *Harvard International Law Journal* 42 (2001): 201–45; Orford, *Reading Humanitarian Intervention*.

19. Chris Cunneen, "State Crime, the Colonial Question and Indigenous Peoples," in *Supranational Criminology: Towards a Criminology of International Crimes*, ed. Alette Smeulers and Roelof Haveman (Antwerp: Intersentia, 2008), 159; Anne Orford, "Commissioning the Truth," *Columbia Journal of Gender and Law* 15, no. 3 (2006): 851–83.

20. In the Australian case, see John Maynard, *Fight for Liberty and Freedom: The Origins of Australian Aboriginal Activism* (Canberra: Aboriginal Studies Press, 2007); Bain Attwood, *Rights for Aborigines* (Crows Nest, NSW: Allen and Unwin, 2003). See also Lauren A. Benton, *Law and Colonial Cultures: Legal Regimes in World History, 1400–1900* (New York: Cambridge University Press, 2002); Saliha Belmessous, *Native Claims: Indigenous Law against Empire, 1500–1920* (New York: Oxford University Press, 2012).

21. A. Dirk Moses, "Official Apologies, Reconciliation and Settler Colonialism: Australian Indigenous Alterity and Political Agency," *Citizenship Studies* 15, no. 2 (2011): 145–59; Nicola Henry, "From Reconciliation to Transitional Justice: The Contours of Redress Politics in Established Democracies," *International Journal of Transitional Justice* 9, no. 2 (2015): 199–218.

22. Jung, "Canada and the Legacy of the Indian Residential Schools."

23. Stephen Harper, "Statement of Apology to Former Students of Indian Residential Schools," Indigenous and Northern Affairs Canada, 2008, https://www.aadnc-aandc.gc.ca/eng/1100100015644/1100100015649; Australian Human Rights and Equal Opportunity Commission, "Bringing Them Home: Report of the National Inquiry into the Separation of Aboriginal and Torres Strait Islander Children from Their Families"; Kevin Rudd, "Apology to Australia's Indigenous Peoples," 2008, http://www.australia.gov.au/about-australia/our-country/our-people/apology-to-australias-indigenous-peoples

24. Maria Rae, "When Reconciliation Means Reparations: Tasmania's Compensation to the Stolen Generations," *Griffith Law Review* 24, no. 4 (2015): 640–56.

25. Johnston, "National Report of the Royal Commission into Aboriginal Deaths in Custody."

26. Jung, "Canada and the Legacy of the Indian Residential Schools"; Bonner and James, "Three R's of Seeking Transitional Justice"; Short, *Reconciliation and Colonial Power*; Orford, "Commissioning the Truth"; Paige Arthur et al., "Strengthening Indigenous Rights through Truth Commissions: A Practitioner's Resource" (New York:

International Center for Transitional Justice, 2012). See also the related conferences and symposia: Alvaro Pop, Esther Attear, and Alcibiades Escué, "Truth Commissions and Indigenous Peoples: Lessons Learned, Future Challenges," *UN Permanent Forum on Indigenous Issues* (New York: International Center for Transitional Justice, 2012); "Indigenous Rights and Transitional Justice: Two Side Events to the UN Permanent Forum," *UN Permanent Forum on Indigenous Issues* (New York: International Center for Transitional Justice, 2012).

27. These include two significant national inquiries (Johnston, "National Report of the Royal Commission into Aboriginal Deaths in Custody"; Australian Human Rights and Equal Opportunity Commission, "Bringing Them Home: Report of the National Inquiry into the Separation of Aboriginal and Torres Strait Islander Children from Their Families"); the High Court decision to overthrow the notion of *terra nullius* in *Mabo* and the highly circumscribed legislative recognition of native title in the subsequent Native Title Act 1993 (Cth) (and Native Title Amendment Act 1998); a now defunct National Council for Aboriginal Reconciliation, which was mandated to operate for ten years from 1991 and now operates minimally as Reconciliation Australia; and, in 2008, a formal apology to "all Aborigines and Stolen Generations" (see Rudd, "Apology to Australia's Indigenous Peoples.") A range of state-based reforms around justice issues followed the Royal Commission into Aboriginal Deaths in Custody, although implementation of recommendations varies markedly across jurisdictions.

28. Michael Humphrey, "Re-Entering History as Suffering Victims: The Reach of Transitional Justice into Past Imperial Violence and Trauma," paper presented at *Human Rights and Imperialism in Historical Perspective*, Sydney, Australia, 11–12 August 2012. See also Arthur, "How 'Transitions' Reshaped Human Rights," 335.

29. UN Secretary-General, "The Rule of Law and Transitional Justice in Conflict and Post-Conflict Societies" (New York: United Nations, 2004), 9, 22.

30. Ibid., 9.

31. For discussion of treaties, see Behrendt, Cunneen, and Libesman, *Indigenous Legal Relations in Australia*; Joanna R. Quinn, "Introductory Essay: Canada's Own Brand of Truth and Reconciliation?," *International Indigenous Policy Journal* 2, no. 3 (2011): 3. See also on the nature of public discussions Birch, "'Invisible Fire'"; Stuart Macintyre and Anna Clark, *The History Wars* (Carlton, VIC: Melbourne University Press, 2004). The state of Victoria in Australia is, at the stage of writing, belatedly negotiating a treaty: see https://www.vic.gov.au/aboriginalvictoria/treaty.html

32. After twenty years of negotiation, the UN General Assembly adopted the declaration in September 2007. Only four negative votes were cast (Canada, Australia, New Zealand, United States). Australia finally adopted the declaration in April 2009 and New Zealand in April 2010.

33. Bonner and James, "Three R's of Seeking Transitional Justice," 3.

34. See Alexander Reilly, "Sovereign Apologies," in *Sovereignty: Frontiers of Possibility*, ed. Julie Evans et al. (Honolulu: University of Hawaii Press, 2013), 196–219. In terms of fostering conduits between the commonly discrete fields of scholarship we outline here, it is interesting to note other transitional justice scholarly interventions in the case of Northern Ireland: see, for example, Anna Eriksson, *Justice in Transition: Community Restorative Justice in Northern Ireland* (Cullompton, Devon: Willan Publishing, 2009). The questions of Ireland's status as a settler colony, and of the influence of its colonial history more generally on contemporary events in Northern Ireland, has long been debated in historical and postcolonial literature: for a controversial intervention in the field, see Stephen Howe, *Ireland and Empire: Colonial Legacies in Irish History and Culture* (New York: Oxford University Press, 2000).

35. The report of the Truth and Reconciliation Commission of South Africa refers to the role of the Commission to "uncover as much as possible of the truth about past gross violations" and ensure the "public acknowledgement" of "untold suffering and injustice": Truth and Reconciliation Commission of South Africa, *Truth and Reconciliation Commission of South Africa Report*. Vol. 1(London: Macmillan Reference, 1999), 49. The report of the Sierra Leone Truth and Reconciliation Commission states that it is "intended to enable Sierra Leoneans to understand the conflict and come to grips with the problems that gave rise to it": Sierra Leone Truth and Reconciliation Commission, "Witness to Truth: Report of the Sierra Leone Truth and Reconciliation Commission," 2004, 2. Meanwhile, although the central focus of the Rwandan *gacaca* courts was to ensure comprehensive accountability for all those implicated in the genocide, it did so through public hearings that local communities were expected to attend and participate in.

36. Bonner and James, "Three R's of Seeking Transitional Justice," 14; Arthur, "How 'Transitions' Reshaped Human Rights," 356.

37. See Bonner and James, "Three R's of Seeking Transitional Justice," 14.

38. Tony Barta, "After the Holocaust: Consciousness of Genocide in Australia," *Australian Journal of Politics & History* 31, no. 1 (1985): 154.

39. See Jung, "Canada and the Legacy of the Indian Residential Schools," 238.

40. Bonner and James, "Three R's of Seeking Transitional Justice," 9.

41. Ibid., 9–10.

42. See, for example, Mark A. Drumbl, "Sclerosis: Retributive Justice and the Rwandan Genocide," *Punishment & Society* 2, no. 3 (2000): 287–307.

43. See, in particular, Teitel, *Transitional Justice*; Huyse, "Justice after Transition"; Minow, *Between Vengeance and Forgiveness*; Kritz, *Transitional Justice*; Hayner, *Unspeakable Truths*; Mark Osiel, *Mass Atrocity, Collective Memory, and the Law* (New Brunswick, NJ: Transaction Publishers, 2000).

44. Adam Czarnota, "Law as Mnemosyne and as Lethe: Quasi-Judicial Institutions and Collective Memories," in *Lethe's Law: Justice, Law and Ethics in Reconciliation*, eds. Emilios Christodoulidis and Scott Veitch (Oxford: Hart Publishing, 2001), 127.

45. Christine Bell notes that this critical reflexivity of transitional justice scholars and practitioners has emerged relatively quickly given the recent establishment of transitional justice as a field: "Transitional Justice, Interdisciplinarity and the State of the 'Field' or 'Non-Field,'" *International Journal of Transitional Justice* 3, no. 1 (2009): 5–27.

46. Leebaw, "Irreconcilable Goals of Transitional Justice."

47. Kieran McEvoy, "Beyond Legalism: Towards a Thicker Understanding of Transitional Justice," *Journal of Law and Society* 34, no. 4 (2007): 411–40; Nagy, "Transitional Justice as Global Project"; Rosalind Shaw, "Memory Frictions: Localizing the Truth and Reconciliation Commission in Sierra Leone," *International Journal of Transitional Justice* 1, no. 2 (2007): 183–207; Kieran McEvoy and Lorna McGregor, eds., *Transitional Justice from Below: Grassroots Activism and the Struggle for Change* (Oxford: Hart Publishing, 2008).

48. Muvingi, "Sitting on Powder Kegs"; David Miller, *National Responsibility and Global Justice* (Oxford: Oxford University Press, 2007); Mani, "Dilemmas of Expanding Transitional Justice," 254.

49. Ratna Kapur, "Normalizing Violence: Transitional Justice and the Gujarat Riots," *Columbia Journal of Gender and Law* 15, no. 3 (2006): 889. See also Nagy, "Transitional Justice as Global Project," 11.

50. Orford, "Commissioning the Truth," 861; Quinn, "Introductory Essay," 1; Kapur, "Normalizing Violence," 926; Nagy, "Transitional Justice as Global Project," 285–86.

51. Through its institutional hearings, the Truth and Reconciliation Commission of South Africa considered the broader institutional framework of apartheid and made recommendations to address it, while the Truth and Reconciliation Commission of Peru and the Commission on Historical Clarification of Guatemala acknowledged the socioeconomic and structural roots of the violence in these countries. For further discussion and examples, see Jennifer Balint and Julie Evans, "Transitional Justice and Settler States," in *ANZCCC: Australian and New Zealand Critical Criminology Conference 2010, Proceedings*, ed. Murray Lee, Gail Mason, and Sanja Milivojevic (Sydney: Sydney Law School, 2011), 4–5; Laplante, "Transitional Justice and Peace Building," 335–36; Vijayalakshmi Teelock, "The Mauritius Truth and Justice Commission: 'Eyewash,' 'Storm in a Teacup' or Promise of a New Future for Mauritians?," in *Emancipation and the Remaking of the British Imperial World*, ed. Catherine Hall, Nicholas Draper, and Keith McClelland (Manchester: Manchester University Press, 2014), 207–22. See also the broad-based CARICOM Reparations Commission, www.caricomreparations.org

52. Balint and Evans, "Transitional Justice and Settler States," 4–5.

53. Kent, *Dynamics of Transitional Justice*.

54. Mani, "Dilemmas of Expanding Transitional Justice," 225.

55. Laplante, "Transitional Justice and Peace Building," 333.

56. Meister, *After Evil*, 24.

57. Arthur, "How 'Transitions' Reshaped Human Rights," 324–26, 343–48.

58. Paige Arthur, "Introduction: Identities in Transition," in *Identities in Transition:*

Challenges for Transitional Justice in Divided Societies, ed. Paige Arthur (Cambridge: Cambridge University Press, 2011), 1.

59. Arthur, "How 'Transitions' Reshaped Human Rights," 326.

60. Nagy, "Transitional Justice as Global Project"; Miller, *National Responsibility and Global Justice*.

61. Moon, *Narrating Political Reconciliation*.

62. Kent, *Dynamics of Transitional Justice*.

63. Hintjens, "Explaining the 1994 Genocide in Rwanda"; Gerard Prunier, *The Rwanda Crisis: History of a Genocide* (New York: Columbia University Press, 1995).

64. For the characterization of transitional justice as a state-building enterprise, see Bell, "Transitional Justice, Interdisciplinarity and the State of the 'Field' or 'Non-Field,'" 13; Richard Wilson, *The Politics of Truth and Reconciliation in South Africa: Legitimizing the Post-Apartheid State* (New York: Cambridge University Press, 2001), xvi.

65. Orford, "Commissioning the Truth," 874, 876–77.

66. Meister, *After Evil*, 24–25.

67. Jung, "Canada and the Legacy of the Indian Residential Schools," 241–42, 245–46.

68. Williams, *American Indian in Western Legal Thought*; Anghie, *Imperialism, Sovereignty and the Making of International Law*.

69. Anthony Pagden, *Lords of All the World: Ideologies of Empire in Spain, Britain, and France* (New Haven: Yale University Press, 1995).

70. Patrick Wolfe, "Corpus Nullius: The Exception of Indians and Other Aliens in US Constitutional Discourse," *Postcolonial Studies* 10, no. 2 (2007): 127–51; Anghie, *Imperialism, Sovereignty and the Making of International Law*.

71. James Anaya, *Indigenous Peoples in International Law* (Oxford: Oxford University Press, 2004); Anghie, *Imperialism, Sovereignty and the Making of International Law*.

72. On the importance of contesting "the state's monopoly over the legitimate exercise of legitimacy" if Indigenous polities are to "cease to be axiomatically enfolded within the ideological and institutional structures of the settler state," see Mark Rifkin, "Indigenizing Agamben: Rethinking Sovereignty in Light of the 'Peculiar' Status of Native Peoples," *Cultural Critique* 73 (2009): 88–124, especially at 111, 115.

73. Cited in Bonner and James, "The Three R's of Seeking Transitional Justice," 19.

74. Evans, "Where Lawlessness Is Law."

75. Nagy, "Transitional Justice as Global Project," 281. See also Jung, "Canada and the Legacy of the Indian Residential Schools," 271, 240–41; Arthur, "How 'Transitions' Reshaped Human Rights," 361–62.

76. Thank you to project partner Rachael Maza for this articulation of what "transitional justice" may mean.

77. UN Secretary-General, "The Rule of Law and Transitional Justice in Conflict and Post-Conflict Societies."

78. Young, "Responsibility and Global Justice"; Young, *Responsibility for Justice*.

79. Lu, "Colonialism as Structural Injustice."

80. Jung, "Canada and the Legacy of the Indian Residential Schools," 254–56.

81. Lambourne, "Transitional Justice and Peacebuilding after Mass Violence"; Paul Gready and Simon Robins, "From Transitional to Transformative Justice: A New Agenda for Practice," *International Journal of Transitional Justice* 8, no. 3 (2014): 339–61.

82. Jung, "Canada and the Legacy of the Indian Residential Schools," 227; Meister, *After Evil*, 42.

83. Arthur, "How 'Transitions' Reshaped Human Rights," 362.

84. Jung, "Canada and the Legacy of the Indian Residential Schools," 239.

85. For a related discussion, see Rifkin, "Indigenizing Agamben"; Black, McVeigh, and Johnstone, "Of the South"; Birch, "'Invisible Fire.'"

Chapter 6

1. Letter from Ndiku Mutua, Paulo Nzili, Jane Muthoni Mara, Wambugu Wa Nyingi, and Susan Ngondi to Gordon Brown, 24 June 2009. The materials in this chapter in relation to the Kenyan case are primarily sourced from the case files from the "Mau Mau" hearings held at the British High Court of Justice in 2011 and 2012, along with archival material at the National Archives in the United Kingdom. We are grateful to Leigh Day & Co. and Richard Hermer QC for allowing access to files on the case.

2. Wadjularbinna Nulyarimma, Supreme Court of the ACT, 17 July 1998. We are grateful to Eleanor Gilbert for access to files from the "genocide" hearing at the ACT Supreme Court in 1998, which Jennifer Balint also attended and wrote an affidavit. We respectfully acknowledge the passing of Wadjularbinna Nulyarimma, Isobell Coe, and Billy Craigie.

3. "Report of the Board Appointed to Enquire into, and Report upon, the Present Condition and Management of the Coranderrk Aboriginal Station, Together with the Minutes of Evidence," 10.

4. Jane Muthoni Mara, Witness Statement, British High Court, 4 November 2010. Full statement available at "The Mau Mau Claims," accessed January 31, 2019, https://www.leighday.co.uk/International/Further-insights/Detailed-case-studies/The-Mau-Mau-claims/The-Mau-Mau-claimants

5. Transcript of Proceedings, Supreme Court of the Australian Capital Territory, Crispin J, SC No 457 of 1998 (hereafter "*Transcript of Proceedings*"), 17 July 1998, 11. Case reported as *In the matter of an application for a writ of mandamus directed to Phillip R Thompson Ex parte Wadjularbinna Nulyarimma, Isobel Coe, Billy Craigie and Robbie Thorpe (Applicants), Tom Trevorrow, Irene Watson, Kevin Buzzacott and Michael J Anderson (Intervenors)* (1998) ACTSC 13 (hereafter "*Thompson et al.*").

6. Ibid., 15.

7. Mariana Valverde, *Chronotopes of Law: Jurisdiction, Scale and Governance* (New York: Routledge, 2015).

8. Renisa Mawani, "Law's Archive," *Annual Review of Law and Social Science* 8 (2012): 337–65; Kirsten Campbell, "The Laws of Memory: The ICTY, the Archive, and Transi-

tional Justice," *Social & Legal Studies* 22, no. 2 (2016): 247–69; Jacques Derrida, *Archive Fever: A Freudian Impression* (Chicago: University of Chicago Press, 1995); Stewart Motha and Honni van Rijswijk, *Law, Memory, Violence: Uncovering the Counter-Archive* (New York: Routledge, 2016); Katherine Biber and Trish Luker, "Evidence and the Archive: Ethics, Aesthetics, and Emotion," *Australian Feminist Law Journal* 40, no. 1 (2014): 1–14; Katherine Biber, "In Crime's Archive: The Cultural Afterlife of Criminal Evidence," *British Journal of Criminology* 53 (2013): 1033–49; Mawani, *Colonial Proximities*.

9. Joan M. Schwartz and Terry Cook, "Archives, Records, and Power: The Making of Modern Memory," *Archival Science* 2, no. 1 (2002): 1–19; Richard Harvey Brown and Beth Davis-Brown, "The Making of Memory: The Politics of Archives, Libraries and Museums in the Construction of National Consciousness," *History of the Human Sciences* 11, no. 4 (1998): 17–32; Michel Foucault, *The Archaeology of Knowledge*, trans. Alan Mark Sheridan-Smith (New York: Pantheon Books, 1972).

10. Emilios Christodoulidis describes these modes of remembering as "a template of interpretative possibilities that are peculiar to it and recalls the remembered event through its vocabularies and the distinctions and attribution that allow it to attribute value": "Law's Immemorial," in *Lethe's Law: Justice, Law and Ethics in Reconciliation*, ed. Emilios A. Christodoulidis and Scott Veitch (Oxford: Hart Publishing, 2001), 223.

11. Kapur, *Erotic Justice*, 3; Williams, "Obliging Shell"; Patricia Williams, *The Alchemy of Race and Rights* (Cambridge: Harvard University Press, 1991); Angela P. Harris, "Critical Race Theory," in *Law and Social Theory*, ed. Reza Banakar and Max Travers (Oxford: Hart, 2013), 147–60; Richard Delgado, "Storytelling for Oppositionists and Others: A Plea for Narrative," *Michigan Law Review* 87, no. 8 (1989): 2411–41.

12. Smart, *Feminism and the Power of Law*, 88.

13. Santos, "Law."

14. Ehrlich, *Fundamental Principles of the Sociology of Law*; see also Nelken, "Eugen Ehrlich, Living Law, and Plural Legalities."

15. Petrażycki, *Law and Morality*; see also Kojder, "Leon Petrażycki's Socio-Legal Ideas and Their Contemporary Continuation."

16. Adam Podgórecki, "Unrecognized Father of Sociology of Law: Leon Petrażycki: Reflections Based on Jan Gorecki's Sociology and Jurisprudence of Leon Petrażycki," *Law & Society Review* 15, no. 1 (1980): 183–202; Adam Podgórecki, *Law and Society* (London: Routledge and Kegan Paul, 1974).

17. Peter Sack and E. J. Minchin, "Legal Pluralism: Proceedings of the Canberra Law Workshop VII" (Canberra: Australian National University, 1986); Sally Engle Merry, "Culture, Power, and the Discourse of Law," *New York Law School Law Review* 37 (1992): 209–25; Merry, "Legal Pluralism"; M. B. Hooker, *Legal Pluralism: An Introduction to Colonial and Neo-Colonial Laws* (Oxford: Clarendon Press, 1975); Franz von Benda-Beckmann, "Who's Afraid of Legal Pluralism?," *Journal of Legal Pluralism and Unofficial Law* 34, no. 47 (2002): 37–82.

18. Sally Falk Moore, "Law and Social Change: The Semi-Autonomous Social Field as an Appropriate Subject of Study," *Law & Society Review* 7, no. 4 (1973): 719–46; Santos,

"Law"; John Griffiths, "What Is Legal Pluralism?," *Journal of Legal Pluralism and Unofficial Law* 18, no. 24 (1986): 1–55; Anne Griffiths, "Legal Pluralism in Botswana: Women's Access to Law," *Journal of Legal Pluralism and Unofficial Law* 30, no. 42 (1998): 123–38; Paul Schiff Berman, "The New Legal Pluralism," *Annual Review of Law and Social Science* 5, no. 1 (2009): 225–42; Emmanuel Melissaris, "The More the Merrier? A New Take on Legal Pluralism," *Social & Legal Studies* 13, no. 1 (2004): 57–79.

19. Mari Matsuda, "Looking to the Bottom: Critical Legal Studies and Reparations," *Harvard Civil Rights–Civil Liberties Law Review* 22, no. 1 (1987): 334.

20. Affidavit of Wadjularbinna Nulyarimma. Submission in *Thompson et al. 1998*, 8 July 1998, para. 3.

21. Letter from P. R. Thompson, Registrar of the ACT Magistrates Court to Wadjularbinna Nulyarimma, 7 July 1998.

22. The case was joined by Tom Trevorrow, Irene Watson, Kevin Buzzacott, Michael Anderson, Alice Hoolihan, Daisy Brown, Albert Hayes, Alister Thorpe, Yaluritja Clarrie Isaacs, and Mingli Wanjurri Nungala. For a detailed discussion of the case, see Jennifer Balint, "Stating Genocide in Law: The Aboriginal Embassy and the ACT Supreme Court," in *The Aboriginal Tent Embassy: Sovereignty, Black Power, Land Rights and the State*, ed. Gary Foley, Andrew Schaap, and Edwina Howell (New York: Routledge, 2014), 235–50.

23. Larissa Behrendt, "Foreword," in *The Aboriginal Tent Embassy: Sovereignty, Black Power, Land Rights and the State*, ed. Gary Foley, Andrew Schaap, and Edwina Howell (New York: Routledge, 2014), xxiii–xxiv.

24. *Transcript of Proceedings*, 20 July 1998.

25. The Native Title Act had come about as a result of the *Mabo* decision, which recognized that Australia was not *terra nullius* ("land belonging to no-one") yet established what was to become an increasingly restrictive regime of access to what was termed "native title."

26. Balint, Evans, and McMillan, "Rethinking Transitional Justice, Redressing Indigenous Harm"; Wolfe, "Nation and MiscegeNation."

27. Damien Short has argued that genocide is a "continuing process in an Australia that has failed to decolonize and continues to assimilate," is "predicated on a victim's understanding of the culturally genocidal dimensions of settler colonialism and the central importance of land to the survival of many Indigenous peoples *as peoples*": "Australia: A Continuing Genocide?," *Journal of Genocide Research* 12, no. 1 (2010): 46. See also Colin Tatz, "Genocide in Australia," *Journal of Genocide Research* 1, no. 3 (1999): 315–52; Colin Tatz, "Confronting Australian Genocide," *Aboriginal History* 25, no. 1 (2001): 16–35; Katherine Bischoping and Natalie Fingerhut, "Border Lines: Indigenous People in Genocide Studies," *Canadian Review of Sociology* 33, no. 4 (1996): 481–506.

28. Wadjularbinna Nulyarimma, *Transcript of Proceedings*, 17 July 1998.

29. Written Submissions of the Aboriginal Genocide Prosecutors and Intervenors, 7 September 1998.

30. Wadjularbinna Nulyarimma, *Transcript of Proceedings*, 17 July 1998, 11.

31. See also Tony Barta: "I think we have to face the fact that historically we have a

relationship of genocide with the Aborigines which cannot be understood only in terms of a clear intention to wipe them out": Barta, "After the Holocaust," 156.

32. Larissa Behrendt, who argues that genocide "is part of the colonisation process that takes place in many guises over many generations, with many attempts, with many policies, with many administrators": Larissa Behrendt, "Genocide: The Distance between Law and Life," *Aboriginal History* 25 (2001): 140. See also Colin Tatz, *Genocide in Australia: By Accident or Design?* (Canberra: Aboriginal Studies Press, 1999).

33. Balint, Evans, and McMillan, "Rethinking Transitional Justice, Redressing Indigenous Harm."

34. Thomas Nagel, speaking at the conference of the Aspen Institute Justice and Society Program in 1988, made the distinction in the context of seeking justice for state crime between knowledge and acknowledgment. As Stanley Cohen noted, drawing on Nagel, "Acknowledgment is what happens to knowledge when it becomes officially sanctioned and enters the public realm": "State Crimes of Previous Regimes: Knowledge, Accountability, and the Policing of the Past," *Law & Social Inquiry* 20, no. 1 (1995): 18.

35. Wadjularbinna Affidavit, 8 July 1998, para. 30.

36. Chris Cunneen, *Conflict, Politics and Crime: Aboriginal Communities and the Police* (Crows Nest, NSW: Allen and Unwin, 2001); Eileen Baldry and Sue Green, "Indigenous Welfare in Australia," in *Neoliberalism and the Australian Welfare State*, ed. Christian Aspalter (Taichung City, Taiwan: Casa Verde Publishing, 2003), 41–60; Chris Cunneen and Terri Libesman, "Removed and Discarded: The Contemporary Legacy of the Stolen Generations," *Australian Indigenous Law Reporter* 7, no. 4 (2002): 1–26; Terri Libesman and Chris Cunneen, "Postcolonial Trauma: The Contemporary Removal of Indigenous Children and Young People from Their Families in Australia," *Australian Journal of Social Issues* 35, no. 2 (2000): 99–115.

37. Isobell Coe, *Transcript of Proceedings*, 23 July 1998.

38. Ibid., 4, paras. 10–20.

39. Ibid., 14, para. 25.

40. Affidavit, Wadjularbinna Nulyarimma, 8 July 1998, para. 10.

41. See Buzzacott testimony at Embassy, *Transcript of Proceedings*, 23 July 1998, paras. 10–35.

42. *Transcript of Proceedings*, 23 July 1998, 6, para. 35.

43. *Transcript of Proceedings*, 17 July 1998, 24–25.

44. *Thompson et al.*, para. 78.

45. There had been partial recognition in *Coe v Commonwealth* in the High Court of Australia. Justice Murphy noted: "[T]he aborigines did not give up their lands peacefully; they were killed or removed forcibly from the lands by United Kingdom forces or the European colonists in what amounted to attempted (and in Tasmania almost complete) genocide": *Coe v Commonwealth* 1979 HCA 68 (5 April 1979), para. 8.

46. Particulars of Claim, 22 October 2009.

47. Telegram to Major General Heyman from unknown, 17 December 1954 (GHQ171254).

48. Letter to the Secretary of State for the Colonies from detainees at Manyani Special Detention Camp, 10 April 1956.

49. Letter to the Chairman of the Commonwealth Parliamentary Association Nairobi, from Njiri d/o Wanjiku, Kamiti Prison Camp, 20 August 1954.

50. This was to be echoed in the claims made later to the British High Court as the first factor as to why there existed a duty of care on the part of the UK government to the claimants, as put by Richard Hermer QC for the claimants: (i) The victims were all Her Majesty's subjects, owing allegiance to the Crown: *Mutua v. Foreign and Commonwealth Office* (2011) 1913 EWHC QB (hereafter "*Mutua I*"); para. 155–156.

51. Petition from detainees at Manyani Special Detention Camp to the Governor of Kenya, 5 January 1958.

52. Ibid.

53. See Ehrlich, *Fundamental Principles of the Sociology of Law*; Podgórecki, *Law and Society*; Moore, "Law and Social Change."

54. See Huw Bennett, *Fighting the Mau Mau: The British Army and Counter-Insurgency in the Kenya Emergency* (New York: Cambridge University Press, 2012). See also his interview with Katie Engelhart, "Empire and the Mau Mau: A Story of Colonialism and Counter-Insurgency," *Los Angeles Review of Books*, 2016, https://lareviewofbooks.org/article/empire-and-the-mau-mau-a-story-of-colonialism-and-counter-insurgency

55. David M. Anderson, "Mau Mau in the High Court and the 'Lost' British Empire Archives: Colonial Conspiracy or Bureaucratic Bungle?," *Journal of Imperial and Commonwealth History* 39, no. 5 (2011): 710.

56. See further, Jennifer Balint, Julie Evans, and Nesam McMillan, "Justice Claims in Colonial Contexts: Commissions of Inquiry in Historical Perspective," *Australian Feminist Law Journal* 42, no. 1 (2016): 75–96. See also Thalia Anthony, "'They Were Treating Me Like a Dog': The Colonial Continuum of State Harms against Indigenous Children in Detention in the Northern Territory, Australia," *State Crime* 7, no. 2 (2018): 251–77.

57. Cited by David Anderson, Expert Witness Statement 2. Submission in *Mutua I*, 1 April 2011, para. 33.

58. Minutes of the Chief Secretary's Complaints Coordinating Committee, 6 December 1954.

59. David Anderson, Expert Witness Statement 3. Submission in *Mutua II*, 18 June 2012, para. 58.

60. Letter from detainees at the Athi River Detention Camp, 29 September 1953.

61. David Anderson, Expert Witness Statement 3. Submission in *Mutua v. Foreign and Commonwealth Office* (2012) 2678 EWHC QB (hereafter "*Mutua II*"), 18 June 2012, para. 36.

62. Caroline Elkins, *Imperial Reckoning: The Untold Story of Britain's Gulag in Kenya* (New York: Henry Holt, 2005), 40.

63. David Anderson, Expert Witness Statement 3. Submission in *Mutua II*, 18 June 2012, paras. 21, 26.

64. Letter from Commissioner of Police to Secretary for African Affairs, 21 April 1954.

65. David Anderson, Expert Witness Statement 1. Submission in *Mutua I*, 21 December 2010, para. 5.

66. Ibid., para. 7.

67. David M Anderson, "British Abuse and Torture in Kenya's Counter-Insurgency, 1952–1960," *Small Wars & Insurgencies* 23, nos. 4–5 (2013): 704.

68. Anderson writes that "the head of military command in Kenya, General Erskine . . . feared that an investigation into the activities of the government's forces in the period from October 1952 to June 1953 'would be shattering'": ibid., 705.

69. Caroline Elkins, Expert Witness Statement 3. Submission in *Mutua II*, 25 May 2012, para. 26.

70. "Glenday Report," AA 45-26-2-2, cited in ibid., 706.

71. David Anderson, Expert Witness Statement 2. Submission in *Mutua I*, 1 April 2011, para. 19.

72. Elkins, *Imperial Reckoning*, 116.

73. Caroline Elkins, Expert Witness Statement 1. Submission in *Mutua I*, 20 February 2011, para. 129.

74. 86 KNA, MSS 115/51, Press Office, Handout no. 142, "Death of Ten Detainees at Hola," 4 March 1959, cited in ibid., para. 127. See also Elkins, *Imperial Reckoning*, 347.

75. Elkins, *Imperial Reckoning*, 348.

76. See Committee on Emergency Detention Camps, *Report of the Committee on Emergency Detention Camps* (Nairobi: Government Printer, 1959).

77. Cited in judgment, *Mutua & Ors v FCO* 2012 EWHC 2678 QB (hereafter "*Mutua & Ors*"), 138.

78. *Mutua & Ors*, para. 139.

79. Elkins, *Imperial Reckoning*.

80. United Kingdom, *Parliamentary Debates*, House of Commons, 16 June 1959, vol. 607, col. 248–384, para. 311.

81. See, further, Balint, *Genocide, State Crime and the Law*, chap. 2.

82. Elkins, *Imperial Reckoning*; David M. Anderson, *Histories of the Hanged: Britain's Dirty War in Kenya and the End of Empire* (London: Weidenfeld and Nicolson, 2005); Bennett, *Fighting the Mau Mau*.

83. *Mutua I*; *Mutua II*.

84. *Mutua II*, para. 117.

85. Claim Form submitted to the High Court of Justice, 23 June 2009.

86. *Mutua I*, para. 2.

87. Ibid., para. 27.

88. The REDRESS Trust was an Intervenor in this hearing.

89. Full statements available at "The Mau Mau Claims," accessed January 31, 2019, https://www.leighday.co.uk/International/Further-insights/Detailed-case-studies/The-Mau-Mau-claims/The-Mau-Mau-claimants

90. *Mutua I*, para. 1.

91. *Mutua II*, para. 86.

92. See, for example, Justice Olney in *Members of the Yorta Yorta Aboriginal Community v Victoria* (2002) HCA 58 who relied upon the memoir of the member of the Board of Protection Edward Curr who had so clearly shown his prejudice against the Aboriginal residents of Coranderrk in his testimony to the Parliamentary Inquiry, rather than the oral evidence of continuity of connection to land by the Yorta Yorta people themselves: see native title claimant Wayne Atkinson, "19 Seconds of Dungudja Wala (Yorta Yorta Word for Big River): Reflections Paper on the Yorta Yorta Native Title Judgment," 2000, http://www.kooriweb.org/sljr/dungudjawala.htm

93. For example, Shoshana Felman argues that the Nuremberg trials had a more significant impact on international law than the Eichmann trial in part due to the former's greater reliance on documentary evidence, as opposed to the latter's more prominent featuring of victim's verbal testimony: *The Juridical Unconscious: Trials and Traumas in the Twentieth Century* (Cambridge: Harvard University Press, 2002), 134.

94. As Michelle Caswell has noted, if claims exist in documentary form, in archival form, they can often be seen as reliable, as non-self-interested, as "fact" rather than "testimony": "Khmer Rouge Archives: Accountability, Truth, and Memory in Cambodia," *Archival Science* 10, no. 1 (2010): 25–44.

95. Criminal Appeals 998 and 989 of 1954, and Criminal Case No. 240 of 1954 (*R v Muiru & Ors*) in *Mutua I*, para. 35.

96. *Mutua II*, para. 123.

97. *Mutua II*, para. 126.

98. *Mutua II*, para. 128.

99. *Mutua II*, para. 129.

100. *Mutua II*, paras. 130–32.

101. *Mutua II*, para. 133.

102. *Mutua II*, para. 138.

103. *Mutua II*, para. 139.

104. *Mutua II*, para. 140.

105. *Mutua I*, para. 125.

106. *Mutua I*, para. 128.

107. *Mutua II*, para. 109.

108. Claimant's Skeleton Argument upon the Preliminary Issues (Richard Hermer QC, Phillippa Kaufmann, Zachary Douglas).

109. Sir Frank Soskice (Newport): "I would remind the Secretary of State that, holding

the high office that he does, he is responsible for the good name of British administration in the Colonies and that the events at Hola have done more than any other single happening to injure that good name. It is a disaster which has taken place in a province of government for which he is under a direct and personal responsibility": United Kingdom, *Parliamentary Debates*, House of Commons, 16 June 1959, vol. 607, col. 248–384, para. 263.

110. See chapter 5 (this volume), and Balint, Evans, and McMillan, "Rethinking Transitional Justice, Redressing Indigenous Harm."

111. *Mutua I*, para. 143.

112. *Mutua I*, para. 132.

113. Transcript, Royal Courts of Justice, 17 July 2012, 23, lines 15–19.

114. *Mutua II*, para. 27.

115. United Kingdom, *Parliamentary Debates*, House of Commons, 6 June 2013, vol. 563, col. 1692.

116. In the apology, Foreign Secretary William Hague stated: "We continue to deny liability on behalf of the Government and British taxpayers today for the actions of the colonial administration in respect of the claims, and indeed the courts have made no finding of liability against the Government in this case. We do not believe that claims relating to events that occurred overseas outside direct British jurisdiction more than 50 years ago can be resolved satisfactorily through the courts without the testimony of key witnesses, which is no longer available. It is therefore right that the Government have defended the case to this point since 2009.": United Kingdom, *Parliamentary Debates*, House of Commons, 6 June 2013, vol. 563, col. 1692.

117. McCombe stated in his judgment: "I have reached the conclusion . . . that a fair trial on this part of the case does remain possible and that the evidence on both sides remains significantly cogent for the Court to complete its task satisfactorily": *Mutua II*, para. 95.

118. See discussion in Jennifer Balint, "The 'Mau Mau' Legal Hearings and Recognizing the Crimes of the British Colonial State: A Limited Constitutive Moment," *Critical Analysis of Law* 3, no. 2 (2016): 261–85.

119. See, for example, Kapur, "Normalizing Violence"; Shaw, "Memory Frictions"; Balint, Evans, and McMillan, "Rethinking Transitional Justice, Redressing Indigenous Harm"; Balint, Evans, and McMillan, "Justice Claims in Colonial Contexts."

120. Priyamvada Gopal, "Redressing Anti-Imperial Amnesia," *Race & Class* 57, no. 3 (2016): 18–30; Balint, "'Mau Mau' Legal Hearings and Recognizing the Crimes of the British Colonial State."

121. Wolfe, "Nation and MiscegeNation," 96.

Chapter 7

1. Ian Lowe, *A Big Fix: Radical Solutions for Australia's Environmental Crisis* (Melbourne: Black Inc., 2005), 108.

2. Young, "Responsibility and Global Justice," 102; see also 114.

3. Ibid., 122; see also 123.

4. Bevernage, "The Past Is Evil/Evil Is Past," 352.

5. Eve Darian-Smith, "Precedents of Injustice: Thinking about History in Law and Society Scholarship," in *Law and Society Reconsidered*, ed. Austin Sarat (Bingley, UK: Emerald, 2008), 62.

6. See, in particular, Dorsett and McVeigh, *Jurisdiction*. See also Black, *Land Is the Source of the Law*; Genovese, "Critical Decision, 1982"; Genovese, "Critical Decision 1983." See further "Lives Lived with Law," ed. Ann Genovese, Shaun McVeigh, and Peter D. Rush, special issue of *Law Text Culture* 20 (2016).

7. See further Julie Evans, "The Ethos of the Historian: The Minutes of Evidence Project, and Lives Lived with Law on the Ground," *Law Text Culture* 20 (2016): 136–64.

8. See further ibid.

9. Ovide Mercredi, Assembly of First Nations leader, Canada, cited in Bonner and James, "The Three R's of Seeking Transitional Justice," 19.

10. Julie Evans in Jennifer Balint et al., "Minutes of Evidence Project: Doing Structural Justice," *State Crime* 7, no. 2 (2018): 391.

11. Lilly Brown in ibid., 405.

12. Julie Evans et al., "Minutes of Evidence Project: Promoting New and Collaborative Ways of Understanding Australia's Past and Engaging with Structural Justice," *Australian Research Council Final Report*, 2015, 11.

13. Ibid.

14. Ibid., 12.

15. Ibid., 14.

SELECT BIBLIOGRAPHY

Legislation Cited

Aboriginal Land Rights (Northern Territory) Act 1976 (Northern Territory).
The Aborigines Protection Act 1886 (Victoria).
Charter of the International Military Tribunal (1945).
Charter of the United Nations (1945).
Native Title Act 1993 (Cth).
Rome Statute of the International Criminal Court (1998).
Statute of the International Criminal Tribunal for the Prosecution of Persons Responsible for Genocide and Other Serious Violations of International Humanitarian Law Committed in the Territory of Rwanda and Rwandan Citizens Responsible for Genocide and Other Such Violations Committed in the Territory of Neighbouring States, between 1 January 1994 and 31 December 1994 (1994).
Traditional Owner Settlement Act 2010 (Victoria).
United Nations Convention on the Prevention and Punishment of the Crime of Genocide (1948).
United Nations General Assembly, Resolution 3103 (XXVIII), Basic Principles of Legal Status of the Combatants Struggling against Colonial and Alien Domination and Racist Regimes.

Cases Cited

Coe v Commonwealth (1979) HCA 68.
In the matter of an application for a writ of mandamus directed to Phillip R Thompson Ex parte Wadjularbinna Nulyarimma, Isobel Coe, Billy Craigie and Robbie Thorpe (Applicants), Tom Trevorrow, Irene Watson, Kevin Buzzacott and Michael J Anderson (Intervenors) (1998) ACTSC 13.
Mabo and Others v Queensland (No. 2) (1992) HCA 23, 175 CLR 1.
Members of the Yorta Yorta Aboriginal Community v Victoria & Ors (1998) FCA 1606.
Members of the Yorta Yorta Aboriginal Community v Victoria (2002) HCA 58, 214 CLR 422.
Mutua & Ors v FCO (2012) EWHC 2678 QB.
Mutua v. Foreign and Commonwealth Office (2011) 1913 EWHC QB.

Mutua v. Foreign and Commonwealth Office (2012) 2678 EWHC QB.

The Prosecutor v. Clément Kayishema and Obed Ruzindana (Trial Judgment) (International Criminal Tribunal for Rwanda, ICTR-95-1-T, 21 May 1999).

The Prosecutor v. Ferdinand Nahimana, Jean-Bosco Barayagwiza, Hassan Ngeze (Appeal Judgment) (International Criminal Tribunal for Rwanda, ICTR-99-52-A, 28 November 2007).

The Prosecutor v. Jean-Paul Akayesu (Trial Judgement) (International Criminal Tribunal for Rwanda, ICTR-96-4-T, 2 September 1998).

R v Johnston, Clarke, Nicholson, Castles, and Crear (1824) NSWSupC 8.

Primary Materials

For primary materials on file with authors, see chapter citations.

Campbell, John Thomas. "Proclamations &c Black Natives Establishment of Institution for Children Government and General Orders Government House Sydney: 10th December 1814." Sydney, 1814.

"Government and General Orders," *Sydney Gazette and New South Wales Advertiser*, 10 December 1814, 1, http://nla.gov.au/nla.news-article629022

Permanent Under Secretary James Stephen's minute, 19 February 1841, Gawler to S/S, no. 12, 15 August 1840, CO 13/16, National Archives, London.

"Proclamation By His Excellency Lachlan Macquarie," *Sydney Gazette and New South Wales Advertiser*, 20 July 1816, 1, http://nla.gov.au/nla.news-article2176728

"Proclamation By His Excellency Lachlan Macquarie," *Sydney Gazette and New South Wales Advertiser*, 4 May 1816, 1, https://trove.nla.gov.au/newspaper/article/2176637

"Proclamation By His Excellency Lachlan Macquarie," *Sydney Gazette and New South Wales Advertiser*, 2 November 1816, http://nla.gov.au/nla.news-article2176884

"Proclamation By His Excellency Sir Thomas Brisbane," *Sydney Gazette and New South Wales Advertiser*, 14 August 1824, 1, http://nla.gov.au/nla.news-article2183147

"Report of the Board Appointed to Enquire into, and Report upon, the Present Condition and Management of the Coranderrk Aboriginal Station, Together with the Minutes of Evidence." Melbourne: Government Printer, 1882.

S/S to Grey, "Confidential," 14 December 1841, CO 396/2, National Archives, London.

"Supreme Court of Criminal Jurisdiction," *Sydney Gazette and New South Wales Advertiser*, 12 August 1824, 2, http://nla.gov.au/nla.news-article2183123

Sydney Gazette and New South Wales Advertiser, 8 January 1824 http://nla.gov.au/nla.news-page494770

Sydney Gazette and New South Wales Advertiser, 10 June 1824 http://trove.nla.gov.au/newspaper/page/494866

Sydney Gazette and New South Wales Advertiser, 22 July 1824 http://nla.gov.au/nla.news-article2183067

United Kingdom, *Parliamentary Debates*, House of Commons, 16 June 1959, vol. 607, col. 248-384.

United Kingdom, *Parliamentary Debates*, House of Commons, 6 June 2013, vol. 563, col. 1692.

Watson, Frederick. *Historical Records of Australia*. Vol. 1. Series 1. Sydney: Library Committee of the Commonwealth Parliament, 1917.

Watson, Frederick. *Historical Records of Australia*. Vol. 9. Series 1. Sydney: Library Committee of the Commonwealth Parliament, 1917.

Watson, Frederick. *Historical Records of Australia*. Vol. 11. Series 1. Sydney: Library Committee of the Commonwealth Parliament, 1917.

Watson, Frederick. *Historical Records of Australia*. Vol. 17. Series 1. Sydney: Library Committee of the Commonwealth Parliament, 1917.

Watson, Frederick. "Introduction." In *Historical Records of Australia*, edited by Frederick Watson, 11:vii–xxvi. Series 1. Sydney: Library Committee of the Commonwealth Parliament, 1917.

Works Cited

"Africa Debate—Is the ICC Targeting Africa Inappropriately?" ICC Forum, 2014. http://iccforum.com/africa

Agamben, Giorgio. *Remnants of Auschwitz: The Witness and the Archive*. Translated by Daniel Heller-Roazen. New York: Zone Books, 1999.

Alfred, Taiaiake. *Wasáse: Indigenous Pathways of Action and Freedom*. Peterborough, UK: Broadview Press, 2005.

Altman, Jon C., and Melinda Hinkson, eds. *Coercive Reconciliation: Stabilise, Normalise, Exit Aboriginal Australia*. North Carlton, VIC: Arena Publications Association, 2007.

Amin, Samir. *Eurocentrism*. Translated by Russell Moore. New York: Monthly Review Press, 1989.

Anaya, James. *Indigenous Peoples in International Law*. Oxford: Oxford University Press, 2004.

Anderson, David M. "British Abuse and Torture in Kenya's Counter-Insurgency, 1952–1960." *Small Wars & Insurgencies* 23, nos. 4–5 (2013): 700–719.

Anderson, David M. *Histories of the Hanged: Britain's Dirty War in Kenya and the End of Empire*. London: Weidenfeld and Nicolson, 2005.

Anderson, David M. "Mau Mau in the High Court and the 'Lost' British Empire Archives: Colonial Conspiracy or Bureaucratic Bungle?" *Journal of Imperial and Commonwealth History* 39, no. 5 (2011): 699–716.

Anghie, Antony. *Imperialism, Sovereignty and the Making of International Law*. Cambridge: Cambridge University Press, 2005.

Anthony, Thalia. "'They Were Treating Me Like a Dog': The Colonial Continuum of State Harms against Indigenous Children in Detention in the Northern Territory, Australia." *State Crime* 7, no. 2 (2018): 251–77.

Arthur, Paige. "How 'Transitions' Reshaped Human Rights: A Conceptual History of Transitional Justice." *Human Rights Quarterly* 31, no. 2 (2009): 321–67.

Arthur, Paige. "Introduction: Identities in Transition." In *Identities in Transition: Challenges for Transitional Justice in Divided Societies*, edited by Paige Arthur, 1–14. Cambridge: Cambridge University Press, 2011.

Arthur, Paige, Eduardo González, Yukyan Lam, Joanna Rice, César Rodríguez-Garavito, and Deborah J. Yashar. "Strengthening Indigenous Rights through Truth Commissions: A Practitioner's Resource." New York: International Center for Transitional Justice, 2012.

Atkinson, Alan. *The Europeans in Australia: A History*. New York: Oxford University Press, 1997.

Atkinson, Wayne. "19 Seconds of Dungudja Wala (Yorta Yorta Word for Big River): Reflections Paper on the Yorta Yorta Native Title Judgment." 2000. http://www.kooriweb.org/sljr/dungudjawala.htm

Atkinson, Wayne. "'Not One Iota' of Land Justice: Reflections on the Yorta Yorta Native Title Claim, 1994–2001." *Indigenous Law Bulletin* 5, no. 6 (2001): 19–23.

Attwood, Bain. *Rights for Aborigines*. Crows Nest, NSW: Allen and Unwin, 2003.

Attwood, Bain, and Helen Doyle. *Possession: Batman's Treaty and the Matter of History*. Carlton, VIC: Miegunyah Press, 2009.

Australian Bureau of Statistics. "4517.0—Prisoners in Australia, 2018: Aboriginal and Torres Strait Islander Prisoner Characteristics." Canberra, 2018. http://www.abs.gov.au/ausstats/abs@.nsf/Lookup/by Subject/4517.0~2018~Main Features~Aboriginal and Torres Strait Islander prisoner characteristics ~13

Australian Electoral Commission. "Electoral Milestones for Indigenous Australians." 2017. https://www.aec.gov.au/indigenous/milestones.htm

Australian Human Rights and Equal Opportunity Commission. "Bringing Them Home: Report of the National Inquiry into the Separation of Aboriginal and Torres Strait Islander Children from Their Families." Sydney, NSW, 1997.

Australian Institute of Aboriginal and Torres Strait Islander Studies. "Day of Mourning and Protest Aborigines Conference—75th Anniversary: 26th January 1938." http://aiatsis.gov.au/exhibitions/day-mourning-26th-january-1938

Australian Institute of Aboriginal and Torres Strait Islander Studies. "Mabo Case." 2015. https://aiatsis.gov.au/explore/articles/mabo-case

Baldry, Eileen, and Sue Green. "Indigenous Welfare in Australia." In *Neoliberalism and the Australian Welfare State*, edited by Christian Aspalter, 41–60. Taichung City, Taiwan: Casa Verde Publishing, 2003.

Balint, Jennifer. *Genocide, State Crime, and the Law: In the Name of the State*. New York: Routledge, 2012.

Balint, Jennifer. "The 'Mau Mau' Legal Hearings and Recognizing the Crimes of the British Colonial State: A Limited Constitutive Moment." *Critical Analysis of Law* 3, no. 2 (2016): 261–85.

Balint, Jennifer. "Stating Genocide in Law: The Aboriginal Embassy and the ACT Supreme Court." In *The Aboriginal Tent Embassy: Sovereignty, Black Power, Land Rights and the State*, edited by Gary Foley, Andrew Schaap, and Edwina Howell, 235–50. New York: Routledge, 2014.

Balint, Jennifer, Lilly Brown, Caitlin Dullard, Julie Evans, Nesam McMillan, and Mark McMillan. "Minutes of Evidence Project: Doing Structural Justice." *State Crime* 7, no. 2 (2018): 389–409.

Balint, Jennifer, and Julie Evans. "Transitional Justice and Settler States." In *ANZCCC: The Australian and New Zealand Critical Criminology Conference 2010, Proceedings*, edited by Murray Lee, Gail Mason, and Sanja Milivojevic. Sydney: Sydney Law School, 2011.

Balint, Jennifer, Julie Evans, and Nesam McMillan. "Justice Claims in Colonial Contexts: Commissions of Inquiry in Historical Perspective." *Australian Feminist Law Journal* 42, no. 1 (2016): 75–96.

Balint, Jennifer, Julie Evans, and Nesam McMillan. "Rethinking Transitional Justice, Redressing Indigenous Harm: A New Conceptual Approach." *International Journal of Transitional Justice* 8, no. 2 (2014): 194–216.

Balint, Jennifer, Julie Evans, Nesam McMillan, Giordano Nanni, and Melodie Reynolds-Diarra. "The 'Minutes of Evidence' Project: Creating Collaborative Fields of Engagement with the Past, Present and Future." In *Settler Colonial Governance in Nineteenth-Century Victoria*, edited by Leigh Boucher and Lynette Russell, 203–24. Canberra, ACT: ANU Press and Aboriginal History Inc., 2015.

Barta, Tony. "After the Holocaust: Consciousness of Genocide in Australia." *Australian Journal of Politics & History* 31, no. 1 (1985): 154–61.

Barta, Tony. "Sorry, and Not Sorry, in Australia: How the Apology to the Stolen Generations Buried a History of Genocide." *Journal of Genocide Research* 10, no. 2 (2008): 201–14.

Barwick, Diane. *Rebellion at Coranderrk*. Edited by Laura E. Barwick and Richard E. Barwick. Canberra, ACT: Aboriginal History Inc., 1998.

Bassiouni, M. Cherif, ed. *The Pursuit of International Criminal Justice: A World Study on Conflicts, Victimization, and Post-Conflict Justice*. Antwerp: Intersentia, 2010.

Behrendt, Larissa. Foreword to *The Aboriginal Tent Embassy: Sovereignty, Black Power, Land Rights and the State*, edited by Gary Foley, Andrew Schaap, and Edwina Howell, xxiii–xxiv. New York: Routledge, 2014.

Behrendt, Larissa. "Genocide: The Distance between Law and Life." *Aboriginal History* 25 (2001): 132–47.

Behrendt, Larissa, Chris Cunneen, and Terri Libesman. *Indigenous Legal Relations in Australia*. South Melbourne, VIC: Oxford University Press, 2009.

Bell, Christine. "Transitional Justice, Interdisciplinarity and the State of the 'Field' or 'Non-Field.'" *International Journal of Transitional Justice* 3, no. 1 (2009): 5–27.

Bell, Derrick A. "Who's Afraid of Critical Race Theory?" *University of Illinois Law Review* 1, no. 4 (1995): 893–910.

Belmessous, Saliha. *Native Claims: Indigenous Law against Empire, 1500–1920*. New York: Oxford University Press, 2012.

Benda-Beckmann, Franz von. "Who's Afraid of Legal Pluralism?" *Journal of Legal Pluralism and Unofficial Law* 34, no. 47 (2002): 37–82.

Bennett, Huw. *Fighting the Mau Mau: The British Army and Counter-Insurgency in the Kenya Emergency*. New York: Cambridge University Press, 2012.

Benton, Lauren A. *Law and Colonial Cultures: Legal Regimes in World History, 1400–1900*. New York: Cambridge University Press, 2002.

Berman, Paul Schiff. "The New Legal Pluralism." *Annual Review of Law and Social Science* 5, no. 1 (2009): 225–42.

Bevernage, Berber. "The Past Is Evil/Evil Is Past: On Retrospective Politics, Philosophy of History and Temporal Manichaeism." *History and Theory* 53, no. 3 (2015): 350–52.

Bevernage, Berber. "Writing the Past Out of the Present: History and the Politics of Time in Transitional Justice." *History Workshop Journal* 69, no. 1 (2010): 111–31.

Bhabha, Homi K. *The Location of Culture*. London: Routledge, 2004.

Biber, Katherine. "In Crime's Archive: The Cultural Afterlife of Criminal Evidence." *British Journal of Criminology* 53 (2013): 1033–49.

Biber, Katherine, and Trish Luker. "Evidence and the Archive: Ethics, Aesthetics, and Emotion." *Australian Feminist Law Journal* 40, no. 1 (2014): 1–14.

Birch, Tony. "Archive Box—Series One: Matters in Relation to Aborigines Act (1886)." *Law Text Culture* 7 (2003): 142–47.

Birch, Tony. "'I Could Feel It in My Body': War on a History War." *Transforming Cultures EJournal* 1, no. 1 (2006): 19–32.

Birch, Tony. "'The Invisible Fire': Indigenous Sovereignty, History and Responsibility." In *Sovereign Subjects: Indigenous Sovereignty Matters*, edited by Aileen Moreton-Robinson, 105–17. Crows Nest, NSW: Allen and Unwin, 2007.

Bird, Deborah Rose. *Dingo Makes Us Human: Life and Land in Australian Aboriginal Culture*. Oakleigh, VIC: Cambridge University Press, 2000.

Bischoping, Katherine, and Natalie Fingerhut. "Border Lines: Indigenous People in Genocide Studies." *Canadian Review of Sociology* 33, no. 4 (1996): 481–506.

Black, Christine. *The Land Is the Source of the Law: A Dialogic Encounter with Indigenous Jurisprudence*. New York: Routledge, 2011.

Black, Christine. "Maturing Australia through Australian Aboriginal Narrative Law." *South Atlantic Quarterly* 110, no. 2 (2011): 347–62.

Black, Christine, Shaun McVeigh, and Richard Johnstone. "Of the South." *Griffith Law Review* 16, no. 2 (2007): 299–309.

Bonner, Michelle, and Matt James. "The Three R's of Seeking Transitional Justice: Reparation, Responsibility, and Reframing in Canada and Argentina." *International Indigenous Policy Journal* 2, no. 3 (2011): 1–29.

Borrows, John. *Drawing Out Law: A Spirit's Guide*. Toronto: Toronto University Press, 2010.

Boucher, Leigh, and Lynette Russell, eds. *Settler Colonial Governance in Nineteenth Century Victoria*. Canberra: ANU Press and Aboriginal History Inc., 2015.

Broome, Richard. *Aboriginal Australians: A History since 1788*. 4th ed. Crows Nest, NSW: Allen and Unwin, 2010.

Broome, Richard. *Aboriginal Victorians: A History since 1800*. Crows Nest, NSW: Allen and Unwin, 2005.

Brown, Richard Harvey, and Beth Davis-Brown. "The Making of Memory: The Politics of Archives, Libraries and Museums in the Construction of National Consciousness." *History of the Human Sciences* 11, no. 4 (1998): 17–32.

Butler, Judith. *Frames of War: When Is Life Grievable?* New York: Verso, 2009.

Butler, Judith. *Precarious Life: The Powers of Mourning and Violence*. London: Verso, 2004.

Campbell, Kirsten. "The Laws of Memory: The ICTY, the Archive, and Transitional Justice." *Social & Legal Studies* 22, no. 2 (2016): 247–69.

Caswell, Michelle. "Khmer Rouge Archives: Accountability, Truth, and Memory in Cambodia." *Archival Science* 10, no. 1 (2010): 25–44.

Césaire, Aimé. *Discourse on Colonialism*. Translated by Joan Pinkham. New York: Monthly Review Press, 2000.

Chakrabarty, Dipesh. *Provincializing Europe: Postcolonial Thought and Historical Difference*. Princeton: Princeton University Press, 2000.

Chaves, Kelly K. "'A Solemn Judicial Farce, the Mere Mockery of a Trial': The Acquittal of Lieutenant Lowe, 1827." *Aboriginal History* 31 (2007): 122–40.

Chesterman, John, and Brian Galligan. *Citizens without Rights: Aborigines and Australian Citizenship*. Cambridge: Cambridge University Press, 1997.

Christodoulidis, Emilios A. "Law's Immemorial." In *Lethe's Law: Justice, Law and Ethics in Reconciliation*, edited by Emilios A. Christodoulidis and Scott Veitch, 207–27. Oxford: Hart Publishing, 2001.

Clarke, Kamari. *Fictions of Justice: The International Criminal Court and the Challenge of Legal Pluralism in Sub-Saharan Africa*. New York: Cambridge University Press, 2009.

Clarke, Kamari. "Rethinking Africa through Its Exclusions: The Politics of Naming Criminal Responsibility." *Anthropological Quarterly* 83, no. 3 (2010): 625–51.

Clarke, Kamari M., Abel S. Knottnerus, and Eefje de Volder. "Africa and the ICC: An Introduction." In *Africa and the ICC: Perceptions of Justice*, edited by Kamari M. Clarke, Abel S. Knottnerus, and Eefje de Volder, 1–35. Cambridge: Cambridge University Press, 2016.

Coe, Mary. *Windradyne, a Wiradjuri Koorie*. Canberra: Aboriginal Studies Press, 1989.

Cohen, Stanley. "State Crimes of Previous Regimes: Knowledge, Accountability, and the Policing of the Past." *Law & Social Inquiry* 20, no. 1 (1995): 7–50.

Committee on Emergency Detention Camps. *Report of the Committee on Emergency Detention Camps*. Nairobi: Government Printer, 1959.

Connor, John. *The Australian Frontier Wars, 1788–1838*. Sydney: University of New South Wales Press, 2002.

Coulthard, Glen Sean. *Red Skin, White Masks: Rejecting the Colonial Politics of Recognition.* Minneapolis: University of Minnesota Press, 2014.

Cruvellier, Thierry. "The ICC, Out of Africa." *New York Times*, 6 November 2016.

Cunneen, Chris. *Conflict, Politics and Crime: Aboriginal Communities and the Police.* Crows Nest, NSW: Allen and Unwin, 2001.

Cunneen, Chris. "State Crime, the Colonial Question and Indigenous Peoples." In *Supranational Criminology: Towards a Criminology of International Crimes*, edited by Alette Smeulers and Roelof Haveman, 159–79. Antwerp: Intersentia, 2008.

Cunneen, Chris, and Terri Libesman. "Removed and Discarded: The Contemporary Legacy of the Stolen Generations." *Australian Indigenous Law Reporter* 7, no. 4 (2002): 1–26.

Curthoys, Ann, Ann Genovese, and Alexander Reilly. *Rights and Redemption: History, Law and Indigenous People.* Sydney, NSW: University of New South Wales Press, 2008.

Czarnota, Adam. "Law as Mnemosyne and as Lethe: Quasi-Judicial Institutions and Collective Memories." In *Lethe's Law: Justice, Law and Ethics in Reconciliation*, edited by Emilios Christodoulidis and Scott Veitch, 115–28. Oxford: Hart Publishing, 2001.

Darian-Smith, Eve. "Precedents of Injustice: Thinking about History in Law and Society Scholarship." In *Law and Society Reconsidered*, edited by Austin Sarat, 61–81. Bingley, UK: Emerald, 2008.

Dawes, James. *That The World May Know: Bearing Witness to Atrocity.* Cambridge: Harvard University Press, 2007.

Delgado, Richard. "Storytelling for Oppositionists and Others: A Plea for Narrative." *Michigan Law Review* 87, no. 8 (1989): 2411–41.

Denoon, Donald. *Settler Capitalism: The Dynamics of Dependent Development in the Southern Hemisphere.* New York: Oxford University Press, 1983.

Derrida, Jacques. *Archive Fever: A Freudian Impression.* Chicago: University of Chicago Press, 1995.

Des Forges, Alison. *"Leave None to Tell the Story": Genocide in Rwanda.* New York: Human Rights Watch, 1999.

Des Forges, Alison, and Timothy Longman. "Legal Responses to Genocide in Rwanda." In *My Neighbor, My Enemy: Justice and Community in the Aftermath of Mass Atrocity*, edited by Eric Stover and Harvey M. Weinstein, 49–68. New York: Cambridge University Press, 2004.

Dorsett, Shaunnagh, and Shaun McVeigh. "Conduct of Laws: Native Title, Responsibility, and Some Limits of Jurisdictional Thinking." *Melbourne University Law Review* 36 (2012): 470–93.

Dorsett, Shaunnagh, and Shaun McVeigh. *Jurisdiction.* Abingdon, Oxon: Routledge, 2012.

Doty, Roxanne Lynn. *Imperial Encounters: The Politics of Representation in North-South Relations.* Minneapolis: University of Minnesota Press, 1996.

Drandic, Isaac (director). *Coranderrk: We Will Show the Country.* Carlton, VIC: La Mama Courthouse Theatre: Ilbijerri Theatre Company, 2011.

Drumbl, Mark A. "Sclerosis: Retributive Justice and the Rwandan Genocide." *Punishment & Society* 2, no. 3 (2000): 287–307.

Durbach, Andrea. "'The Cost of a Wounded Society': Reparations and the Illusion of Reconciliation." *Australian Indigenous Law Review* 12, no. 1 (2008): 22–40.

Edmonds, Penelope. "Theatre of Evidence." *History Australia* 9, no. 2 (2012): 205–7.

Ehrlich, Eugen. *Fundamental Principles of the Sociology of Law*. Translated by Walter L. Moll. Cambridge: Harvard University Press, 1936.

Elder, Bruce. *Blood on the Wattle: Massacres and Maltreatment of Australian Aborigines since 1788*. Frenchs Forest, NSW: Child and Associates, 1988.

Elkins, Caroline. *Imperial Reckoning: The Untold Story of Britain's Gulag in Kenya*. New York: Henry Holt, 2005.

Engelhart, Katie. "Empire and the Mau Mau: A Story of Colonialism and Counter-Insurgency." *Los Angeles Review of Books*, 2016. https://lareviewofbooks.org/article/empire-and-the-mau-mau-a-story-of-colonialism-and-counter-insurgency

Eriksson, Anna. *Justice in Transition: Community Restorative Justice in Northern Ireland*. Cullompton, Devon: Willan Publishing, 2009.

Evans, Julie. "Colonialism and the Rule of Law: The Case of South Australia." In *Crime and Empire, 1840–1940: Criminal Justice in Local and Global Context*, edited by Barry S. Godfrey and Graeme Dunstall, 57–75. Cullompton, Devon: Willan Publishing, 2005.

Evans, Julie. "The Ethos of the Historian: The Minutes of Evidence Project, and Lives Lived with Law on the Ground." *Law Text Culture* 20 (2016): 136–64.

Evans, Julie. "Where Lawlessness Is Law: The Settler-Colonial Frontier as a Legal Space of Violence." *Australian Feminist Law Journal* 30, no. 1 (2009): 3–22.

Evans, Julie, Jennifer Balint, Nesam McMillan, Joanna Cruickshank, Patricia Grimshaw, and Mark McMillan. "Minutes of Evidence Project: Promoting New and Collaborative Ways of Understanding Australia's Past and Engaging with Structural Justice." *Australian Research Council Final Report* (2015).

Evans, Julie, and Tessa Fluence. "Securing the Settler Polity: Martial Law and the Aboriginal Peoples of Van Diemen's Land." *Journal of Australian Colonial History* 15 (2013): 1–22.

Evans, Julie, Ann Genovese, Alexander Reilly, and Patrick Wolfe, eds. *Sovereignty: Frontiers of Possibility*. Honolulu: University of Hawaii Press, 2013.

Fanon, Frantz. *The Wretched of the Earth*. Translated by Constance Farrington. New York: Grove Press, 1966.

Farmer, Paul. *Pathologies of Power: Health, Human Rights, and the New War on the Poor*. Berkeley: University of California Press, 2003.

Felman, Shoshana. *The Juridical Unconscious: Trials and Traumas in the Twentieth Century*. Cambridge: Harvard University Press, 2002.

Felman, Shoshana, and Dori Laub. *Testimony: Crises of Witnessing in Literature, Psychoanalysis, and History*. New York: Routledge, 1992.

Ford, Lisa. *Settler Sovereignty: Jurisdiction and Indigenous Peoples in America and Australia, 1788–1836*. Cambridge: Harvard University Press, 2010.

Foucault, Michel. *The Archaeology of Knowledge*. Translated by Alan Mark Sheridan-Smith. New York: Pantheon Books, 1972.

Furphy, Samuel. *Edward M. Curr and the Tide of History*. Canberra: ANU Press, 2013.

Galanter, Marc. "The Radiating Effects of Courts." In *Empirical Theories about Courts*, edited by Keith O. Boyum and Lynn M. Mather, 117–42. New York: Longman, 1983.

Galanter, Marc. "Why the 'Haves' Come Out Ahead: Speculations on the Limits of Legal Change." *Law & Society Review* 9, no. 1 (1974): 95–160.

Galtung, Johan. "Violence, Peace, and Peace Research." *Journal of Peace Research* 6, no. 3 (1969): 167–91.

Genovese, Ann. "Critical Decision, 1982: Remembering *Koowarta v Bjelke-Petersen*." *Griffith Law Review* 23, no. 1 (2014): 1–15.

Genovese, Ann. "Critical Decision 1983: Remembering *Commonwealth v Tasmania*." *Griffith Law Review* 24, no. 1 (2015): 1–15.

Genovese, Ann. "On Australian Feminist Tradition: Three Notes on Conduct, Inheritance and the Relations of Historiography and Jurisprudence." *Journal of Australian Studies* 38, no. 4 (2014): 430–44.

Genovese, Ann, Shaun McVeigh, and Peter D. Rush, eds. "Lives Lived with Law: An Introduction." *Law Text Culture* 20 (2016): 1–13.

Giannacopoulos, Maria. "Offshore Hospitality: Law, Asylum and Colonisation." *Law Text Culture* 17 (2013): 163–83.

Gillison, Joan. "Bon, Ann Fraser (1838–1936)." *Australian Dictionary of Biography*. Carlton, VIC: Melbourne University Press, 1979.

Goodall, Heather. *Invasion to Embassy: Land in Aboriginal Politics in New South Wales*. St. Leonards, NSW: Allen and Unwin, 1996.

Goodrich, Peter. *Languages of Law: From Logics of Memory to Nomadic Masks*. London: Weidenfeld and Nicolson, 1990.

Goodrich, Peter. *Reading the Law: A Critical Introduction to Legal Method and Techniques*. New York: Blackwell, 1986.

Gopal, Priyamvada. "Redressing Anti-Imperial Amnesia." *Race & Class* 57, no. 3 (2016): 18–30.

Grant, Stan. "At Poisoned Waterhole Creek I Tell My Son about the Slaughter of Our People." *Guardian*, 12 October 2015.

Grassby, Albert Jaime, and Marji Hill. *Six Australian Battlefields: The Black Resistance to Invasion and the White Struggle against Colonial Oppression*. North Ryde, NSW: Angus and Robertson, 1988.

Graybill, Lyn S. "Pursuit of Truth and Reconciliation in South Africa." *Africa Today* 45, no. 1 (1998): 103–33.

Gready, Paul, and Simon Robins. "From Transitional to Transformative Justice: A New Agenda for Practice." *International Journal of Transitional Justice* 8, no. 3 (2014): 339–61.

Green, Penny, and Tony Ward. *State Crime: Governments, Violence and Corruption*. London: Pluto Press, 2004.

Griffiths, Anne. "Legal Pluralism in Botswana: Women's Access to Law." *Journal of Legal Pluralism and Unofficial Law* 30, no. 42 (1998): 123–38.

Griffiths, John. "What Is Legal Pluralism?" *Journal of Legal Pluralism and Unofficial Law* 18, no. 24 (1986): 1–55.

Haebich, Anna. *Broken Circles: Fragmenting Indigenous Families 1800–2000*. Fremantle, WA: Fremantle Arts Centre Press, 2000.

Harper, Stephen. "Statement of Apology to Former Students of Indian Residential Schools." Indigenous and Northern Affairs Canada, 2008. https://www.aadnc-aandc.gc.ca/eng/1100100015644/1100100015649

Harring, Sidney L. "The Killing Time: A History of Aboriginal Resistance in Colonial Australia." *Ottawa Law Review* 26, no. 2 (1994): 385–424.

Harris, Angela P. "Critical Race Theory." In *Law and Social Theory*, edited by Reza Banakar and Max Travers, 147–60. Oxford: Hart, 2013.

Hayner, Priscilla B. *Unspeakable Truths: Facing the Challenge of Truth Commissions*. New York: Routledge, 2002.

Healy, Chris. *From the Ruins of Colonialism: History as Social Memory*. Cambridge: Cambridge University Press, 1997.

Henry, Nicola. "From Reconciliation to Transitional Justice: The Contours of Redress Politics in Established Democracies." *International Journal of Transitional Justice* 9, no. 2 (2015): 199–218.

Hesford, Wendy S. "Documenting Violations: Rhetorical Witnessing and the Spectacle of Distant Suffering." *Biography* 27, no. 1 (2004): 104–44.

Hillyard, Paddy, and Steve Tombs, eds. *Beyond Criminology: Taking Harm Seriously*. London: Pluto Press, 2004.

Hintjens, Helen M. "Explaining the 1994 Genocide in Rwanda." *Journal of Modern African Studies* 37, no. 2 (1999): 241–86.

Hoff, Joan. *Law, Gender, and Injustice: A Legal History of U.S. Women*. New York: New York University Press, 1991.

Hooker, M. B. *Legal Pluralism: An Introduction to Colonial and Neo-Colonial Laws*. Oxford: Clarendon Press, 1975.

Howe, Stephen. *Ireland and Empire: Colonial Legacies in Irish History and Culture*. New York: Oxford University Press, 2000.

Humphrey, Michael. "Re-Entering History as Suffering Victims: The Reach of Transitional Justice into Past Imperial Violence and Trauma." Paper presented at the Human Rights and Imperialism in Historical Perspective conference, Sydney, 11–12 August 2012.

Hunt, Nancy Rose. "An Acoustic Register, Tenacious Images, and Congolese Scenes of Rape and Repetition." *Cultural Anthropology* 23, no. 2 (2008): 220–53.

Huyse, Luc. "Justice after Transition: On the Choices Successor Elites Make in Dealing with the Past." *Law & Social Inquiry* 20, no. 1 (1995): 51–78.

"Indigenous Rights and Transitional Justice: Two Side Events to the UN Permanent Forum," *UN Permanent Forum on Indigenous Issues*. New York: International Center for Transitional Justice, 2012.

International Law Commission. *Yearbook of the International Law Commission, 1984: Report of the Commission to the General Assembly on the Work of Its 36th Session*. Vol. 2, part 2. New York: United Nations, 1985.

International Law Commission. *Yearbook of the International Law Commission, 1991: Report of the Commission to the General Assembly on the Work of Its 43rd Session*. Vol. 2, part 2. New York: United Nations, 1994.

International Law Commission. *Yearbook of the International Law Commission, 1992: Summary Records of the Meetings of the 44th Session, 4 May-24 July 1992*. Vol. 1. New York: United Nations, 1994.

International Law Commission. *Yearbook of the International Law Commission, 1993: Documents of the 45th Session*. Vol. 2, part 1. New York: United Nations, 2000.

International Law Commission. *Yearbook of the International Law Commission, 1995: Report of the Commission to the General Assembly on the Work of Its 47th Session*. Vol. 2, part 2. New York: United Nations, 1998.

International Law Commission. *Yearbook of the International Law Commission, 1995: Summary Records of the Meetings of the 47th Session, 2 May-21 July 1995*. Vol. 1. New York: United Nations, 1997.

Johnston, Elliott. *National Report of the Royal Commission into Aboriginal Deaths in Custody*. Canberra, 1991.

Jung, Courtney. "Canada and the Legacy of the Indian Residential Schools: Transitional Justice for Indigenous People in a Nontransitional Society." In *Identities in Transition: Challenges for Transitional Justice in Divided Societies*, edited by Paige Arthur, 217–50. Cambridge: Cambridge University Press, 2011.

Kagame, Paul. "Speech by President Kagame at the 15th Commemoration of the Genocide against the Tutsi at the Nyanza Memorial Site in Kicukiro." 7 April 2009.

Kagame, Paul. "Speech by President Paul Kagame at the 20th Commemoration of the Genocide against the Tutsi." 7 April 2014.

Kamatali, Jean-Marie. "The Challenge of Linking International Criminal Justice and National Reconciliation: The Case of the ICTR." *Leiden Journal of International Law* 16 (2003): 115–33.

Kantorowicz, Ernst Hartwig. *The Kings' Two Bodies: A Study in Mediaeval Political Theology*. Princeton: Princeton University Press, 1957.

Kapur, Ratna. *Erotic Justice: Law and the New Politics of Colonialism*. London: Glasshouse Press, 2005.

Kapur, Ratna. "Normalizing Violence: Transitional Justice and the Gujarat Riots." *Columbia Journal of Gender and Law* 15, no. 3 (2006): 885–927.

Kapur, Ratna. "Precarious Desires and Ungrievable Lives: Human Rights and Postcolonial Critiques of Legal Justice." *London Review of International Law* 3, no. 2 (2015): 267–94.

Karskens, Grace. *The Colony: A History of Early Sydney*. Crows Nest, NSW: Allen and Unwin, 2009.

Katzenstein, Suzanne. "Hybrid Tribunals: Searching for Justice in East Timor." *Harvard Human Rights Journal* 16, no. 6 (2003): 245–78.

Kearns, Thomas R., and Austin Sarat. "Legal Justice and Injustice: Toward a Situated Perspective." In *Justice and Injustice in Law and Legal Theory*, edited by Austin Sarat and Thomas R. Kearns, 1–18. Ann Arbor: University of Michigan Press, 1996.

Kennedy, Dane. "Imperial History and Post-Colonial Theory." *Journal of Imperial and Commonwealth History* 24, no. 3 (1996): 345–63.

Kent, Lia. *The Dynamics of Transitional Justice: International Models and Local Realities in East Timor*. Abingdon, Oxon: Routledge, 2012.

Kingston, Jeffrey. "Balancing Justice and Reconciliation in East Timor." *Critical Asian Studies* 38, no. 3 (2006): 271–302.

Kojder, Andrzej. "Leon Petrażycki's Socio-Legal Ideas and Their Contemporary Continuation." *Journal of Classical Sociology* 6, no. 3 (2006): 333–58.

Kolsky, Elizabeth. *Colonial Justice in British India: White Violence and the Rule of Law*. New York: Cambridge University Press, 2011.

Kostal, Rande W. *A Jurisprudence of Power: Victorian Empire and the Rule of Law*. New York: Oxford University Press, 2005.

Kritz, Neil J., ed. *Transitional Justice: How Emerging Democracies Reckon with Former Regimes*. Washington, DC: United States Institute of Peace Press, 1995.

Kurasawa, Fuyuki. *The Work of Global Justice: Human Rights as Practices*. New York: Cambridge University Press, 2007.

Kymlicka, Will. *Multicultural Citizenship: A Liberal Theory of Minority Rights*. New York: Oxford University Press, 1995.

Laidlaw, Zoë. "Breaking Britannia's Bounds? Law, Settlers, and Space in Britain's Imperial Historiography." *Historical Journal* 55, no. 3 (2012): 807–30.

Laidlaw, Zoë, and Alan Lester, eds. *Indigenous Communities and Settler Colonialism: Land Holding, Loss and Survival in an Interconnected World*. Houndmills, Basingstoke: Palgrave Macmillan, 2015.

Lambourne, Wendy. "Transitional Justice and Peacebuilding after Mass Violence." *International Journal of Transitional Justice* 3 (2009): 28–48.

Langton, Marcia. "Dominion and Dishonour: A Treaty between Our Nations?" *Postcolonial Studies* 4, no. 1 (2001): 13–26.

Laplante, Lisa J. "Transitional Justice and Peace Building: Diagnosing and Addressing the Socioeconomic Roots of Violence through a Human Rights Framework." *International Journal of Transitional Justice* 2 (2008): 331–55.

Leebaw, Bronwyn. "The Irreconcilable Goals of Transitional Justice." *Human Rights Quarterly* 95 (2008): 98–106.

Leith, Denise. *Bearing Witness: The Lives of War Correspondents and Photojournalists*. Milsons Point, NSW: Random House, 2004.

Lendrum, S. D. "The 'Coorong Massacre': Martial Law and the Aborigines at First Settlement." *Adelaide Law Review* 6, no. 1 (1977): 26–43.

Lester, Alan, and Fae Dussart. *Colonization and the Origins of Humanitarian Governance: Protecting Aborigines across the Nineteenth-Century British Empire.* Cambridge: Cambridge University Press, 2014.

Levi, Primo. *The Drowned and the Saved.* Translated by Raymond Rosenthal. London: Abacus, 1989.

Libesman, Terri, and Chris Cunneen. "Postcolonial Trauma: The Contemporary Removal of Indigenous Children and Young People from Their Families in Australia." *Australian Journal of Social Issues* 35, no. 2 (2000): 99–115.

Little, Adrian, and Mark McMillan. "Invisibility and the Politics of Reconciliation in Australia: Keeping the Conflict in View." *Ethnopolitics* 16, no. 5 (2016): 519–37.

Lowe, Ian. *A Big Fix: Radical Solutions for Australia's Environmental Crisis.* Melbourne: BlackInc., 2005.

Lu, Catherine. "Colonialism as Structural Injustice: Historical Responsibility and Contemporary Redress." *Journal of Political Philosophy* 19, no. 3 (2011): 261–81.

Macintyre, Stuart, and Anna Clark. *The History Wars.* Carlton, VIC: Melbourne University Press, 2004.

Mamdani, Mahmood. "From Conquest to Consent as the Basis of State Formation: Reflections on Rwanda." *New Left Review* 216 (1996): 3–36.

Mamdani, Mahmood. "Responsibility to Protect or Right to Punish?" *Journal of Intervention and Statebuilding* 4, no. 1 (2010): 53–67.

Mamdani, Mahmood. "The New Humanitarian Order." *New Nation*, September 2008.

Mani, Rama. *Beyond Retribution: Seeking Justice in the Shadows of War.* Cambridge: Polity Press, 2002.

Mani, Rama. "Dilemmas of Expanding Transitional Justice, or Forging the Nexus between Transitional Justice and Development." *International Journal of Transitional Justice* 2 (2008): 253–65.

Matsuda, Mari. "Looking to the Bottom: Critical Legal Studies and Reparations." *Harvard Civil Rights–Civil Liberties Law Review* 22, no. 1 (1987): 323–400.

Matsuda, Mari. "When the First Quail Calls: Multiple Consciousness as Jurisprudential Method." *Women's Rights Law Reporter* 11 (1989): 7–10.

"The Mau Mau Claims." https://www.leighday.co.uk/International/Further-insights/Detailed-case-studies/The-Mau-Mau-claims/The-Mau-Mau-claimants

Mawani, Renisa. *Colonial Proximities: Crossracial Encounters and Juridical Truths in British Columbia, 1871–1921.* Vancouver: UBC Press, 2009.

Mawani, Renisa. "Law's Archive." *Annual Review of Law and Social Science* 8 (2012): 337–65.

Maynard, John. *Fight for Liberty and Freedom: The Origins of Australian Aboriginal Activism.* Canberra: Aboriginal Studies Press, 2007.

Mbembé, Achille. *On the Postcolony.* Berkeley: University of California Press, 2001.

McEvoy, Kieran. "Beyond Legalism: Towards a Thicker Understanding of Transitional Justice." *Journal of Law and Society* 34, no. 4 (2007): 411–40.
McEvoy, Kieran, and Lorna McGregor, eds. *Transitional Justice from Below: Grassroots Activism and the Struggle for Change*. Oxford: Hart Publishing, 2008.
McHugh, Paul G. *Aboriginal Societies and the Common Law: A History of Sovereignty, Status, and Self-Determination*. New York: Oxford University Press, 2004.
McMillan, Mark, and Martin Clark. "Making Sense of Indigeneity, Aboriginality and Identity: Race as a Constitutional Conundrum since 1983." *Griffith Law Review* 24, no. 1 (2015): 106–26.
McMillan, Nesam. *Imagining the International: Crime, Justice, and the Promise of Community*. Stanford: Stanford University Press, 2020.
Meister, Robert. *After Evil: A Politics of Human Rights*. New York: Columbia University Press, 2011.
Melissaris, Emmanuel. "The More the Merrier? A New Take on Legal Pluralism." *Social & Legal Studies* 13, no. 1 (2004): 57–79.
Merry, Sally Engle. "Culture, Power, and the Discourse of Law." *New York Law School Law Review* 37 (1992): 209–25.
Merry, Sally Engle. "Legal Pluralism." *Law & Society Review* 22, no. 5 (1988): 869–96.
Mertens, Charlotte. "Frames of Empire: Congo and Sexual Violence." PhD diss., University of Melbourne, 2017.
Miller, David. *National Responsibility and Global Justice*. Oxford: Oxford University Press, 2007.
Miller, Robert J., Jacinta Ruru, Larissa Behrendt, and Tracey Lindberg. *Discovering Indigenous Lands: The Doctrine of Discovery in the English Colonies*. Oxford: Oxford University Press, 2010.
Minow, Martha. *Between Vengeance and Forgiveness: Facing History after Genocide and Mass Violence*. Boston: Beacon Press, 1998.
Moon, Claire. *Narrating Political Reconciliation: South Africa's Truth and Reconciliation Commission*. Lanham, MD: Lexington Books, 2008.
Moore, Sally Falk. "Law and Social Change: The Semi-Autonomous Social Field as an Appropriate Subject of Study." *Law & Society Review* 7, no. 4 (1973): 719–46.
Moran, Leslie. *The Homosexual(ity) of Law*. London: Routledge, 1996.
Moreton-Robinson, Aileen. "Imagining the Good Indigenous Citizen: Race War and the Pathology of Patriarchal White Sovereignty." *Cultural Studies Review* 15, no. 2 (2009): 61–79.
Moreton-Robinson, Aileen, ed. *Sovereign Subjects: Indigenous Sovereignty Matters*. Crows Nest, NSW: Allen and Unwin, 2007.
Moreton-Robinson, Aileen. *Talkin' Up to the White Woman: Aboriginal Women and Feminism*. St. Lucia, QLD: University of Queensland Press, 2000.
Moreton-Robinson, Aileen. *The White Possessive: Property, Power, and Indigenous Sovereignty*. Minneapolis: University of Minnesota Press, 2015.
Moreton-Robinson, Aileen. "Writing Off Indigenous Sovereignty: The Discourse of Se-

curity and Patriarchal White Sovereignty." In *Sovereign Subjects: Indigenous Sovereignty Matters*, 86–102. Crows Nest, NSW: Allen and Unwin, 2007.

Moses, A. Dirk. "Official Apologies, Reconciliation and Settler Colonialism: Australian Indigenous Alterity and Political Agency." *Citizenship Studies* 15, no. 2 (2011): 145–59.

Motha, Stewart. *Archiving Sovereignty: Law, History, Violence*. Ann Arbor: University of Michigan Press, 2018.

Motha, Stewart. "The Failure of Postcolonial Sovereignty in Australia." *Australian Feminist Law Journal* 22 (2005): 107–26.

Motha, Stewart, and Honni van Rijswijk. *Law, Memory, Violence: Uncovering the Counter-Archive*. New York: Routledge, 2016.

Mutua, Makau W. "Savages, Victims, and Saviors: The Metaphor of Human Rights." *Harvard International Law Journal* 42 (2001): 201–45.

Muvingi, Ismael. "Sitting on Powder Kegs: Socioeconomic Rights in Transitional Societies." *International Journal of Transitional Justice* 3 (2009): 163–82.

Nagy, Rosemary. "Transitional Justice as Global Project: Critical Reflections." *Third World Quarterly* 29, no. 2 (2008): 275–89.

Nanni, Giordano, and Andrea James. *Coranderrk: We Will Show the Country*. Canberra, ACT: Aboriginal Studies Press, 2013.

National Native Title Tribunal. "Tribunal's Role." N.d. http://www.nntt.gov.au/aboutus/Pages/default.aspx

Nelken, David. "Eugen Ehrlich, Living Law, and Plural Legalities." *Theoretical Inquiries in Law* 9, no. 2 (2008): 443–71.

Nelson, Elizabeth, Sandra Smith, and Patricia Grimshaw, eds. *Letters from Aboriginal Women in Victoria, 1867–1926*. Melbourne: History Department, University of Melbourne, 2002.

Nettelbeck, Amanda. "'Keep the Magistrates Straight': Magistrates and Aboriginal 'Management' on Australia's North-West Frontiers, 1883–1905." *Aboriginal History* 38 (2014): 19–37.

Nettelbeck, Amanda, and Lyndall Ryan. "Salutary Lessons: Native Police and the 'Civilising' Role of Legalised Violence in Colonial Australia." *Journal of Imperial and Commonwealth History* 46, no. 1 (2018): 47–68.

Nouwen, Sarah M. H., and Wouter G. Werner. "Doing Justice to the Political: The International Criminal Court in Uganda and Sudan." *European Journal of International Law* 21, no. 4 (2010): 941–65.

Nugent, Maria. *Captain Cook Was Here*. Port Melbourne, VIC: Cambridge University Press, 2009.

Ohlmann, Aaron. *20 Years Challenging Impunity*. United Nations International Criminal Tribunal for Rwanda, 2014. http://unictr.irmct.org

Olsen, Tricia D., Leigh A. Payne, and Andrew G. Reiter. *Transitional Justice in Balance: Comparing Processes, Weighing Efficacy*. Washington, DC: US Institute of Peace Press, 2010.

Orford, Anne. "Commissioning the Truth." *Columbia Journal of Gender and Law* 15, no. 3 (2006): 851–83.

Orford, Anne. *Reading Humanitarian Intervention: Human Rights and the Use of Force in International Law*. Cambridge: Cambridge University Press, 2003.

Osiel, Mark. *Mass Atrocity, Collective Memory, and the Law*. New Brunswick, NJ: Transaction Publishers, 2000.

Pagden, Anthony. *Lords of All the World: Ideologies of Empire in Spain, Britain, and France*. New Haven: Yale University Press, 1995.

Pearson, Noel. "Mabo Lecture: Where We've Come From and Where We're at with the Opportunity That Is Koiki Mabo's Legacy to Australia." In *Dialogue about Land Justice: Papers from the National Native Title Conferences*, 33–51. Arrernte Country: Aboriginal Studies Press, 2003.

Petrażycki, Leon. *Law and Morality*. Cambridge: Harvard University Press, 1955.

Philips, David. "Defining 'Reconciliation': A Critical Analysis of the Understanding and Use of the Word in South Africa's Truth and Reconciliation Commission." In *Biennial Conference of the South African Historical Society*. Cape Town, South Africa: University of Cape Town, 2005.

Podgórecki, Adam. *Law and Society*. London: Routledge and Kegan Paul, 1974.

Podgórecki, Adam. "Unrecognized Father of Sociology of Law, Leon Petrażycki: Reflections Based on Jan Gorecki's Sociology and Jurisprudence of Leon Petrażycki." *Law & Society Review* 15, no. 1 (1980): 183–202.

Pogge, Thomas. "Priorities of Global Justice." *Metaphilosophy* 32, nos. 1–2 (2001): 6–24.

Pop, Alvaro, Esther Attear, and Alcibiades Escué. "Truth Commissions and Indigenous Peoples: Lessons Learned, Future Challenges," *UN Permanent Forum on Indigenous Issues*. New York: International Center for Transitional Justice, 2012.

Presland, Gary. *First People: The Eastern Kulin of Melbourne, Port Phillip & Central Victoria*. Melbourne: Museum Victoria Publishing, 2010.

Prunier, Gerard. *The Rwanda Crisis: History of a Genocide*. New York: Columbia University Press, 1995.

Quinn, Joanna R. "Introductory Essay: Canada's Own Brand of Truth and Reconciliation?" *International Indigenous Policy Journal* 2, no. 3 (2011): 1–3.

Rae, Maria. "When Reconciliation Means Reparations: Tasmania's Compensation to the Stolen Generations." *Griffith Law Review* 24, no. 4 (2015): 640–56.

Reilly, Alexander. "Sovereign Apologies." In *Sovereignty: Frontiers of Possibility*, edited by Julie Evans, Ann Genovese, Alexander Reilly, and Patrick Wolfe, 196–219. Honolulu: University of Hawaii Press, 2013.

Reynolds, Henry. *The Forgotten War*. Sydney: NewSouth Publishing, 2013.

Reynolds, Henry. *The Other Side of the Frontier: Aboriginal Resistance to the European Invasion of Australia*. Ringwood, VIC: Penguin, 1982.

Rifkin, Mark. "Indigenizing Agamben: Rethinking Sovereignty in Light of the 'Peculiar' Status of Native Peoples." *Cultural Critique* 73 (2009): 88–124.

Roberts, David. "Bells Falls Massacre and Bathurst's History of Violence: Local Tradition and Australian Historiography." *Australian Historical Studies* 26, no. 105 (1995): 615–33.

Roberts, David. "Windradyne (1800–1829)." *Australian Dictionary of Biography*. Canberra: National Centre of Biography, Australian National University, 2005.

Roht-Arriaza, Naomi, and Javier Mariecurrena, eds. *Transitional Justice in the Twenty-First Century: Beyond Truth versus Justice*. Cambridge: Cambridge University Press, 2006.

Ross, Fiona C. *Bearing Witness: Women and the Truth and Reconciliation Commission in South Africa*. London: Pluto Press, 2003.

Roth, Kenneth. "Africa Attacks the International Criminal Court." *New York Review of Books*, 6 February 2014.

Rothberg, Michael. *Multidirectional Memory: Remembering the Holocaust in the Age of Decolonization*. Stanford, CA: Stanford University Press, 2009.

Rudd, Kevin. "Apology to Australia's Indigenous Peoples." 2008. http://www.australia.gov.au/about-australia/our-country/our-people/apology-to-australias-indigenous-peoples

Rush, Peter. "An Altered Jurisdiction: Corporeal Traces of Law." *Griffith Law Review* 6 (1997): 144–68.

Sack, Peter, and E. J. Minchin. "Legal Pluralism: Proceedings of the Canberra Law Workshop VII." Canberra: Australian National University, 1986.

Said, Edward W. *Orientalism*. New York: Pantheon Books, 1978.

Salisbury, T., and Percy J. Gresser. *Windrayne of the Wiradjuri: Martial Law at Bathurst in 1824*. Sydney: Wentworth Books, 1971.

Santos, Boaventura de Sousa. "Law: A Map of Misreading: Toward a Postmodern Conception of Law." *Journal of Law and Society* 14, no. 3 (1987): 279–302.

Sarat, Austin, and Thomas R. Kearns, eds. *Justice and Injustice in Law and Legal Theory*. Ann Arbor: University of Michigan Press, 1996.

Savelsberg, Joachim J., and Hollie Nyseth. "Collective Representations of Atrocities and National Identity: The Case of Darfur." In *Crossing Borders, Shifting Boundaries: National and Transnational Identities in Europe and Beyond*, edited by Franz Höllinger and Markus Hadler. Frankfurt: Campus Verlag, 2012.

Scheper-Hughes, Nancy, and Philippe Bourgois. "Introduction: Making Sense of Violence." In *Violence in War and Peace: An Anthology*, edited by Nancy Scheper-Hughes and Philippe Bourgois, 1–16. Malden, MA: Blackwell Publishing, 2004.

Schwartz, Joan M., and Terry Cook. "Archives, Records, and Power: The Making of Modern Memory." *Archival Science* 2, no. 1 (2002): 1–19.

Schwöbel-Patel, Christine. "International Criminal Court Must Not Ignore Threats of an African Mass Withdrawal." *The Conversation*, 8 February 2017.

Shaw, Rosalind. "Memory Frictions: Localizing the Truth and Reconciliation Commission in Sierra Leone." *International Journal of Transitional Justice* 1, no. 2 (2007): 183–207.

Shohat, Ella. "Notes on the 'Post-Colonial.'" *Social Text*, nos. 31–32 (1992): 99–113.

Shohat, Ella, and Robert Stam. *Unthinking Eurocentrism: Multiculturalism and the Media*. 2nd ed. New York: Routledge, 2014.

Short, Damien. "Australia: A Continuing Genocide?" *Journal of Genocide Research* 12, no. 1 (2010): 45–68.

Short, Damien. *Reconciliation and Colonial Power: Indigenous Rights in Australia*. Aldershot: Ashgate, 2008.

Short, Damien. "The Social Construction of Indigenous 'Native Title' Land Rights in Australia." *Current Sociology* 55, no. 6 (2007): 857–76.

Short, Damien. "When Sorry Isn't Good Enough: Official Remembrance and Reconciliation in Australia." *Memory Studies* 5, no. 3 (2012): 293–304.

Sierra Leone Truth and Reconciliation Commission. "Witness to Truth: Report of the Sierra Leone Truth and Reconciliation Commission." 2004.

Simpson, Gerry. "Mabo, International Law, Terra Nullius and the Stories of Settlement: An Unresolved Jurisprudence." *Melbourne University Law Review* 19 (1993): 195–210.

Smart, Carol. *Feminism and the Power of Law*. London: Routledge, 1989.

Spivak, Gayatri Chakravorty. "Can the Subaltern Speak?" In *Marxism and the Interpretation of Culture*, edited by Cary Nelson and Lawrence Grossberg, 271–312. London: Macmillan, 1988.

Sriram, Chandra Lekha. *Confronting Past Human Rights Violations: Justice vs. Peace in Times of Transition*. New York: Frank Cass, 2004.

Stanley, Elizabeth. *Torture, Truth and Justice: The Case of Timor-Leste*. London: Routledge, 2009.

Stasiulis, Daiva, and Nira Yuval-Davis, eds. *Unsettling Settler Societies: Articulations of Gender, Race, Ethnicity and Class*. London: SAGE Publications, 1995.

Stauffer, Jill. *Ethical Loneliness: The Injustice of Not Being Heard*. New York: Columbia University Press, 2015.

Stoler, Ann Laura. "Imperial Debris: Reflections on Ruins and Ruination." *Cultural Anthropology* 23, no. 2 (2008): 191–219.

Stychin, Carl, and Didi Herman, eds. *Sexuality in the Legal Arena*. London: Athlone, 2000.

Taggart, Michael. "Ruled by Law?" *Modern Law Review* 69, no. 6 (2006): 1006–25.

Tatz, Colin. "Confronting Australian Genocide." *Aboriginal History* 25, no. 1 (2001): 16–35.

Tatz, Colin. "Genocide in Australia." *Journal of Genocide Research* 1, no. 3 (1999): 315–52.

Tatz, Colin. *Genocide in Australia: By Accident or Design?* Canberra: Aboriginal Studies Press, 1999.

Teelock, Vijayalakshmi. "The Mauritius Truth and Justice Commission: 'Eyewash,' 'Storm in a Teacup' or Promise of a New Future for Mauritians?" In *Emancipation and the Remaking of the British Imperial World*, edited by Catherine Hall, Nicholas Draper, and Keith McClelland, 207–22. Manchester: Manchester University Press, 2014.

Teitel, Ruti G. *Humanity's Law*. New York: Oxford University Press, 2011.

Teitel, Ruti G. *Transitional Justice*. New York: Oxford University Press, 2000.

Thakur, Ramesh, and Peter Macontent. *From Sovereign Impunity to International Accountability: The Search for Justice in a World of States*. Tokyo: United Nations University Press, 2004.

Thornton, Margaret. "Feminism and the Contradictions of Law Reform." *International Journal of the Sociology of Law* 19 (1991): 453–74.

Tomas, Nin. "Maori Concepts and Practices of Rangatiratanga: 'Sovereignty?'" In *Sover-*

eignty: Frontiers of Possibility, edited by Julie Evans, Ann Genovese, Alexander Reilly, and Patrick Wolfe, 220–49. Honolulu: University of Hawaii Press, 2013.

Truth and Reconciliation Commission of South Africa. *Truth and Reconciliation Commission of South Africa Report*. London: Macmillan Reference, 1999.

Tuathail, Gearóid Ó. *Critical Geopolitics: The Politics of Writing Global Space*. Minneapolis: University of Minnesota Press, 1996.

Unger, Roberto Mangabeira. *The Critical Legal Studies Movement*. Cambridge: Harvard University Press, 1986.

United Nations. "The Genocide — Timeline." Legacy Website for the International Criminal Tribunal for Rwanda. http://unictr.irmct.org/en/genocide#timeline

United Nations International Criminal Tribunal for Rwanda. "The Genocide." 1994. https://unictr.irmct.org/en/genocide

UN Secretary-General. "The Rule of Law and Transitional Justice in Conflict and Post-Conflict Societies." New York: United Nations, 2004.

Valverde, Mariana. *Chronotopes of Law: Jurisdiction, Scale and Governance*. New York: Routledge, 2015.

Valverde, Mariana. "From Persons and Their Acts to Webs of Relationships: Some Theoretical Resources for Environmental Justice." *Crime, Law and Social Change* 68, no. 5 (2017): 547–62.

Valverde, Mariana. "Jurisdiction and Scale: Legal 'Technicalities' as Resources for Theory." *Social and Legal Studies* 18, no. 2 (2009): 139–57.

Veracini, Lorenzo. *Settler Colonialism: A Theoretical Overview*. Basingstoke: Palgrave Macmillan, 2010.

Vernon, Richard. "What Is Crime against Humanity?" *Journal of Political Philosophy* 10, no. 3 (2002): 231–49.

Victorian Government. "Treaty Legislation: The Advancing the Treaty Process with Aboriginal Victorians Act 2018." N.d. https://www.vic.gov.au/aboriginalvictoria/treaty/treaty-legislation.html

Ward, Damen. "A Means and Measure of Civilisation: Colonial Authorities and Indigenous Law in Australasia." *History Compass* 1, no. 1 (2003): 1–24.

Watson, Nicole. "Justice in Whose Eyes? Why Lawyers Should Read Black Australian Literature." *Griffith Law Review* 23, no. 1 (2014): 44–60.

Watson, Nicole. "The Northern Territory Emergency Response—Has It Really Improved the Lives of Aboriginal Women and Children?" *Australian Feminist Law Journal* 35, no. 1 (2011): 147–63.

Watson, Nicole. "What Do We Want? Not Native Title, That's for Bloody Sure." In *The Aboriginal Tent Embassy: Sovereignty, Black Power, Land Rights and the State*, edited by Gary Foley, Andrew Schaap, and Edwina Howell, 284–98. New York: Routledge, 2014.

Williams, Huw Lloyd. "Wacky Races: Miller, Pogge and Rawls, and Conceptions of Development in the Global Justice Debate." *Journal of International Political Theory* 10, no. 2 (2014): 206–28.

Williams, Patricia. *The Alchemy of Race and Rights*. Cambridge: Harvard University Press, 1991.

Williams, Patricia. "The Obliging Shell: An Informal Essay on Formal Equal Opportunity." *Michigan Law Review* 87, no. 8 (1989): 2128–51.

Williams, Robert A. *The American Indian in Western Legal Thought: The Discourses of Conquest*. New York: Oxford University Press, 1990.

Wilson, Richard. *The Politics of Truth and Reconciliation in South Africa: Legitimizing the Post-Apartheid State*. New York: Cambridge University Press, 2001.

Wilson, Richard Ashby. "When Humanity Sits in Judgment: Crimes against Humanity and the Conundrum of Race and Ethnicity at the International Criminal Tribunal for Rwanda." In *In the Name of Humanity: The Government of Threat and Care*, edited by Ilana Feldman and Miriam Ticktin, 27–57. Durham, NC: Duke University Press, 2010.

Wolfe, Patrick. "Corpus Nullius: The Exception of Indians and Other Aliens in US Constitutional Discourse." *Postcolonial Studies* 10, no. 2 (2007): 127–51.

Wolfe, Patrick. "History and Imperialism: A Century of Theory, from Marx to Postcolonialism." *American Historical Review* 102, no. 2 (1997): 388–420.

Wolfe, Patrick. "Land, Labor, and Difference: Elementary Structures of Race." *American Historical Review* 106, no. 3 (2001): 866–905.

Wolfe, Patrick. "Nation and MiscegeNation: Discursive Continuity in the Post-Mabo Era." *Social Analysis* 36 (1994): 99–152.

Wolfe, Patrick. "Recuperating Binarism: A Heretical Introduction." *Settler Colonial Studies* 3, no. 3 (2013): 257–79.

Wolfe, Patrick. *Settler Colonialism and the Transformation of Anthropology: The Politics and Poetics of an Ethnographic Event*. London: Cassell, 1999.

Wolfe, Patrick. *Traces of History: Elementary Structures of Race*. London: Verso, 2016.

Young, Iris Marion. "Responsibility and Global Justice: A Social Connection Model." *Social Philosophy and Policy* 23, no. 1 (2006): 102–30.

Young, Iris Marion. *Responsibility for Justice*. New York: Oxford University Press, 2011.

Young, Robert. *White Mythologies: Writing History and the West*. New York: Routledge, 1990.

Žižek, Slavoj. *Violence: Six Sideways Reflections*. New York: Picador, 2008.

INDEX

In this index, page references in *italic type* refer to illustrations.

Printed and bound by CPI Group (UK) Ltd, Croydon, CR0 4YY
16/09/2026
14963491-0002